GET ON WITH IT

GET ON WITH IT

THE GAY AND LESBIAN GUIDE TO GETTING ONLINE

Richard Laermer

BROADWAY BOOKS | NEW YORK

BROADWAY

GET ON WITH IT. Copyright © 1997 by Richard Laermer. All rights reserved. Printed in the United States of America. No part of this book may be reproduced or transmitted in any form or by any means, electronic or mechanical, including photocopying, recording, or by any information storage and retrieval system, without written permission from the publisher. For information, address Broadway Books, a division of Bantam Doubleday Dell Publishing Group, Inc., 1540 Broadway, New York, NY 10036.

Broadway Books titles may be purchased for business or promotional use or for special sales. For information, please write to: Special Markets Department, Bantam Doubleday Dell Publishing Group, Inc., 1540 Broadway, New York, NY 10036.

BROADWAY BOOKS and its logo, a letter B bisected on the diagonal, are trademarks of Broadway Books, a division of Bantam Doubleday Dell Publishing Group, Inc.

Library of Congress Cataloging-in-Publication Data

Laermer, Richard
    Get on with it : the gay and lesbian guide to getting online/
Richard Laermer.—1st ed.
    p. cm.
    Includes index.
    ISBN 0-553-06934-9 (PB)
    1. Gay men—United States—Computer network resources.
    2. Lesbians—United States—Computer network resources.
    3. Homosexuality—United States—Computer network resources.
    4. Internet (Computer network)—United States. I. Title.
HQ76.2.U5L34   1997
004.67'8'086'64—dc21   97-491
                                                          CIP

FIRST EDITION

Designed by Stanley S. Drate / Folio Graphics Co. Inc.

97 98 99 00 01 10 9 8 7 6 5 4 3 2 1

To Steve,
who let me work late
(and stuff)

Information's easy
Tapping at my PC
That is the frame of the game

—PET SHOP BOYS

CONTENTS

CONTENTS

ACKNOWLEDGMENTS

This was tough. And, although a lot of people helped out, most people didn't even bother to return an e-mail! So . . . thank you to those who did. Really.

Extreme thanks: Ken Legins, for his incredible research skills, grace and needed humor, style as a writer, and mostly, patience; virtuous Doug Loewe, for introducing me to CompuServe way back when he was shocked I knew what it was (Nightline: "Transcripts for this broadcast available via CompuServe . . ."); Greg Cassagnol, for serious legwork, and Jonah Copiaco, for last-minute great late work; Lauren Marino and Kati Steele, for this thing's final appearance; Lisa Swayne, for saying of course it will; e-mail repliers: amazed you bothered (I mean, we were only offering promotion of your work . . .); Bob Richter, for constant support in the office! Thanks to Glenn Herman of Prodigy Internet for the art.

Just thanks: My lawyer Jonathan C. Herzog; Suki John, Ilene Diamond, Tom Samiljan, Michael Kaminer, Mr. DeCola, Natalie, David Culbertson and Kim Jones at CIS; Jennifer B. Sander; Steven Rivers and AOL's press offices (!); Michelle Almeyda, John Flinn, Rick Christel, Morgenstern, Mom, Dad; and you, the one at home.

INTRODUCTION

A Primer for Everyone on (and about) the Web

NO MORE television for you.

It's not that you've been bad. You just don't need it anymore. Thanks to the internet, and an invention called the World Wide Web (WWW), nobody has to worry whether or not the cable is working. The point is now connectivity. Are you on, that is, are you online? To paraphrase Bill Gates, how fast do you want to go?

That is the point of this book: to get you up, on, and out—so you will find yourself learning more, communicating more, meeting more, and of course, just becoming more of a part of this grand citizenry we call the gay and lesbian community.

The gay and lesbian internet is strong, due in part to people who had the foresight to get on early. The best story is the history of **www.out.com.** *Out* magazine is not the journalistic wunderkind everyone thought it would be, but it got an early start on the Web in 1994 by hiring Mediapolis, a company in Los Angeles, to create a site that is reminiscent of music videos from the early 1980s. Clunky, slow, and ridiculously colorful, the first pass gave way to a streamlined Web site that now includes a database on gay news that assisted my research for this book.

Until it was abruptly shut down in March, out.com, circa 1997, seemed promising. A press release from *Out* magazine simply quoted its president: "No magazine that we know of has found a way to profitably publish on the Web." Regardless of this hyperbole, *Out*'s Website was on its way to helping middle America cope with the coming out process.

Out.com became well known for its "Gratuitous, Anonymous Intriguing Surveys," first posted in early 1996. One survey, answered by a thousand young men, provided a stunning series of statistics, among them that more than half of out.com's users got more than half their information from the WWW. Nearly everyone surveyed felt the Web would "grow in importance, competing with televised media."

The out.com survey that introduced me to the importance of internet access to gay users was one posted in mid-1996 on favorite sites. Surprisingly, the men looked to **www.cnn.com., www.hrcusa.org** (the homepage of Human Rights Campaign), the various search engines—Yahoo!, Netscape, AltaVista—the picture (porn) sites, and the ever-so-user-friendly **www.windows95.com.**

Each morning, 13 percent exercised, 46 percent drank coffee, 61 percent ate a useful breakfast and 47 *percent* checked e-mail. More than half surfed the Web for pleasure at work; over 70 percent used the Web at home. Sixty-six percent of the respondents were happy with what they're doing on the job. Yet only 4 percent of these men "ordered dinner in" with regularity. Sixty-one percent stayed at home most weeknights with a partner or roommates. Fifty percent surfed the Web while home with that special person. More than half slept in the nude. For 76 percent, high school would have been "more positive" if the student-run organizations had included a gay group. Seventy-one percent said monogamy was necessary for a committed relationship. These were not computer nerds. Few of them helped to buy computers for their companies, but they had been using the net for a while: 30 percent of them between one to two years and 18 percent (the fewest) for between seven and twelve months.

Reading this, I thought that gays on the Web must be open, comfortable, and settled about their sexuality. Then I read on. When asked what age they came out to mother, a whopping 32 percent admitted that they were still waiting for her to ask.

Women were not surveyed for this one; however, at **www.qworld.com,** a site that focused on women, its owner, Becky Boone, conducted similar research and discovered that "80 percent of the users wanted relationships, worked to get together both on and offline, and were particularly good at maintaining strong online alliances."

In gathering information about the net from the perspective of the user, I am hoping to thwart confusion. After all, the internet is the one place you can go if, in the words of Jeff Walsh, the twenty-six-year-old creator of **www.oasis.com,** you feel confused about your place in the world, or if your "life is an empty shell." While [I was] growing up," Walsh explained, "Penylwyn, Pennsylvania, was not exactly gay mecca for me. Online I stumbled onto a planet I didn't know existed."

The so-called digital revolution is brand new to most gay men and lesbians. Cyberspace is a place that the author, William Gibson, calls "consensual hallucination." Walsh continues: "I was an eighteen-year-old in a world called 'Hot Young

Gay Teens,' a chat room on AOL [America Online] meant for us! There I could discuss feelings I had, where I was made to feel content, finally, about my homosexuality."

Walsh tells the quintessential first-time story, one I heard over and over again in researching this book. Early one summer, at age eighteen, Walsh encountered someone on the fledgling service America Online with whom he had a conversation in which they both asked and answered a lot of questions. Suddenly, he discovered he was talking to someone who wanted to know if he was gay. The Pennsylvania boy had merely thought he wanted to lose some flab on his body—"I wanted to look like body-builders. I had never *pictured* anything sexual with men," he said without irony. Walsh and his newfound friend discussed general sexuality, and five hours later, Walsh and friend admitted they were "definitely gay."

While he was making friends online all over the world, Walsh noted, "AOL ate my paycheck that summer and I went into debt worse than I ever thought possible." Although he lost sleep over money woes, his tale, like those of most early online enthusiasts, had a happy ending: Today, he runs his own classy Webzine for youngsters and helps kids who feel as uncomfortable as he did back then.

All over the country, people are either uncomfortable about some aspect of their sexuality or confused about the net. Then again, I got tired of hearing moaning and groaning from my brothers and sisters who muttered how there was nothing on the internet.

"If there is something on, it's probably all a bunch of ads anyway," goes the lament. Matthew Bank concurs. Bank, a copublisher and Webmaster for *HomoExtra,* an overwhelmingly advertiser-supported bar rag from Manhattan, says he has no intention of "reinventing the world. We give this magazine the same spin every week. And online, they go and check out info, then leave."

Natalie R. Davis, a lesbian scribe from Baltimore, believes that "the Web can be a big time-waster if you think it's going to be a Miss Lonelyhearts service. What people have to realize is the distilled information on chat rooms is not the Web. It's a lot of talk."

When asked about the big Web sites **www.planetout.com, www.out.com, www.gaywired.com,** et al.), Davis lets out a low laugh. "There doesn't seem to be any voice saying anything . . . that is not found in magazines. But," she says, "the Web is a great place to talk to people, [to] *interact* with the whole world."

Davis says the online services are brimming with thousands of users who, when asked if they use the net, will answer, "I'm on America Online." Because of the service's insistent television advertising exposure, AOL users think that they are "using the net" while they are only typing in hard-and-horny chat rooms.

AOL and the net are distinct animals. Throughout the book you will see references to the ''big gimmick'' of AOL. I feel that the largest online service is phony in its dealings with gays and lesbians. People who visit AOL's Gay and Lesbian Community Forum may think that the money they spend by chatting in the People Connection rooms is somehow going to QView, which is a gay-run firm. But P-C rooms, guided by moderators who will not let you use certain words (the penalty is dismissal from AOL class) are owned wholly by AOL. Only *some* areas of the Forum make money for gay people.

The Web may be a great place to hang out. But you have to know how to use it. I spent eleven months, or nearly the lifetime of the Web, meandering through the corridors of an electronic medium I now call home. I discussed the pros and cons of Web watching with dozens of Webmasters (the creators), a few hundred ''addicted'' users, and some internet types so technically inept that they made people like you and me look like technology innovators.

I started this project as the least technical guy you might meet. I was enticed by the idea that if *I* could conquer this thing called the Web, then anyone had a shot. I discovered that the internet is a lot bigger than most people think it is: It allowed me to learn more than anyone told me it would. I met friends, waved to enemies, even got my passport renewed by downloading software.

The net is just a spiderweb of computers. That's all. The software that takes you into cyberspace consists of browsers that let you find what you're looking for. But *the software isn't the net*. The computers on the net are not organized in any specific way. One is simply attached to another and that to several others, and where they are located in cyberspace is defined by the address. Information travels much as it does by word of mouth: two friends tell two friends who . . . and so on.

Meanwhile, technology is *not* what this is about. Imagination is. If you get a good Web browser and locate that one Web site or chat area you admire and love, you can go there and remain pretty happy for a while. Or, if you wish, you can go there and be pretty down—there are sites (listed in Chapter 7) for getting you down too.

Every person you meet online and every link you make by clicking on a brightly lit word (a hot link or hypertext) will take you to the next level. Each layer you unveil as you head up the learning curve of the internet makes it more fascinating and, sometimes, a little frustrating. But stick with it. Don't let it overwhelm you. Imagine that it's just another step in the evolution of the phone: from tin cans to huge servers. People often ask how to start, or where to go after they've plateaued. Learn as much as you can from the thousands of offerings on the net, bookmark[1]

---

[1]Bookmarking means you save the address so you only have to click on it once to get to it. This is something you do instead of having to retype http://www.yeahwhatever.com every time.

those sites that turn you on, make sure your software is strong enough to handle your desires—and suddenly you're surfin' safari, baby.

AUTHOR'S NOTE

I chose to eliminate the "http://" prefix since it stands for hypertext transport protocol. In the old days (1994) people referred to the World Wide Web as "the exciting land of http sites." Most sites exist in this area of the internet. Be aware of that before you look for the http:// preceding site names.

Internet address that *change* often leave forwarding addresses.

Take notes.

DOT. COM. WHATEVER:
Questions and Answers
from Web World

Welcome to the internet. If you know precisely what you're doing, then leave this chapter and go on to the next. Nah, I take that back. There is something in here for everyone and there'll be a quiz. So:

Q: So what is this Web? And what's the internet? And which word do you capitalize?

A: The Web, or World Wide Web, was started as a mechanism for scientists to speak to one another in 1990; a way for them to look up one another's e-mail addresses and to research statistics.

The Web is pretty much a system of regional hubs that loosely direct traffic and speed communications using high-speed phone lines. Most internet communications will eventually be routed toward those lines. A person whose computer is attached to one site on the Web can have access to the internet (the net).

The Web works on a client/server model where client software (the browser) runs on a local computer. The server software runs on a Web host. First you connect to the internet and then you launch your browser.

The internet is much larger in scope and should not be confused with WWW addresses. I chuckled when a friend of the Web's inventor, Tim Berners-Lee, told me that Tim is upset because this system was seriously meant for professors, not the rest of us.

The internet is the system of networks that makes it possible for computers to talk to each other. Television or phone systems have a network or infrastructure, and so does the internet. If you're teleconferencing using a Telnet address, Gopher, e-mail from system to system—you name it—that is all the internet. (I'll tell you what these are in a minute; hold your horses.)

Everyone thinks the online services *are* the net. But those online services, such as America Online (AOL), are separate entities and are not on the internet. You call

7

into them as you would call someone's office. You can also Telnet to places, which is like one computer calling another up for a date.

Everyone and his sister disagrees with this, but hell it's my book: You capitalize World Wide Web, because it is a proper name; internet is lower case because it's a noun. So there.

Q: How do you get on?

A: Pretty much any way you can. Find an online service with a browser you can use. The online service can be CompuServe (CIS), or AOL, or Netcom, or any other service that provides connectivity. Browsers are the tools that allow you access to everything on the Web.

Get an internet provider or hook into a service. They are cheap (between ten and twenty dollars per month) and easy to use. Usually, technical support is available—if not twenty-four hours a day, at least eight.

AOL software can be gotten by calling (800) 827-6364; CIS at (800) 848-8199; Prodigy at (800) 776-3449. Microsoft Network (MSN) did offer a free month but if they are still operating, call (800) FREE-MSN.

Or, find a library or a school that makes surfing free.

Or, go to a café or a cybercafe or even nightclubs in major cities. Cybercafes can rent you time for a few dollars an hour—then you will see if Web watching is something you like. (See Chapter 11 for a list of cafés.) Nightclubs have cyberrooms for people to zone in and see what's happening outside while they stay at home watching Nick at Nite. (Use those computers, if you dare, to check out the net.)

Q: How difficult is it to ''do'' the internet? And should I be afraid that I will be overwhelmed? On the flipside, once you get onto a site, don't you basically get bored quickly and leave? I mean, what's the point of discovering all the good stuff if you are going to get bored and log off in a few seconds?

A: Demanding questions. The only way you will get overwhelmed is if you never get offline. In which case, you are probably obsessive about most things. Yes, you are going to be bored, and often it's difficult to stay online because you get distracted by real live people. But, all in all, you will be glad you learned even a little. Said a new-to-the-net publisher, *Wisconsin Lite*'s Terry Boughner, after he started submitting Web listings from the paper to a site called www.gayuniverse.com in 1996: ''It's so intriguing. Last year I knew absolutely nothing about the internet. This year I know nothing.''[1]

Q: What is the most efficient way to use the net?

A: The most basic is through a delicious organization of newsgroups known as the Usenet system. Usenet is the set of people who exchange articles tagged with one

---

[1]Later, when quizzed, he explained: ''I'm an eighty-year-old man, and I don't want to go learn this arcane, esoteric language.''

or more universally recognized labels, called newsgroups. Those are also called "groups" for short.

Usenet is discussion-group central, truly cool, a place with approximately eighteen thousand (and growing) different subjects to choose from. And the best part of the Usenet system is its lack of censorship. The content of these discussions does not undergo peer review or have citations for claims! It's a lot of fun and, yes, it's a lot of bull too. I would also advise you to be careful who you speak to, or what you post, on Usenet, because it could end up on the screen of someone you know . . . who will then know you a lot better. Finally, you must remember that, although Usenet is not censored by any defined group of people, materials that appear on Usenet, if found to be offensive to any one person, can be reported, and if you are posting "morally questionable" material, you may have some explaining to do.

Q: What's your favorite way to get connected?

A: The Listserv system, another variation on popular e-mail. Instead of being a central repository, however, the host computer of some majordomo (that's the person or place all lists start at) distributes e-mail messages to everyone on . . . a list! This computer contains all of the names of the members of the list. As e-mail messages are received, they are reflected, or sent, only to the addresses contained in the listserve membership list. Listservs tend to be limited to narrow topics. These are not Usenet groups. And, because mail can come quickly, members of an internet-service provider that charges by the number can have costly bills. To become a member, you subscribe. To become LOST from the list you have to unsubscribe. The information in the first message you send (to subscribe) will give you lots of information on methods to contribute to each group. This is an unusual way to meet and discuss ideas.

Q: What software do I need?

A: To be on the net you don't need that much. Yet this is where most people lose it, thinking that they have to go out and get everything. Nope. First, get yourself a personal computer (PC) that's 386 or better. (Macs are terrific machines but only the Power PC now; to be able to use IBM and Mac files on a single machine is heavenly.) Then get a browser. I recommend Netscape 3.0 Gold because it was Netscape that invented and supported the idea of a commercial net that regular people could use.[2] Microsoft's Internet Explorer 3.0 (**www.microsoft.com**) is as good, but I don't fully trust a company that came in at the last minute.

Software buying is a problem. Most people who use the newsgroups want to go out and get lots of tools. Things like Freeagent, a news reader, are crucial if you wish to participate extensively on the newsgroup scene! And you will need to ensure your

---

[2]Netscape Navigator, made by Netscape Communications Corp. can be downloaded at **www.netscape.com**.

computer has the right modem. Go out and buy a decent modem and—if you are a newbie—wait on the rest.

My favorite hint: Don't buy what you won't need. Start with the basics and add as you go along. People go out and buy things, indiscriminately. What a waste.

Q: Tell me about "shareware." It's all the rage.

A: If you don't use shareware you waste time on the net. cNet, the computer network that is available on **www.cnet.com**—and discussed throughout the book—supports the site that lets you get what you need, on a trial basis. I needed Quick Time for Windows (video, sound, graphics, and animation in one) and there it was. The download time: twelve minutes on a 28.8 kbs modem. Then I wanted a Quick Time movie player. I got it—eleven minutes. tops!

Granted all these are ninety-day trials,[3] but I kept getting new ones, recaps of the oldies, until one day I finally bought the suckers for around forty-nine dollars. (Quick Time is available on most machines with Windows 95; mine seems to work strangely!)

Why do they do this? To show ads—they make money on those adverts, and know many eyeballs roam over pages of freebies.

You can find software for newsgroups, something called nslide21,[4] which is a Windows-compatible sideshow application for all your fancy dirty photos. Plus, you can just find a host of others. I always try something on Shareware before buying. Then you save yourself lots of time returning stuff you hate.

Second to lastly, many files are zipped files, which is WinZip for Windows and also available as an Unfolder on Mac. Zip is also available—and forever—on your favorite software finder, **www.shareware.com**, known to experts as **www.download.com.**

Finally, so as not to anger the shareware people, note the prefix *share*. That means you ought to pay 29 bucks for registration of software. I did it for the slide-show application and not only did they profusely thank me for being "honest and upright," but also gave me their secret site for more updates and further info.

Q: Where do I go for free information on modem software?

A: Special software can enhance modems. To help, download Trumpet Winstock made by Trumpet Software International, which can be reached at the site called **oak.oakland.edu/SimTel/win3/winstock.** Its primary applications are as TCP/IP and modem software. Pay the $20 registration fee—bill it to your Amex card.

Q: Speaking of software, what can I get if I want to sort my e-mail?

[3]Sometimes these are thirty days. Whatever. Then you get annoying messages telling you that your software's days are numbered (you can find computer people to get rid of these messages), and then they disintegrate! Which is a cool operation in itself: Watch as your software goes, "I'm melting!"

[4]ftp://ftp.simtel.net/pub/simtelnet/win95/inet/nslide21.zip

A: If you want to get special software for receiving and sorting e-mail, Pegasus, Eudora, and Qualcomm are the best. They are available on the Web, and are pretty darn great because they let you skip the pain of getting, sorting, and filing e-mail. (See Chapter 3 for more on the many brilliant uses of e-mail.)

Q: What are news readers, and how do I use them?

A: News readers are ways to read the newsgroups and get the news and Usenet messages. Newsgroups are better served through readers outside your browser. The best is Freeagent, I think, which is found (and may be downloaded) at **www.forteinc.-com/forte/agent/freeagent.htm.**

Q: What is Archie?

A: Some people may want to ''get on the Archie bandwagon. Archie is a tool (software) for finding files stored on anonymous File Transfer Protocol (FTP) sites. You need to know the exact file name or a substring of it in order to get those files. You can start your descent into Archieland by dialing up **www.csra.net/junodj/ws_ftp.htm.** (Archie software is available on Shareware and another share-oriented site called Freeware.)

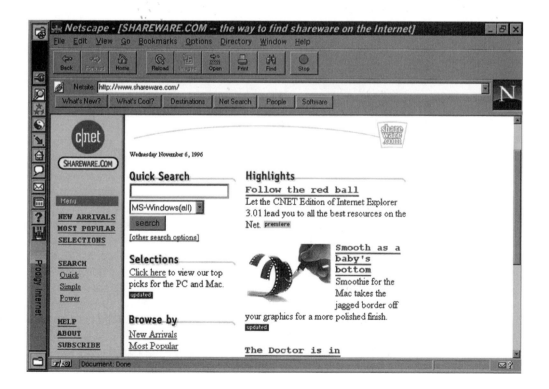

Q: What is Gopher?

A: The Gopher system is a widely successful method of making menus of material available over the internet. Gopher is a client-and-server-style program, which requires the user to have a Gopher client program. Although Gopher spread rapidly across the globe in only a couple of years, it has been largely supplanted by hypertext. Gopher is considered old hat by many experts, but there are still thousands of Gopher servers on the internet and we can expect that they will remain for a while.

    WS Gopher, reachable at **dewey.tis.inel.gov/pub/wsgopher/,** is a Gopher you can download and keep via Freeware. BC Gopher, reachable at **ns.uam.es/pub/ms-windows/com/,** is also a Gopher available through Freeware. Both programs are Windows-based, point-and-click navigators of the internet Gopher world.

Q: Can I do something besides use Netscape and Explorer?

A: Besides Netscape and Explorer, the old standbys, try out NCSA Mosaic, made by the National Center for Supercomputing Applications, reachable at **ftp.ncsa.uiuc.edu/Web/Mosaic/.**

Q: I saw the Glossary and laughed at how silly some of the terminology is. What is the origination of the term *spamming*?

A: Spamming, which is the act of repeating a message (often vitriolic) by sending it to tens, hundreds, or sometimes thousands of e-mail addresses, is frowned upon. The term comes from a notorious skit on the BBC's program, *Monty Python's Flying Circus* (later used in the film *And Now for Something Completely Different*) that takes place in a coffee shop where people order nothing but Spamspamspamspamspam! It's a stretch.

Q: What about commercial service providers?

A: You can get on the net via AOL, CompuServe, Prodigy or even MSN, which is the newest and least-tested of the four—or use a local service provider that you trust. (See the ads for your neighborhood freebie that charges $16.95 a month for unlimited access; or call your telephone company, which may be able to provide some sort of deal.) Or call Netcom at 800-NETCOM1. These people will give you the best service in the business, and it's about 20 bucks. IDT (telephone 1 (800) 245-8000) has just started charging $15.95, and the customer service is pretty good if not overworked.

    Remember that internet providers which are *not* "proprietary services," like CompuServe, will have to set you up. That means you need to spend time installing IP addresses or DNS names into dialer programs—a little complicated if you're unsure of yourself.

    The absolute best thing to do for a test is to grab a free month on CIS, AOL, MSN, or Prodigy. (Prodigy has a $19.95-per-month internet service *and content* as a new service, what it calls Prodigy Internet. MSN offers a similar service. Both give a month free on these services.) This way you try it out on them. In January '97, AOL introduced AOL Lite: Spend less than five dollars and get a few hours free. (I wonder what AOL Fat would be.)

Q: Why is AOL so popular and why is it that you can't set up a chat room called Hot Young Gay Teens on the service anymore?

A: America Online, those ambitious little marketers, sends formattable disks to more people than 3M would during a warehouse closing! (My advice is, when they arrive in the mail, to turn them into a stockpile of diskettes!)

Gay people are taken in by the overt marketing efforts ("Come join our community") because they know that the Gay and Lesbian Community Forum on AOL is simply *the* place to get hard and get off. Furthermore, GLCF is not moderated and you can basically say what you will, at any time, though it is never private. (See Chapter 5 to change that opinion that it's private.) However unmoderated the chat rooms are, "AOL police" still patrol the place, so don't attack anyone and don't use the wrong words while you type, or you will receive a warning letter through "snail mail." A friend of an acquaintance was bounced off AOL for entering a so-called gay chat room and typing "Greetings, fellow faggots"—an unremarkable salutation among gays but one that did offend AOL's underinformed cyberexaminers.

The cancellation of the Hot Young Gay Teens room a young person could use is easily explained: Commanders at AOL today disallow you to open up rooms they imagine to be offensive to some. The 1996 Terms of Service that you click "Agree" to join contains such a disclosure, even though the government recently explained that litigious actions against online services' content are unconstitutional. Anyway, nobody under eighteen can talk about sex on AOL. (Real world.) Marketing sources working with AOL tell me that about 30 percent of the online membership is queer! Some argue that AOL treats gay members like second-class citizens, as you cannot find the word *gay* in their searchable terms! See Chapter 5.

Q: Now let's see about the Web itself. What is a hot link? And is hypertext really useful?

A: Hot links and hypertext allow you to click onto something relevant to the subject at hand. Both hot links and hypertext are lit up so you can easily see them on a color screen. (Monochrome monitor users—be wary of the net or visit Radio Shack.) Using hypertext or hot links is felt to be a fast way to get more information and if it turns out you hate what you link to, then click on the word Back and it will return you to the place you started.

Hypertext is arranged by the current page's Webmaster, so you can take advantage of extra definitions of whatever word you are clicking on. For instance, in a site where the words *hyper-text* or *hot links* are featured in blue type rather than black, you would click on them and suddenly you'd be whooshed away to a page that gave you this:

The Cool Hyper-Text Page by Richard Laermer

The most important thing about hyper-text or hot links is that it goes on forever. Click on the word *forever* and watch your pages fly! Continual clicking of the mouse makes for great experiences on the internet. But you can get carried away by clicking and forget the subject you intended to search!

In a unique twist that continually fascinates me, the WWW knows where you've been: After you click onto a site, no matter where you entered it from, a link to that site will never light up again. It won't be, even if you see the link to that site on *another* site . . . seven years from now! Your computer knows where you've been; it's the record-keeping brilliance of the Web. This is attributed to the browser's cache, where Web pages, graphics, etc. are being temporarily stored, that way when a user returns to a page, the browser gets it from the cache instead of the original server.

Last cool thing about linking mania: if you use the mail feature on Netscape or MS Explorer and you type in http://whatever.com that address (or any online address) will, if the recipient is using Netscape or MS Explorer mail, show up in his or her mailbox as a hypertexted link.

Q: Okay, so now I know about mail and stuff. What about pics? How do I get a jpeg. or gif. picture of me, or a picture that I want to represent as little ole me? (Jpeg/gif images are types of digital photos.)

A: Go to any copy center that provides computer use and scan the picture or ask them to do it; save it on a disk; go to town. These can be sent via e-mail or you can always drop the disk in the mail. When scanning, it's helpful to know what size you want the picture to be, because some proprietary (commercial) services handle only a small scanned image. And you want to be handled.

Q: There you are going on and on about chat. Um, what exactly is this "IRC" you're so eager about?

A: These are the Internet Relay channels that are available as soon as you phone up. IRC is easy and attracts many thousands of gays and lesbians all over the world because you make up the rules and you set the FAQ (frequently asked questions) that are "right" for the group that participates.

In the United States, everyone is nervous about the monitoring of chat by online services; IRC is not monitored here because the majority of the IRC channels are gone tomorrow. *Get On with It* will introduce you to newsgroups and Usenet areas that are known to be popular enough to stick around.

Nobody's "moral values" will cut them off.

Read Chapter 6 and learn more about Inter Relay and eventually Direct Contact Channel, the photo-enhanced area built to show off your new Rembrandt™-enhanced smile! Or, use it to show off not-so-brightly-lit parts.

Q: Who can I depend on other than you?

A: No one. Okay, I think books and magazines are great sources but I depend on online Webzines, which ensure that you become more invested in the World Wide Web and the internet on the whole. The last part of this book has Web-oriented print mags listed, but the best for novices is *NetGuide* magazine; for gay men, there's a twenty-something mag called *XY* (almost entirely for gay Web cruisers) and for women, *Lesbian News* and *Curve*. (*LN* is available on the rainbowmall.com service, too, and *Curve* is being built on planetout.com.) I also am quite impressed with listings sections of most high-circulation newspapers around the country, which are great places to start learning what's available on the net: Daily papers cram their pages with listings of great chat areas and their special guests.

Q: I suppose I should ask about modems. Is 28.8 the best modem speed I can do right now? And how does it work? What should I pay for a modem?

A: First, why obsess about speed? Like size, modems are viewed philosophically. Do the best you can use with the one you've got.

A modem works when you plug it in and allow it to talk to another computer; it works like a telephone, only here the data is talking. The modem carries sound through the phone. On a "28.8 modem," 28.8 thousand bits per second are traveling through the system per second. (Bits are binary digits that computers use to communicate—the *ffehhyiewi* sound that you hear from the speaker.)

For phoneaholics like me, Telnet is a real joy. Regardless of speed of modem, Telnet is a function that allows you to connect with the computer on the internet, or a server, which in turn dials up an address for you. Telnet is fun because you are actually calling a phone that then does all the work! Computers are big toys. Don't let them intimidate you.

Every modem user asks about cost. It varies somewhere between 5 bucks for a 1980-era 240-bit antique, to $400 for a super duper 33.6 Hayes-compatible model. (Hayes and U.S. Robotics issued a "56 bit" modem in 1997. I saw that Honeywell has released one as fast. It works on regular phones, but actually delivers at faster speeds. Way too cool.)

Q: I know I have heard about cellular modems and satellite hookups? What gives?

A: A product named Ricochet, which costs $299 for the modem or a mere $10 to rent, has been produced by the Metricom company. The speed of Ricochet is somewhere between 14.4 and 28.8 and, by the time you read this, will have spread out nationwide. It's only fourteen ounces, too. *How does it work?* should be this question! It blinks an LED in various colors and emits urgent tones and even installs a special edition of Netscape Navigator. Hidden charges: a $45 setup fee, $29.95 per month for service, and you never have to worry about a busy signal (damn!) because the whole thing is really wireless.

Q: Such hype in the papers about Ma Bell's subsidiaries going the internet route. Will the Baby Bell local telephone companies and cable television corporations make it easier for us to connect, or are these just empty promises?

A: First, it's important to note that interactive cable TV was invented in the 1980s by the late Steve Ross, chairman of Warner Communications. He was laughed out of the interactive field by nonbelievers; Warner squandered beaucoup bucks on technology that consumers didn't want. Today, the conglomerate Time Warner wants to make modem-speed cable boxes for the phone, merely connections to the net. Cable people have a history of overcharging, so the government probably will need to step in and regulate all this. Stick with a modem.

The almighty dollar will force telephone companies to offer free internet access by late 1997. "Free" means that connections will be free; the call will cost. Thus homeowners will be more inclined at least to try the internet.

The boxes being plotted by cable companies can give us ISDN-like speed (see Glossary). They get a big thumbs down from me. Do you think that, after I'm charged $3.95 to sit through *Fair Game,* they might undercharge me for a *new* technology?

Q: Does the whole world use the Web the way Americans do?

A: The rest of the world sees *internetivity* as an opportunity. I think of the United States as a media-cracy, with newspapers shouting out about this "great technology" but with no real information available on how to make it work for your home or office. Currently only the most moneyed, educated, and sick-of-TV-types are using the Web. Most colleges and universities give it to students for free and, until recently, it was an upper-middle-class, white, techno-savvy, and male thing. Now I'm happy to report it's more of a cross-section of the population, the people who I think of it as a big adventure, minus Pee Wee!

But how about a story to illustrate the above?

In mid-1996, I contacted fifty U.S. cafés and fifty European cafés about helping inaugurate the world's largest cybercast. This was the Tibetan Freedom Concert, which was actually held in Golden Gate Park in San Francisco—we're talking wires hanging from the trees! Anyway, only a handful of the U.S. cafés bothered getting in touch. Every single European café manager e-mailed asking for directions and specifically wanting to know—How can /help?

The majority of Americans will only get online every day after the shopping channels transfer their allegiance and purchases are considered secure. Or Oprah and Kathie Lee get their own sites.

Q: Why is cellular service cheaper and in more homes than regular phone service in Poland?

A: While it may seem like a silly topic, it's crucial to note that inexpensive service providers are bringing more pagers and cell phones to Eastern Europe than any other technology right now. In small towns outside Warsaw, people without home phones are using these little phone contraptions!

Cheap service is all we need to start a revolution. In the United States, when the Baby Bells, Time Warner Cable, and AT&T get their acts together and start charging pennies per month for internet access, I guarantee you will use the darn thing to call your mother on Sunday afternoons. (Internet phone is here, and not great.)

Q: Is there one thing you've seen to shock you about the gay and lesbian aspects of the Web?

A: The number of people who signed the guest book on Gay CyberSlut Homepage (UK). I always thought that England was hung up on sex; wrong! :) (See the list of emoticons to be found in the e-mail chapter.)

Q: What advice would you give someone who has never been on the net before and is scared out of his or her wits?

A: Don't be scared to cruise the Web, which is the most colorful part of the net. The worst that can happen is that you get thrown off by your service provider. Nobody will know you are an amateur unless you let it out. Remember: the Web became commercially feasible only in 1994!

But don't go on the Gay CyberSlut page **www.users.dircon.co.u.k./cyberslut/ index2.htm** or pornography sites or links yet. The porn culture, I found, isn't for the uninitiated.

Q: Okay—so let's get down to it! What about porn online? And is it just like the videos you (or I) see when we go to one of those video hangouts?

A: Porno can be much more exciting when you interact with the people who are simultaneously using the sites. Sure, you can go and download and view lots of photos of naked men and women. You can read about sexual experiences, stories like the ones printed in dozens of dirty magazines. And you can even see some films, though most of the time you must pay for the privilege. Just as in any capitalist situation, the most technologically advanced sites are ones that charge, and get, the money.

There's even one strange site called Tangled (see Chapter 12) with photographs of intertwining bodies of men and women. Demented, accessible fun found at **www. mxm.com/tangled,** but the address was changing in mid-'97.

Q: I wonder. Is the health information on the Web potentially harmful, or is that a hyped lie?

A: Health information, depicted with studious effort in this book, is not regulated on the net. This is scary. Have you ever watched infomercials late at night selling diet, aging, fitness appliances, Ginzu knives? The same products are indeed on the internet. Health is a growing business in the United States (that's why they call it health *business,* darling) and the net allows entrepreneurs to take advantage of uneducated consumers. However, there are a few protections. Some national health agencies, such as The Alzheimer's Foundation and The American Cancer Society, have their own sites, and these organizations have a strong reputation in the public health and medical communities. And although entrepreneurs are sometimes misleading, they are concerned with liability—and particularly with jail sentences—so most advice given on the internet is qualified. So, read the small print, take two aspirins, and e-mail me in the morning.

Q: What's your favorite site?

A: **Badpuppy.com** is among the faves, and I admit I'm hooked on **www.pointcast.com,** which is a site for sore eyes (ads, info, media, links galore). But the puppy-ites have it totally together—not only because of its highly charged sexuality, but because the site is original. The couple behind it (Bill and Steve, who have become my friends) are in it for fun. They make money on BP, but they also listen to the people who are their beloved members: changes, new technology, humorous sites on tap, the whole kit and kaboodle. The site has lots of areas to go and meet people, it's unpretentious, and the artwork is quite pretty. Lastly, you can download a variety of video clips—lots of unique porn—for free. And you can pay monthly for some other services, too! A big 10 bucks a month! I also love www.suck.com, a cynical info site.

Q: What about serious information?

A: More and more well-intentioned Webmasters are coming out with new info-seekers. The Rainbow Mall was one of the first, started by Dan Zeitman in 1995 but I now realize that, nah, he hadn't done much except offer commercial transactions. Then I got to know gay newspaper services (**www.qspec.com**), which work a little to help us stay informed, and a whole mess of crucial areas you will find reviewed in Chapter 7, such as the gay military site, and www.gaywired.com, and the whole health chapter!

Meanwhile, QRD (Queer Resources Directory, **www.grd.com**), now part of **www. planetout.com,** catalogues how to find all the gay news that's fit to post. Some groups, such as the *Washington Blade* **(washblade.com),** had the wherewithal to get material on the Web early enough (1996) to be pioneers in new technology. Blade allows gays and lesbians to search through legislation from state to state; the editor was a newbie when he jumped in; he now excels.

Q: Since the Web is one large ad anyway, what's the best slogan you've heard so far?

A: A new gay community has been described by the ubermaster of gay Web surfing, Tom Rielly, the cofounder of a technology charity group, the Digital Queers, and the present of Planetout (www.planetout.com), which can be found on the Web, on AOL, and on the Microsoft Network (MSN).

Rielly—whose service is ubiquitous and contains a lot of information that you may want to look at—claims that he wants to form "an international online gay community so strong that hotels will suffer because every member of Planetout stays with cyberfriends instead of in hotel rooms!" While Planetout, in its first months on the Web, has yet to gather a community *that* large, I guess Rielly is the one to make this pledge. Indeed, he was quoted a few years ago saying, "The computer is the one place where you can escape from predominantly heterosexual role models." His is a noncommercial idea that, luckily for him, is funded to the hilt. But it is a notion that goes right to the heart of the matter.

Q: What's with Planetout?

A: It seems to be everywhere—and buying everyone—reminding me of AT&T in the 1970s. As Frank Rich of the *New York Times* put it, "Even as the dizzying proliferation of media outlets promises a great variety of content, how much variety will there be if all the new 'channels' . . . ultimately have the same few owners."

Q: Something I need to clear up. Can checking your e-mail be obsessive?

A: I'm in trouble if it is. (And please, if all you're doing on the Web is checking e-mail, don't pay for e-mail—try **www.juno.com** for a free service.

Q: Is there a downside to the Web?

A: Yes, there's a downside to anything good—except chocolate. Online, people don't have to join the gay culture. They learn the language, understand the very world they live in, yet never leave the house. I read in *Cosmo*— yes, *Cosmo:* "Cyberspace enables people to enter secret worlds without having to go to a gay bar and posture as a gay. [Surfers] join the culture without having to buy a drink, talk to anyone, or engage in a homosexual act."

The other negative fact is that many gay or lesbian Web sites promote an "us-versus-them" sensibility. Some sites actually proclaim, in their FAQ's or opening statements, a purpose to promote "our own values"—a need for queers to take over the Web in order to help one another. This does not sit well with freethinkers. While the right wing may spend its waking hours plotting against gays, that doesn't mean our outlook has to be mean spirited. Our glass is half full. Look at the how many gay and lesbian Web users there are.

Plus, as Mike Signorile explains in his rambling book on, a-hem, being queer in America:[5] "The [right wing] may never be as fluid or as advanced in computer technology as gays. The more we communicate [our message] the more we win."

Then there's the fakeness thing. As discussed in "Privacy, Talk, and the Dirty Secrets of the Inter Relay" (Chapter 6), it is impossible to know who's yanking your chain when you chat! Don't trust that the person you are speaking to is describing himself correctly.

A scientist I spoke to, "Mr. B.," uses the internet for research and yet told me he goes onto the IRC to masquerade as a thirteen-year-old and trap older men into the act of playing with young boys. After they get hooked on their young fantasy lover, he drops them. Playacting like that is a major part of the attraction; getting duped is easy.

Q: What bodes poorly for the future?

A: The Communications Decency Act (**www.eff.org/blueribbon.com**) holds a threat over the internet and is an act of government censorship that you should keep in mind

---

[5]Yes, we have a winner. *Queer in America: Sex, the Media, and the Closets of Power* is by M. Signorile, and was published originally in 1993 by Random House and later by Anchor Books.

when enjoying the freedom of the Web. The bill's existence is a downside to all this fun.

Perhaps decisions in two lower courts in 1996—two that proclaimed that this is a free speech issue—will help calm people's fears of the Web as some terrible place that needs policing. P.S.: It's back, and haunting us again.

A little history: James Exon (D-Nebr) introduced a bill that would protect children from pornography in cyberspace. As currently written, the Decency Act aims to stop "obscene, indecent, lewd, lascivious, and filthy communications" on computer networks by making creators legally and criminally liable for those communications. Fines would be up to $250,000.

The bill's allies are the usual suspects: Christian Coalition, American Family Association, and Traditional Values Coalition, the same firebrands who went after the Walt Disney Corporation for allowing domestic partners to have insurance benefits last year. The bill's adversaries are the courts, which wrote that no one has the right to tell people what they can publish. Or, "Hello! There's a Constitution in this country!"

The consensus of the internet community (and specifically the Electronic Frontier Foundation, which runs the anticensorship campaign via links on hundreds of sites over the World Wide Web) is that kids really need to be watched after by their parents—not by Web publishers and not by any government that I know of.

Q: The obvious dilemma facing public libraries is, "If we have the Web open to everyone, won't boys automatically hit **www.playboy.com?** And how can we stop that?"

A: I go to libraries. Nobody stops kids from taking down sexually explicit books from the shelves! So why has the fuss suddenly hit the fan? Because the Web is a huge, untapped universe and the net an even larger one. What a scary thought to controlling types. Imagine—children satisfying a hunger for knowledge with no one stopping them. True, they shouldn't be on porn lines, but overseeing one's kids is not a new issue.

Summation: The possibilities of discovering what we didn't know before are endless. Goodbye, huddled and ignorant masses. As early as 1995, even the Cubans had a Web site.

Q: Can you stop being so serious?

A: Sure. The best way to see the gay fun on the Web is to check our "alt.sex.boredom," a group of wild and nutty fetishists who share secrets with one another in a highly unusual newsgroup.[6] Every time I'm incensed or perplexed by something on the net, I go to alt.sex.boredom and recall how much fun this can be.

---

[6]AltaVista is the search engine that features alt.sex.boredom. Use your browser to go to **altavista. digital.com** and ask for this unique newsgroup by name.

A good time can be had by sending an e-mail. Both Walsh and "Mr. B." told me they only decided to stay addicted after they saw they could send e-mail to people as diverse as John Hinkley and even Barney (**asylum.cid.com/barney**). (Mister Hinkley you can find on your own.)

"The online world offers a lot more than just a chance to make friends," said Walsh in an article for *The Advocate,* in 1994. "With even the most basic computer, anyone can e-mail President Clinton and talk about gay issues on message boards."

Q: Okay, I'm hooked. But does this really make TV irrelevant?

A: You bet. Why would people be drawn to the tube when the world is at their fingertips, whether for library searches, titillation, or interaction with new friends or romantic conquests? In the words of Bill Rivers, Webmaster of the aforementioned site Bad-puppy, insists there is more humor than smut to his pages: "Come and see us for a laugh. And we, unlike many of my colleagues, will write back if you have a question about ANYTHING!" he told me.

Q: Then what's going to happen to Must See TV?

A: Ask the president of NBC Entertainment. He's sweating that question right about now.

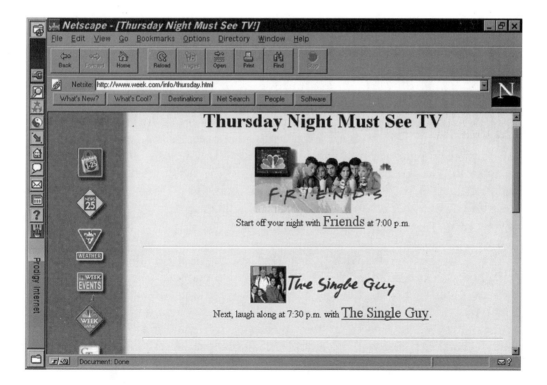

Now you have had a very basic introduction to the internet and all of the systems located within it. I feel you are ready to become a cyberperson. But before you begin, let's get one thing clear: You cannot learn the internet without making a few mistakes. This thing called the internet is filled with notices, ideas, new software, advertisements, and vendors trying to control the future of the system. And then you will be distracted, no doubt, by all the "cuties on the net" (see Chapter 8 for cuties).

You may turn yourself into an educated consumer by simply thinking through options as new software and hardware are needed. *Needed.* Not wanted. The options become apparent as you try to complete a task and you are unable to. Advertisers have figured out how to make themselves known when you need them most, especially on Netscape. Suddenly, the actual software link will appear. It's like magic. Yeah.

Use that to your advantage to gain knowledge about the type of application you find *necessary.* Once you know what you are looking for, then you can simply use one of the infamous search engines to get more details. Trust me, it won't be painful.

In order to survive cyberspace, you must also remember not to believe the hype that your life must center around "keeping up" with all the internet magazines, such as the ones mentioned in Chapter 12, for example. The evolution of the internet is also bringing with it sophisticated educational mediums. You should never use excuses such as, "I'm computer illiterate," or "I am too old," or "I do not have the time." Don't even think of saying "I can't type." That's like saying, "Please don't give me that Maserati because I can't drive."

The internet is evolving into a medium with knowledge that is more understandable, more accessible, and less time consuming to find and enjoy.

I hope that I have now convinced you that you don't have any reasons *not* to begin surfing queer cyberspace, especially if you are gay, lesbian, bisexual, transsexual, or questioning your sexuality. The internet is a unique and exciting endeavor in many ways and the more you find time to use the net, the more uses you will undoubtedly find for it. And the more excuses you will find to use it!

I feel the internet is a tool that can help in either furthering your understanding of your sexuality, or make your sexual development a group experience by interaction with the millions of gays and lesbians on the internet around the world.

In a culture obsessed with sophisticated methods of communication to avoid being harassed or discriminated against, gays and lesbians are rulers on the internet. We have taken hold of this unique medium of communication and brought it to a new level. We are using it to influence politics, create communities in what some might call "cyber civil space," and meet colleagues, friends, and potential intimates though chatting, transferring data or ideas, sharing pics, or going to the video!

As much as you might not want to get involved in the high-tech aspects of the computer revolution, we gays and lesbians are, in a large part, responsible for many of its advances. You have family out there ready to comfort you, admire you, and most of all teach you. So enjoy it.

It's a bizarre ride. Get on with it. Thank me later.

2

USENET—OR LOSE IT

Usenet is a system for sending messages out on the Web, a system that includes postings on the internet and a way to exchange articles tagged with one or more universally recognized labels, often called newsgroups, or groups for short. Note the term *newsgroup*. The terms *area, base, board, bboard, conference, round table, SIG* and all others are incorrect.[1]

Why should you care about Usenet? Because everyone is on it. And the easiest way to learn how to use Usenet is to watch how others use it. Start reading the news and try to figure out what people are doing and why. After a couple of weeks you will start understanding why certain things are done and what things shouldn't be done. There are documents available describing the technical details of how to use the software. Look through the internet's many search engines for **alt.newusers. Usenet,** and find out what you want, and who you want to reach, by using the few rules that follow in this chapter:

First thing to remember: *The computer on the other end is human!* You are going to be talking to people who may turn out to be actual flesh and blood.

Second. The most exacting thing about Usenet is the subject line. For example, Subject: Re: What This Is About is a subject line that really works. This is how you start a message. This enables a person with a limited amount of time to decide whether or not to read your article. It tells people what the article is about before they read it. To the group **alt.binary.sell.bodies** a title like "Man For Sale" does not help as much as "Boy in Need of Daddy." Some sites limit the length of the subject line to forty characters so keep your subjects short and to the point. Thus you

---

[1] If you want to be understood, be accurate. So says Usenet system called **news.announce. newuser,** a popular and useful newsgroup.

will be thinking about your audience. Don't expect people to read your article to find out what it is about because many of them won't bother.

The third rule: because you are going to find yourself in many newsgroups, avoid posting the same message to more than one newsgroup unless you are sure it is appropriate. If you do post to several newsgroups, do not post to each group separately. Instead, specify all the groups on a single copy of the message. One of my personal complaints about Usenet's network is that, when people ask a question, everyone thinks he or she should answer it, even if it is meant for only one person!

I always tell people (as do experts) to send your answers through e-mail rather than posting them on the big system of this Usenet thing. This way the net will only see a single copy of the answers, no matter how many people answer the question.

Also remember that, once something is posted onto the Usenet, it is in the public domain unless you own the appropriate rights (most notably, if you wrote the thing yourself) and you post it with a valid copyright notice. A court would have to decide the specifics, and that has yet to be done. Wanna set a precedent? Be my guest.

Rule number four. Usenet is not a resource for homework or class assignments. Commonly, new users, learning of all the people out there holding discussions, view them as a great resource for gathering information for reports and papers.

Five. Advertisements on Usenet are rarely appreciated. In general, the louder or more inappropriate the ad is, the more antagonism it will stir up. Few things annoy Usenet readers as much as multiple copies of a posting appearing in multiple newsgroups (called *spamming,* as in "spamspamspam" in Monty Python's famous skit). See the Glossary for the skinny on spam.

And thus, the basic New Users' Rules:

1. Never forget that the person on the other side is human. (Really? Somebody told me I was talking to the Beastmaster :).)
2. Don't blame system admins for their users' behavior (don't cry!).
3. Be brief.
4. Your postings reflect on you; be proud of them. (I always am, especially the shots of Debbie and . . . well, anyway.)
5. Use descriptive titles.
6. Think about your audience (they are not twinks or children).
7. Be careful with humor and sarcasm (bitch!).
8. Post a message only once.
9. Please do not thrust out material with questionable content (that is, encrypt it so that Grandma doesn't have a cow). Most of all, regarding questionable content, please don't use Usenet as an advertising medium. They will go after you!

I could go on and on but these are sufficient for now. You'll figure out the rest as you go along. Usenet is definitely learn as you play. At least for me it was play.

So, what are we doing on the Usenet, you and I? And why is this different from Listserv and the e-mail world? Well, Usenet is not at all private, and although Listservs are for many people, messages are sent to a private list. (E-mail, of course, is private; ha ha; see Chapter 3 for the reason I guffaw.)

Besides so much talk that it can drive you insane, Usenet is where you can find internet directions to some of the most obscene pornography on the internet. And that is why gay people flock to it. In a recent study I read that most people used the Usenet system to see binary files, which unlike the regular ones, are sent binary-style, meaning you can get any format possible. That is, you can get pictures. That is, you can get real dirty pictures.

Usenet acts like a huge BBS (bulletin board system: a forum or area where you can post information), allowing surfers to post images, applications, and articles on anything they choose (if they want to test the law), including internet directions to dirty matter. (For the whole scoop on things dirty, see Chapter 8.)

There is one thing to clear up about Usenet. Everyone thinks the net is one big happy family—unlike places such as AOL and CompuServe, which tempt you, and then hook you (and then tell you to stop it!). And it's true that IRC—see Chapter 6—is certainly a free place, but you're not entirely free from censorship on the net. You can get busted on Usenet; in fact, the plethora of "do gooder" computer geeks on Usenet have, compared to WWW users, been around for quite some time and will not only bust you, but also track your fake address down and bomb your memory!

The private sites are accessible only by private modem numbers, and can be quite a treat if you have the connections, :), and are willing to pay for the likely long-distance call. Although some material is illegal no matter what the medium, these private sites are less likely to get busted.

Private modem sites were the predecessors of the first pirate sites. Pirate sites are sites that contain illegal copies of software or, nowadays, pornography that contravenes current regulations. You can get their material just by chatting it up on Usenet and showing some interest in whatever nasty stuff floats your immoral boat:).

If you are interested in the dirty stuff, you basically have two choices. You can (1) try to find these private modems by making yourself known in dirty newsgroups (some alt. groups are listed below) and making friends who appreciate the same stuff you do, and (2) get the hell off Usenet. Most of the directions for Usenet reflect the "up-tight" attitude of people addicted to this kind of forum.

Note that Usenet and newsgroup areas of the net also include some fine groups that talk about real stuff. These are all over the map and are too many to number.

Because it's public, people are indeed being their most polite selves. And whoa! that can be très boring.

I was determined to prove that the whole idea of being polite is not always the case. I checked in with Savoynet, a group of nearly a thousand who speak about Gilbert and Sullivan operettas and the like. Because the majority were straight or in the closet, a member shared the following two newsie items from a thread. The thread got nasty when something homo got brought up. All in all, it showed people's true colors—when they're not being polite.

This thread is called "For I Am Blythe, Among Other Things" and refers to the line in the opera *Patience*: "For she is blythe and she is gay." It's a reference, says my friend, to a ridiculous young maiden who claims she has never known the pain of love. The thread begin:

MEMBER 1: "I saw this article by . . . which appeared in the San Francisco Sentinel in 1994: 'Appreciation of Gilbert & Sullivan operettas is one of the linking characteristics that they've recognized in connection with the new gay gene. . . . This question is one of the few things they got right in the script for the great gay epic Making Love. As soon as Michael Ontkean launched into the HMS PINAFORE, Kate Jackson should have started packing.' My question then is simple: How many of you out there go to my church, play on my team, hang your hat on my rack, etc.? How many consider Dorothy a personal friend? Who, besides myself, carries a big pink membership card?"

MEMBER 2: Gilbert is recorded as once saying, "I don't presume to brandish my private affairs at you; you will please observe the same reticence with regard to mine." Allow me to paraphrase: "I don't presume to brandish my private affairs at you; you will please observe the same reticence with regard to yours."

MEMBER 3: "There was a wonderful Seinfeld program about him being over thirty, thin and neat, and a Broadway fan, ergo . . . Beware of stereotypes, genetic or otherwise. There ARE straight people who love music, theater and The Wizard of Oz."

MEMBER 4: "Why should G&S lovers get off any easier than the rest of the musical theater loving world. rec.arts.theatre.musicals has a permanent thread on homosexuality, actually it's one of the more interesting threads on that newsgroup. . . . I don't give a damn what a performer's—or anyone else's, unless I'm planning to go to bed with him—sexual proclivity is . . . Some subjects are fun to discuss. It gives a chance to practice one's debating skills while remaining disinterested in the subject."

MEMBER 4: "There has been an awful lot of bandwidth wasted on the sexual preferences of both the characters and performers of G & S."

MEMBER 5: "I would like to defend the view that some of Gilbert's characters can be seen as homosexuals. Sam asked a question that could be answered privately, to satisfy his own curiosity and to see if a stereotype was (as far as stereotypes go) more or less accurate. There were no accusations. Or generalizations. And judging from the venehement [*sic*] reactions that greeted [it] I think we ALL know that most of the outspoken members of this Net are not gay, or at least not prepared to admit it . . ."

Friends. Hah!

Here's more, a good example of someone who will definitely not pass the test written by the "professionals" who authored Usenet rules. I would recommend hooking up with these wahoos only to try and find some fascinating stuff out there on the internet.

Subject: I am not gay but obsessed with cocks ∼∼∼∼ Hi all you people that are obsessed with cocks but are not gay . . . My boyfriend, without my knowledge, went to a roadway rest stop this past weekend to see "what it felt like for me to give him head" so he in turn sucked seven guys off in the woods . . . It was the first gay adventure he has had. Now he would like me to go there with him to get the guys real excited as he sucks them and he also wants me to suck him in front of all the gay men. I do feel a little excitement about it, but I feel funny doing something like that.

He now tells me that it is good for him to know just what it feels like to have a nice hard cock in my mouth after him doing the seven gay men.

Signed, Cathy from Long Island

My advice: Stick with the World Wide Web for fun and excitement.

You have heard me mention "alt." And of course your friends may have said they go to something like **alt.messmeup.binary.** You now know what binary is, but what's alt about? The newsgroups denoted by alt., or the alt. newsgroups, contain the dirt you are probably looking for (unless you are in search of dirt on another planet—that would be under sci. for science). The codeword *binaries* means you will most likely be getting pictures rather than bathroom stories.

P.S.: Alt. is where it's at.

We could list alt.binaries from now until next week, but here are a few to get you on the road to Usenet addiction:

```
alt.binaries.pictures.erotica.amateur.male
alt.binaries.pictures.erotica.black.male
alt.binaries.pictures.erotica.furry
```

```
alt.binaries.pictures.erotica.gaymen
alt.binaries.pictures.erotica.male
alt.binaries.pictures.erotica.male.anal
alt.binaries.pictures.erotica.teen.male
alt.binaries.pictures.nudism
alt.pictures.erotica
```

Newsgroups. This is important. Take a deep breath and learn how to create a newsgroup: There's a site called **www.cs.ruu.nl/wais/html/na-bng/alt. config.html** from which you can learn the protocol.

There are about eighteen thousand newsgroups now; there are more sites on the WWW than newsgroups pertaining to gay porn on Usenet. Although Usenet is huge, it doesn't contain the diversity of the WWW. I recommend the Web.

Then there are bulletin board lists (BBS). I mention BBS mechanisms here because they are the "other" Usenet—truly the place to go to post things in a private manner. A great place for BBS-ers is **www.qrd.org/QRD/electronic/queer. bbs.list.** Go there *now.*

Usenet can be wonderful but it is a slightly less intriguing and dynamic medium than the Web, if you are into talking politics, sex, or art. Usenet can fulfill those desires, but you should head to the Web and the many chat rooms if you want to interact with the mainstream gay and lesbian computer using population. The one "kewl" (or cool) aspect of Usenet is that it is the place to find the gay and lesbian cybergeeks. And if you spend the time hanging out at the dirty alt. sites, you will undoubtedly make connections with your favorite freaks. If you want fun, just stick to the boys and girls on the Web.

3

E-MAIL:

Where It's @

Paperless world, my foot. It hasn't happened quite yet. Paper, no matter how many computers are at hand, is still a force to be reckoned with. E-mail, or electronic mail, was an attempt to change that. E-mail was going to be the way to get everyone on line. And maybe one day it will do that.

Nowadays e-mail is merely another electronic thing for people to contend with. The e-pistle is the way to a person's heart or wallet. It is the e-zeest way to get someone to respond to you, the tidiest manner in which to talk back to anyone or any thing. The idea of e-mail being yet another form of communication is a miscalculation, and to relate it to myself I will now tell the story of something I did to make like better for my fellow New Yorkers.

I wrote to Mark Green, the Public Advocate of New York City. (E-mail: mgreen-@pubadvocate.nyc.gov.) Now, perhaps you don't know this, but manicures for men cost $8.50 whereas females get charged $6. "Why?" I asked Green through e-mail. "If you're supposed to be the [high-profile, constantly publicized] advocate for consumers in our town, go find out why men's nails are discriminated against." What gives? I wondered. "It seems (to an out-of-the-closet freak) wholly unfair."

Green got my e- and responded with: "Why not?" I hear he is going to announce his "Gypped by Gender" findings any day now. The moral of the story is that you can get a lot done with e-mail; lots and lots.

For those who can't be bothered, imagine that President Bill, Russ Solomon (the owner of Tower Records), and one-handed Pee Wee Herman himself, not to mention Señor Gates and tons of tech-heads, read every e- they get. Well, maybe not the first Bill. It is a direct connection—you can ask whomever you want whatever you want, as long as you have the address. I wrote Solomon to inquire about his interest in "an available space for a record shop on a totally trendy block"—that is, on my block. He responded thank you and allegedly went on to bid on it! Who's a happy camper?

You don't have to have as big a mouth or the grandiose ideas that I seem to have in good supply. You can write buddies, prospective dates, a high school English teacher, that brother you don't appreciate, or even a talkative friend who, thankfully, moved overseas.

What about the downside of e-mail? One of my least-favorite experiences came from e-pulse, a magazine I subscribe to (free online subscriptions are aplenty) about the wonderful world of music and video. One day Netcom (the internet service provider that handles the listserve for e-pulse) accidentally forwarded nonlistserve mail to my e-mail box and sent mine all over cyberspace. That means I got a thousand e-mails in my crowded box and a zillion complaints from pissed-off subscribers who were receiving my e-mail. The overflow of e-mail crashed my server and irritated internet music fans. I wrote e-pulse, via e-mail, demanding satisfaction for my hardship. They sent me a free CD of New Age music. Whoop-de-do.

Today's e- problem is to enable sexless romances with cyberinformation. This is a world in which television has made many of us think vacuous thoughts nightly—not to mention the predisposition to discuss innocuous situations ("Did you hear what happened to Chandler last night?") at the watercooler every single day.

The promulgators of the internet have successfully found us a new way, in addition to your television-watching habits, and mine, to spend or waste time: Go on line and answer or send e-s to so-called friends in far-off places, mostly people you may never meet and some who (says everyone I've interviewed) are never going to know who you really are. That's fine, until your e-flirtations creep into life and affect your *real* relationships. Then you can have trouble.

Still, users disagree. They say, "Why not play on the net? What good is anonymous talk without anonymity or fiction?" But, seriously, how many times can you describe yourself falsely before it backfires? And, because e-mail allows you to be anything you say you are, you could forget who that is. An e-letter is any letter you can compose, not unlike the storybook, letter-writing romances of the nineteenth century. If only intentions were so pure. So, the moral of e-mail is: Everyone's rubber and you're glue, so don't piss me off and I won't bother you.

E-MAIL 101

If you have never used e-mail before, this is where you will find out how to do it. If you have used e-mail, don't think that there is nothing in this chapter for you; I have hints up the whazoo. Check out the Staying Power section, below, which outlines where e-mail will be sending you in the not-so-far-away future.

In order to send an e-mail message, you write a letter, address it correctly, and it gets to the person addressed in a short time, depending on how you send it. If it goes directly from one address to another on the same Web site, it should be there in seconds. Correspondence going through CompuServe to AOL takes a few hours. (AOL gets overloaded; during Christmas 1995 it actually refused correspondence. So what you write might get lost in the cyber post office.)

You must know the e-mail address of the person who is destined to receive your message. An e-mail address consists of two parts: a user name and a domain name, separated by the symbol @.

For example, if your e-mail address happens to be ethel@merman.com, then ethel is the (your) user name and merman.com is the domain name (the domain is where the user's account resides). Most domain names end in a three-letter code, such as com, edu, or gov, which indicates something about the user's location:

.com	A company or business
.edu	A college or university
.gov	A government office
.mil	A military institution
.net	A network node (usually an internet service provider)
.org	An organization (e.g., professional societies, nonprofit groups)
.bitnet	A BITNET node (BITNET is a university network connected to the internet)

Here are some examples of e-mail addresses using the various domain names.

ken@hq.bigbutt.com	A user at the company, Bigbutt, Inc.
john@biomed.med.yale.edu	A computer user in a department of the Yale medical school
bill@whitehouse.gov	Someone named Bill at some white house

Addresses outside the United States. Those end in two-digit country codes and are usually preceded by .ac (for a university) or .co (for a company). For example:

steen@cu.ac.dk	A student at a Danish university
nikisha@ap.nna.co.au	A user at an Australian company

To send your mail all that you have to do is access the Mail options provided by all of the online services. If you are a student you can usually access Mail by typing mail at the DOS prompt. (Government systems work the same way.) If you have a private shell account (an account that can be obtained from internet providers for minimal cost and allows basic e-mail functions), follow the instructions provided. See Choosing an Online Service later in this chapter.

Here the basic steps to sending e-mail are outlined in this brief task of sending yourself an e-mail.

1. Log on to your account. It can be an online service, a university or government account, or an account from an internet provider.

2. After you are at the host prompt (% or $), type the word mail. If you have an online-service account, you need only click on the Mail icon. (Online accounts also have tons of directions because they charge for time spent sending and receiving e-mail and are desperate for you to learn.)

3. Choose to read, send, edit, or whatever you intend on doing while using your e-mail account. On online services, e-mail options are located in pull-down command boxes. Other types of e-mail software from internet providers simply list e-mail options and ask you to select one. To select the Send option, type send or type edit, or select the appropriate letter, as indicated by your specific e-mail service, to send a message.

4. You are almost there. After you select a Send Mail command, type in the recipient's address. If you are using an online service, you may need to specify that you are mailing to someone outside the service's membership. Don't be afraid to use the help boxes that outline protocol for sending mail outside the service. In all but the latest software offerings, CompuServe says you must use internet: before sending to an address outside CIS; most ask you to write the name "@" the provider's domain address. If you are using DOS, you may need to preface your address with in%ethel@merman. com, to tell the mail software that the address is located on the internet. Because you are sending a message to yourself, you need to type in your own e-mail address at the To: prompt.

5. The Subject: field is important to some e-mail users. If you are sending messages to new individuals, it is wise to use the Subject: field to describe your e-mail. If you want to convey that your message is urgent or important, the Subject: field is the place to do that. To screen out junk mail, some corporations require subjects, so if your friend is a corporate type, it is best to fill out the Subject: field. Also, you need to remember that, in being transferred from one serve to another, your subjectless Subject: field reads, simply, "Message From The Internet." Bo-oring.

6. Now send it. Move the curser to the Send option or the Send icon and click the button. If you are using DOS, hold down the CTRL key and press "z." It is that simple.

A note to the wise: Be careful of what you might send because, once you send it (unless you typed the address incorrectly), you are responsible for what you wrote, and there is no getting it back. The online service, Prodigy, was held accountable—and fined heavily—after someone posted an e-mail that falsely claimed that a stock-broker was breaking SEC rules. The judge ruled that Prodigy was liable for the incorrect information posted in its system. The resulting action was an outspoken need for more legal attention to a newly emerging area of internet litigation.

Consider, too, that angry e-mails are much like angry letters. Experts on netiquette (of which there is little in internet land) say that, when bloated with anger, correspondents should wait for two hours before hitting the SEND key.

CHOOSING AN ONLINE SERVICE

E-mail is cheap, friends. The trick to using this inexpensive device is to get the ultimate out of the ever-changing e-world. Choosing an e-mail provider is a no-brainer. Go with the service that you think will outfit you with what you need: disks, a starter password, groovy contraptions within the system itself, and *lots of* technical support. You may choose a national server, such as IDT, GNN, or Netcom or a local one whose Web site you are attached to—either physically or mentally. It does not matter which you choose, as long as you stick with one address for a while. Changing your address and leaving a dead end for someone who writes you is a no-no. (According to Cybertimes at **www.nytimes.com,** there are inventive companies with names such as Smart Mail who sign you up for e-mail delivery no matter how often you change providers: For upward of $50 per month, you get e-mail forwarded for life. It's expensive so I say feh. You're better off having a smart pigeon deliver it.)

The master list of internet access providers available on the World Wide Web—the address is **www.herbison.com/herbison/iap_meta_list.html**—is a way for you to become educated. Check out the thousands of providers on this site and find one that accommodates your software and economic and geographic needs.

Just like any fairly new technological advance, e-mail costs are all over the playing field. AOL has $19.95 flat fee; CompuServe charges a monthly connection fee of $9.95 for five hours plus $2.95 per extra hour. Prodigy has just announced a plan to charge $19.95 per month, too, for Prodigy Internet. In late 1996 IDT (800-245-8000) offered Netscape and tons of twenty-four-hour customer service for $15.95. AOL, MSN, and CIS are not far behind with offers like that. For most companies, circa 1997, it's around $10; for some, it's about $5. You can even get it free,

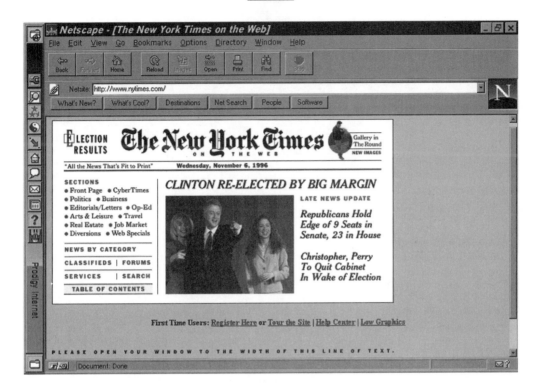

notably if your company has its own Web site or if you are friendly with a provider, café,[1] or tech nerd. (Check out Chapter 1 for online service phone numbers to obtain price quotes specific for your internet needs.) A firm called Juno started a service last year that gives users free e-mail in return for eyes glued to advertisements along the bottom of the screen.

STAYING POWER: OR, E-MAIL DOS AND DONT'S

- What more can we expect from the all powerful e-mail? Not a whole lot. It can only get worse from here. You send a letter to someone you rarely know and he or she responds whenever he or she feels like it. (Receipts let you know your letter was opened, but they cost you and are only valid between same-set servers, that is, within the same provider.)

[1]See Chapter 11, Get Off the Internet.

- Faxing by e-mail: Most services charge a great deal of money for a service that turns e-mail into a fax. (One company started an operation where you can fax into e-mail; it gives the illusion that you're computer literate. Try **www.jfax.com** for a way to fax directly from the net for a few bucks. This is for emergencies only: Online services rip you off faxing. CompuServe sends all faxes out of Columbus, Ohio. For a brief fax you are paying connect time and long-distance charges from area code 614; do the math. AOL has discontinued the flat-fee fax approach and promises to do something soon with faxes! (The Public Relations Department exclaimed, ''Really? No faxes?'') The best thing is to learn how to fax from word processing software (Word, WordPerfect 5.2, 6.0, or 6.1, WinFax, or DragonFax for Macintosh).

- Paging by e-mail: Introduced last year, this is for people with alphanumeric pagers. (For CIS and AOL use the keyword ''pager'' to learn more.) You ask the person sending the e-mail to add the prefix pager: to the address. Suddenly you are paged with e-mail text (186 characters max). You will be buzzing the whole day. CIS started a service, ''calling for e-mails,'' using voice recognition software, as a loss-leader promotion for its long-distance phonecard.

- The feds are not our friends, or privacy means nothing. An article in the *Village Voice,* published while this book was being rushed to the press, reported that two people were snail-mailed (sent by the Postal Service) a dispatch from two fiercely solicitous FBI agents about their American Online IDs were being copied by some porno freaks. These pornophiles were looking for kids on the prowl, those currently roaming AOL or others, photographs of whom had been uploaded to the AOL archives. The Feds happened to be cruising by the very chat room in which the ID holder displayed his desires. The online ID belonged to a middle-aged lady who claimed that she did *not* lend it to anyone.

  After the story was released, an official at the Washington-based Electronic Frontier Foundation (**www.eff.org/blueribbon.com**) was quoted saying, ''Child porn is going to be the McCarthyism of the 90s,'' since the woman in question was not a card-carrying member of the kiddie club.

  In fact, AOL keeps records of zillions of chat-room conversations, e-mail, and possibly more, for days and sometimes months.

  I asked a marketing director of CompuServe, in casual conversation, about ''giving away e-mail or chat-room copy.'' She muttered: ''Do you think we have room at our headquarters for all that drivel?'' In a manner of speaking, no.

  Privacy can be achieved through encryption: You may code e-mail through Pretty Good Privacy (PGP) software available at the local mall's Software Etc. or at a site on the Web called **www.shareware.com** (free!).

- Lists: You can request a subscription to a wide assortment of e-mail lists, commonly known as listservs. I recommend **www.grd.ord/QRD/electronic/email. contacts** for lists of lots of these. A computer address adds your e-mail address to a (usually gigantic) list of recipients for information sent out daily or weekly. In case you are worried about hating the list it is easy to unsubscribe. Sometimes you have to ask them twice. Lists are always free. You pay them only attention.

  To start a subscription, type subscribe on an e-mail (just as you would subscribe to an online magazine). To stop the sub, type unsubscribe and reply via an e-mail; listserv goes both ways!

  One popular but barely known subscription list is from American Airlines. To get this, visit the Netsaver Fares Web site, **www2.amrcorp.com/cgi-bin/aans.** Register and get a list of fares that are published only on internet e-mail. Lists are sent on Wednesday. Tickets must be purchased within twenty-four hours of making reservations. The fares are often one-third off the regular, listed price, but these flights are for departure that Saturday, returning Monday or Tuesday. Several other airlines have similar services.

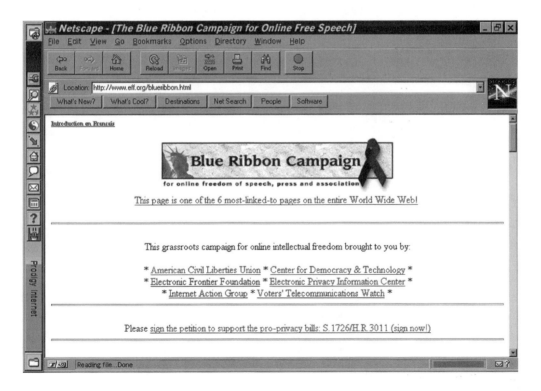

Gay lists include one that comes three or four times a day to my box. Don't subscribe to this unless gay and lesbian news in the media really intrigues you. You are warned. **BSC41@aol.com** belongs in the internet hall of fame. It is an uncannily well collected gay research list that accommodates whatever the so-called straight media will or won't report on, even uploading the gif-image photos. The manager of this changes intermittently, so ask Bill Stosine at this address; he started gay-o-l, an e-mail newsgroup on AOL about all things gay. It seems that once he got going he was hard to stop.

It is important to know what to avoid in the future, as you become more of a cyberqueer and are inundated with e-mail messages. Gay Listservs, though not highly recommended:

> **GLB_Press@listserv.blue.aol.com**—press releases for any-thing gay and lesbian
>
> **GLB_DISCUSS@listserve.aol.com**—discussion of gay and les-bian topics
>
> **chorus@physics.utoronto.ca**—discussion list for members of gay and lesbian choruses; obscure; clean fun
>
> **www.queerplanet@abacus.oxy.edu**—information and discus-sions of gay and lesbian issues; more political (calls for action and that kind of thing) and more global than other lists

- E-mailability: You want to be more popular? Sure you do. Here's an easy way to get more friends and influence people daily. Find out who might—sometimes—be fun to talk to and ask for his or her address. But do this carefully or you may end up sifting through unwanted responses to queer-ies, often hundreds of them. And that is truly a time waster.

    Answer the e-mails you most want to answer, stockpile the others into two categories: (1) those from the people most likely to do something for you (even if that means become a decent social drinking partner) and (2) those you must answer.

- E-mail nuttiness: You and I might get carried away by our e-mail fancies. Recently, a *Wall Street Journal* story noted that "checking your e-mail more than once a day" is the ultimate time waster. What an exaggeration. I mean, really—excuse me a minute while I check my e-mail—doing too much of this good thing cannot happen. Why not? (Oh, look, a letter from Mom!) Just imagine constantly seeing how popular you are. I do understand that some people might feel sad because they don't *get* any mail. The coffee-shop guy I met wrote me first for a change!

    You get the idea.

Sign up with a service provider that includes a Send and Receive All Mail function in its software. It downloads everything into an in basket while you go for milk. It saves time—particularly online time, which is charged by the minute.

- Spamming: It's the craze, all the rage, and it pretty much sucks. Spamming is "the sending of an inappropriate message to a large audience." It is often called mail bombing because unsolicited e-s are sent by every marketer who has a ten-dollar e-mail address. Mail-bombing is something you must be careful of, because one sender can dispatch so many spams as to single-handedly kill a server with overload. Then you're in trouble. Angry mail comes your way. Flames are messages that go after you, specifically to bug you. In newsgroups often someone will misspell a common word and thus a spelling flame erupts, with everyone in the group attempting to prove his or her spelling prowess. What to do? Don't sign up for anything on the Web that gives your e-mail address to weirdos; go after subscriptions to online magazines (see Chapter 7) and only well-maintained lists.
- Watching out: People can act strangely when they write an e-. You may think that's their personality, or better yet, you might think that's the way they write letters. An e-mail letter is *not* the same as a letter our grammar school teacher taught us to write. These people are typing and wanting to get it out of the way. As one scribe said to another: "I'm a writer, you're a typist."

    So, be careful: The recipient might read what you write. People often duplicate the messages you send. (Am I scaring you?) And don't forget that a message that is read once can be saved and read again.
- Length. Space. Time. And wasted length, space, and time: Let's just leave this one to Mark Twain who once said, "If I had more time I would have written less." Apt.
- Cleaning out: Just like hard drives, e-mail boxes can crash. I implore you, as a public service, to get rid of the junk you have saved in your in basket and don't be intimidated by the DELETE key. I have no desire to keep all my friends' cherished recipes when I don't ever cook.
- Cheap Tricks (Three): Most e-mail providers will provide session settings that include Preferences. Click the box that says Auto File and, presto chango, a copy of what you wrote remains in the file cabinet. Netscape gives you the option of copying letters to yourself.

    Always unclick the box that, in the CIS system, reads Show Recipients. (Other systems will have similar wording.) CompuServe, which allows you to affix any type of file when sending an e-pistle, was the first to figure out how to make every person feel special, even if a group of fifty receives the same message. Unclicking the Recipients box is a way to prevent recipients from seeing if anyone else got the same letter.

    Some cybersmarties have developed software for users of e-mail-on-the-Web to include a hyperlink right off e-mail to a site. Accessorize, darling: "You can never have enough hats, gloves and shoes."[2]

- Junk E-: People get your address if you sign onto anything—gay or otherwise. With gay sign-ons you have joined all those guys and gals with disposable income for sellers, yada-yada, one of the most exciting modem-using classes to date. Congratulations. Now hawkers will go after you and sell like crazy. These are examples of what I call *oy-mail*. According to popular wisdom, we'll buy anything . . . vacuum cleaners started it.

I got the strangest e-mail from a prospective congressman, no less. He went on AOL and found or was sold the address of every gay person who had logged onto chat schedules for a month. He wrote us a long letter that I will mercifully excerpt.

> I am writing to introduce myself. My name is Brian Steel, and I am a candidate in the Democratic Primary for the U.S. House of Representatives from the 8th Congressional District in Manhattan and Brooklyn.
>
> I cannot tell if you are a voter who is eligible to vote in the Democratic Primary this September 10. My campaign is hopeful that our computers might provide one way that you can communicate with me, and me with you.
>
> I have a Web Page—"www.briansteel.com." There you will find information about me and the campaign. Please take a moment to download my campaign photo. Don't forget to vote on September 10.

And so it began: One volatile recipient of his solicitation reminded Brian of the AOL Terms of Service one agrees to when becoming a member:

> You may not use AOL to send unsolicited advertising, promotional material, or other forms of solicitation to other members except in those specified areas that are designated for such a purpose (e.g., the classified area) unless you receive the express permission of the Member. You may not use AOL to collect or "harvest" screen names of other Members without the express prior permission of the Member. AOL Inc. reserves the right to block or filter mass e-mail solicitations on or through AOL.

Another member added, "Think about it for a moment: Why should you vote for any politician who campaigns by breaking the Terms of Service that he agreed to with the medium (AOL) that he is using to solicit your vote? AOL doesn't allow this!"

Brian lost.

---

[2]"Absolutely Fabulous," darling.

- Boxes: In. Out. Addresses. Easy. Make sure you keep an online Address Book; nothing is worse than calling someone more than once for his address. Don't ask, "Do you have an e-mail address?" because that's like asking "Do you have a fax?" If someone doesn't have both, find a new person to date, write to, or even call.

  Great tip for dating: how to find someone's address. The expensive way is to go on AOL (ten dollars) and look them up in the directory; then, if that does not work, go on CIS and look them up (ten dollars). I'd even download Netscape (see Chapter 7) and look up e-mail addresses on the World Wide Web information service, aka **www.four11.com/**.

- Lively e-mail of the future ("Did you say post office?"): In 1997 cyberlopes are going to make a splash for thirty-five cents per piece. Just like stamps by mail, a 'lope will be the first officially sanctioned online U.S. Postal goodie. The USPS got smart and issued its e-service with privacy attached. They guarantee it. . . . [joke]

  Cyberlopes are also going to be advertising vehicles. These are beautiful for marketers because recipients decide whether or not to open the mail. If they say no, it goes back. If they choose to accept, the marketer has met his mark and will begin bombing them with e-mail offers. It's the newest letter bomb: An unsuspecting naif gets besieged with direct e-hawking.

- Cellular e-mail and satellite e-mail: Cellular e-mail is simply this: Buy a cell-phone cable (AT&T sells this for forty dollars), hook the computer into the cell communicator, and connect to your provider. The venture can be expensive, because it takes time and, at sixty-five cents per minute, this adds up. Punch in your code through an ASCII dialer or terminal emulator and get your e-mail. There are other systems, too, including satellite systems for as little as twenty dollars per month, but they have not been proven totally effective as yet.

  The future cellular will be. Soon you won't have to add anything to your computer because new models will come equipped with built-in cellular modems. Our lives will be more like the Jetsons' lives than ever before, (without AOL commercials).

- All those ads. How can I avoid them?: First, don't respond to anything like this:

A FREE BUSINESS ON-LINE MAGAZINE . . . .
   Hot business Web sites!
   How to make more money!
   How to write killer ads!

Scam city. Online users get besieged by mail that hits all-time marketing lows. Go with brands you know (such as, *e-pulse* from Tower Records) and avoid the blitz when your address gets picked up.

   Second, remember that sometimes people are pulling your leg. Pull theirs back. Here's an allegory: In the book business smarmy marketers have figured out what I call the "Post-it theory of selling." They send you a typeset article, ostensibly torn from the pages of a business magazine, that raves about a reference set selling for $400. On it is a Post-it note: "I loved this. Thought you would too. Best, J." It's postmarked Santa Rosa CA. Who do you know with the initial J in Santa Rosa? Yeah, right.

These days you'll find "J" working overtime on the internet. The same company—or a cheap imitator—sent me this:

Hi,
Came across this Web site and thought you might be interested. It's about the best selling recording of all time. You can find it at [the name of a bogus site].
Talk with you soon.

J.

I replied: "We know your number and how to reach you." The company (e-mail express at **www.empxp.emxp.com**) told me I was off their list. Small wonder.

- Fake-mail is a company now: To make things worse, you can now change the identity and thus the integrity of mail you send. Click onto **www.fakemail.com** or use a search engine and look up "fakemail" for a better URL. to discover how to disguise your return address when sending e-mail. This is an amusing concept until it is done to you.

- What can be added to e-s: Your service probably allows you to "say something" at the end of each e-mail you write. These cute, lines are called *signatures* (sigs) and can be found in the setup commands of almost all internet e-mail providers, but not, for now, on CompuServe, AOL, or MSN, though the latter promises it any day now. Prodigy has net mail in its just-launched Prodigy Internet browser, which is content on a browser (see Online Services for more on this).[3] A sig, may be an address, a slogan, your saying-of-the-day, whatever you wish. Once arranged, it will be automatically pasted at the bottom of your message as an afterthought. Some people have done wonders with this; others have embarrassed me. For instance, I laughed when I got a wonderfully snarky e-mail from **www.suck.com,** a Web site that derides the WWW each day. Their afterthought was: *Have you told someone you love to suck today?* People will define you by what you put on the bottom of your mail. Don't advertise—unless it's funny. The afterthought ad for **www.-sonicnet.com,** the top alternative-music Web site, always leaves 'em with a smile: *We drink more coffee and smoke more cigarettes before 9 A.M.* than you do in a single day.

---

[3]"Net mail" is internet mail that you can access anywhere but is set up by a provider, e.g., Prodigy.

- Voice your e-mail: Show the world how gay you sound! Or sound off about being gay. They, AOL and CIS, have introduced a very complicated voice mail, so don't bother. Call your local phone company. It allows the sound cards in your computer to sound like you do. This is not very different from forwarding voice mail.[4]
- Emoticons and the language: Listed below are emoticons, little cryptic codes used in e-mail messages to express the emotion of spoken words, and words that users find helpful in typed conversation. Many are taken from the online services Prodigy, CompuServe, and AOL. For more gay-friendly ones, do what I do: Make them up. And I kid you not about any of these. (Okay, there is *one*.)

Emoticon (noun). A figure created with the symbols on the keyboard.

Emoticon	Meaning

How are you smiling

:–1	Smiley blockhead
:–i	Semi-Smiley
:–p	User is sticking tongue out (at you!)
:–#	User's lips are sealed.
:–9	User licking its lips
:–(	Drama
:–)	Comedy
:–\	Popeye's smiling face, for people who look like Popeye
:–c	Bummed-out Smiley
:–)	Winking Smiley

Tell me about your anatomy

.–)	User has one eye
:–	User is male
:–)–{8	User is a big girl
= = = = = =>	Feeling excited
: =)	User has two noses
(–:	User is left-handed
:>)	User has a big nose
:)8 =	Female

---

[4]AT&T can forward voice mail at later date; just ask the operator on the company's 800 number. It costs several dollars, though.

Bad or good hair day, your option

:–%	User has beard
:–{	User has mustache
:–=)	Older user with mustache
–:–)	User sports a mohawk and admires Mr. T
{[:–)	User is wearing toupee.
:–@	User's beard has permanent wave, or, was drawn by Picasso
{:–)	Smiley with hair parted in the middle
(–)	User needs a haircut

Some habits, no nuns

:–o	Doing something with mouth open
:–?	User smoking a pipe
:–)'	User tends to drool
:–D	User talks too much

Bad-d experience

:–'|	User has a cold
:–t	User is cross
:–*	User just ate a sour pickle
:–&	User is tongue-tied
:–(	Sad
:–s	User after a BIZARRE comment
:–|	BORING
:–@	User face screaming
<:|	Dunce

Feeling gorgeous

:–)8	User is well dressed
:–X	User wearing a bow tie
:–}	User wears lipstick
:–X	User changed sex
:–Q	Smoker

Feeling beastly

8:]	Normal smiling face except that user is a gorilla
#–)	User partied all night

@–)	User is Cyclops
= :–)	User is a hosehead
:%)%	User has acne
:~)	User's face needs a nose job; no explanation necessary

Feeling sacreligious or religious or just blasphemous

+ :–)	Smiley priest
+–(:–)	User is the pope
*:o)	User is a bozo

Feeling dramatic

8–|	Suspense
8–#	Death
,–}	Wry and winking
:–P	Yuk
>:–<	Mad

Four Eyes

8–)	User wears glasses
8:–)	User wears glasses on forehead
B–)	Horn-rims
B–|	User wearing cheap sunglasses
g–)	Smiley with pince-nez glasses

The following acronyms were collected from hundreds of e-mail and chat addicts. These are used as e-mail accoutrements.

Where are you going?

BFN	Bye For Now
BBL	Be Back Later
BRB	Be Right Back
OTL	Out To Lunch
FB	Files Busy
RNA	Ring, No Answer (communication or telephone term for a problem; this is something all telephone users should remember, because it answers a time-wasting problem concisely

Conveying what you really mean

LOL	Laugh Out Loud (most popular phrase in acrolanguage)
BTW	By The Way
FUBAR	"Fouled" Up Beyond All Recognition
FWIW	For What It's Worth
FYI	For Your Information

Feeling like a cutie pie

g	Grin—usually in brackets [g] or angle brackets <g>
gd&h	Grinning, ducking, and hiding
gd&r	Grinning, ducking, and running
gd&r, vvf	Grinning, ducking, and running, very very fast

. . . bitchy!! . . .

HSIK	How Should I Know?
IAE	In Any Event
INAL	I'm Not A Lawyer
IMO	In My Opinion
NOYB	None Of Your Business
PITA	Pain In The Ass
PMJI	Pardon My Jumping In
RTFM	Read The Fine Manual

Avoiding conflict

IMHO	In My Humble Opinion
IOW	In Other Words
JFYI	Just For Your Information
LMAO	Laughing My Ass Off
NBD	No Big Deal
OIC	Oh, I See
OTOH	On The Other Hand

Too much!

ROFL	Rolling On Floor Laughing [very popular]
ROTF	Rolling On The Floor
ROTF,L	Rolling On The Floor, Laughing

As if!

TTFN	Ta Ta For Now
WYSIWYG	What You See Is What You Get
WTH	What The H—
WOA	Work Of Art
RSN	Real Soon Now

- Be a pal, Richard: "Like, if I'm an e-mail virgin, what can I do to try this out?" Try **infobot@infomania.com.** You send them mail and the server sends you one back. It's like learning what number you dial to find out automatically what number you're calling from (dial 958). This will give you something to do while you're reading the following.
- The Final Word on E-Mail:

  I think most people are afraid that once they connect to e-mail they will never stop. That's probably true. Silly and needless fears arise from one's lack of knowledge about computers. Starting an e-mail habit makes even the shyest mortal a more communicative person. And every stay-at-home shuttered in by his own fears can learn a great deal about the outside world, by giving in and getting online.

  Meanwhile, I don't really care because e-mail is here to stay. I know it for a fact. I got one today from my sixty-four-year-old mother. She learned how to use a computer a month ago, so it has to be *that* easy. If you use it only sporadically, you can make it a habit by creating an address book that includes everyone you know or by adding their e-mail addresses to a new address book. The process is a helluva lot cheaper than using stamps.

  My mom'll tell you. Just e-mail her at **mom@yeahwhatever.com.**

4

COMMERCIALLY SERVICEABLE

What is an online service? It is most assuredly not the world. If we can be real about it, and most services would rather not have you think this, they are nothing compared to the world of the net. A famous computer geek once said, "A person who is attached to the internet has access to every other computer in the world that is attached to the internet and the available information on those computers." How daunting is that?

I took a survey (which was covered by our friends at the *New York Post* last year) in which I asked about a hundred people why they chose to accept the free ten, fifteen, and now fifty (call (800) 414-8811, AOL's offer may run out) hours from CompuServe (CIS), American Online (AOL), Microsoft Network (MSN), and Prodigy.

What can online services do for you in relation to the internet? Online services are not the internet although, commercial breadwinners that they are, they would like you to believe that they are. They only give you access to the internet. AOL and CIS work hard to ensure your connection to the internet and therefore hope you'll think that they are all you need.

Online services are useful because, in addition to granting access to the internet, they allow access to information databases that are not accessible to the general internet users. These databases range in topics from the weather to the latest advances in biotechnology in Europe. Additionally, they provide forums from print and other media (National Geographic, Time Warner, the ever-popular Pets Forum—we kid you not) that allow communication with other subscribers to the service. The forums are, however, monitored and regulated by people who want you to "be good" and not speak about the things on your mind—if the things on your mind are not PG rated.

What do the services have that people want? In this day and age, where for 20 bucks you can have unlimited access to all things Web, why should people care in the least about the three-dollars-an-hour stuff on the ancient services? Or even 20 bucks for a month on them?

Turns out there's a lot going on.

In the early days of CompuServe and Prodigy (before AOL joined up), this was the only way for the not-so-computer-savvy to get anything done. The services provided text-based systems on which you typed away and eventually got the information you needed. Prodigy even had a color-bar at the bottom. That was an ad.

Soon Bill Gates's Windows exploded on the scene and CompuServe, which had already developed its Information Manager to some acclaim, offered WinCim, the Windows CompuServe Information Manager. What happened next was revolutionary: graphic images and lots more, right on your screen, from your 2,400-bps modem . . . unbelievable.

The rest of the story is easy to swallow: AOL improved on WinCim with its own Windows version and the world became hooked on online services.

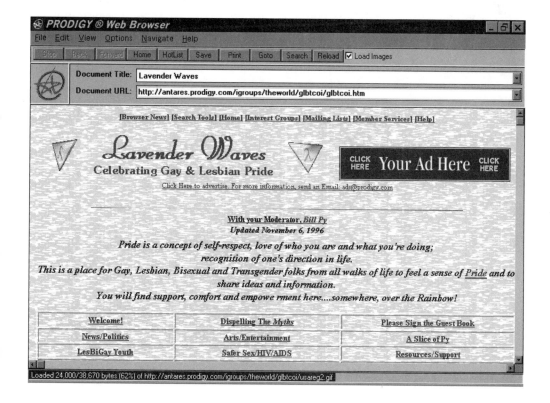

But what about 1997? Why use them now? The answer: There is a feeling of community that comes with being on such services as MSN. (In the early stages of MSN, our group felt that this was a product developed by someone who, like Linda Ronstadt during her "standards" phase, was doing songs known to every radio listener through the ages—and yet sang as though she was the one who wrote them.)

The following year Macintosh loyalists got their own MacCim and Mac software from AOL. And Mac users were hit hard in the mail to use the system. (Both AOL and CIS offer horrible internet connectivity for the Mac.) Currently, everyone including Prodigy is rushing to help Mac users get their net. Prodigy was first with Windows/MAC all-in-one CD-ROM in late 1996.

In the online world, people stick around because they want safety. Your comrades will use it, at the very least, for the five free hours. I interviewed a host of users who told me they wanted a place they could call home. One user told me, "This online service gives me something that isn't in the least difficult to attain, and we know how to do it." It explains why millions stay on AOL, when, in the words of one member, "I feel as though I'm in a place I can't get out of. I hate the service but it's the e-mail address I've given everyone."

Why hate a service? AOL, unlike the other services, is a sales-oriented operation. When you enter the others (CompuServe, Prodigy, MSN), you are given options of what you want to do, but as soon as you go onto AOL, you are asked to buy something. When you try to leave, they want to know if you are sure and you have to exit three separate times.

The fabulous new software of 1997 (AOL 3.0 and CIS 3.0.1) allows people to connect directly to the World Wide Web, then transfer *back* to the online services. This is an agreeable notion because people want online services for forums, information and chatting, connecting to the internet, and e-mail. (CIS 3.0.1. is tough to configure though.)

E-mail is often the reason that many people use a computer in the first place. CompuServe's rules and AOL's rules are basically the same, except for the wording. AOL doesn't think of its members as computer geeks so it spells everything out: Send Mail Later is how AOL puts it; CompuServe says Outbox. CIS, MSN, and Prodigy are from the old school and believe that people should not think of e-mail as anything but computer mail. MSN has funny symbols that read Compose Reply to Sender—a little stuffy but definitely computerese. MSN and AOL let you call yourself anything you want—a Screen Name that really makes life easy for you and those who send you mail. Prodigy has an obnoxious code-number system—mine is xvcq0 for God's sake—but they are straining to change to word names. CompuServe just finally added a personal ID system to replace its admittedly antiquated numbers. CIS customers probably hate it. Unlike Prodigy, on which you would write to **laermer@prodigy.net,** until recently CompuServe asked you to scribble **rlmedia@ cis.compuserve.com.** (These are real IDs; use them mercifully.)

To make matters worse, the CompuServe software demands in recent versions of CIM that you write in the recipient's name first, then the internet address. (CIS was in January taking the name out, leaving the address in.)

In a CompuServe discussion group about sending a message, I unearthed the following Q & A:

Q: How do I send a CompuServe Mail message after I have finished composing or uploading it?

A: If you have composed your message online, select Send or Send with Receipt($) from the CompuServe Mail Send Menu. You will be prompted:

Send to (Name or User ID):

Carefully type the User ID number or name of the person to whom you want to send the message. (Note: you can only enter a person's name at this prompt if you have previously entered their name and User ID number into your CompuServe Mail Address Book.) CompuServe Mail will prompt you to enter a subject. Type the subject of the message (which can be up to 32 characters long) and press ENTER or RETURN key.

If you have entered your own name in your Address Book, CompuServe Mail will automatically sign your name to the message. If you have not, you will be asked to type in your name for that message.

Next, your To:, From:, and Subject: entries are redisplayed and you are asked to verify them. If you enter NO, you will be returned to the Send Menu where you can choose the option SEND and enter the correct sending information.

If at any time—even after you have entered the addressee's name or User ID number and are at the Subject: prompt—you want to return to the Send Menu, just press the ENTER or RETURN key.

CompuServe Mail will respond with the prompt ''% Message Not sent; Press <CR>!'' Press the ENTER or RETURN key to display the Send Menu.

Lastly, a bit on software. For those who remember DOS—the software for those who like to type commands from the C prompt—there is still a version of CompuServe for DOS. I recommend that beginners who are not already hooked on either Mac or Windows use DosCim. People say DOS is antiquated; it is. Still, I can retrieve my mail from DosCim in about ten seconds.

And now, the services as they stand.

COMPUSERVE (CIS)

Though it is relatively easy to manage CompuServe, it is still written as though code for computer geeks. For instance, instead of options such as Read Mail or Old Mail (as AOL has it), CompuServe still uses the term Outbasket. Also, there's a space for the name of the person to whom you are writing, even though an internet address is all you need. You, once again, need a person's name here—Richard Laermer—followed by the e-mail address.

As on all online services, the chat areas on CompuServe are the most popular. Within the chat areas, there are channels. Channels are simply designated chatting areas that are usually labeled by topic. For example, a popular channel in a gay or lesbian area might be Gay Marriage. Some online services let you create the channel topics yourself or recommend channel topics to others. On the IRC you can create your own entire channel (see Chapter 6).

The Gender Alternatives/Gay and Lesbian Lifestyles channel on CB is where the queers used to go. That was when people had few or no alternatives. As on AOL and most "proprietary services," these channels do not permit obscene or sexually explicit language. Nowadays most people are on CompuServe's fag lifesaver called Pride, and some men still hang out on what was once called Alternative Line, now the Gay Channel. It's Channel 33, where men feel that the best way to win friends is to keep telling the world how big their dicks are. The action is in rooms and once in a while you can get some long-distance, one-hand action from platonic (overtly sexual) friends.

A channel is something you dial up very much like the CB channels that were a craze of the 1970s. Everyone has them—except MSN, the new boy in town, which has a new "channels" system for all their content, and it's a way for people to dial up someone else comfortably.

On Channel 34 lesbians trade stories, constantly. Channel 13 is for transvestites—empty space. The people who show here are usually there to find friendship, not to perform (ha). CompuServe is a more international service than the others so you can find lots of Europeans and Asians here.

Until the 1997 introduction of "Café Q," Pride Central is your spot on CompuServe for all the gay and lesbian chat, news, celebrity appearances, and personal therapy you can handle. Once you have logged onto CompuServe, pull down Services, click Go, type pride, and you're on your way.

As the introduction of Pride states, "Here we offer a complete range of online content for the Gay, Lesbian, Bisexual and Transgendered [sic] communities." (Tran . . . what?) This is definitely true, and the Get On with It journey through their site proved to be quite cute, at times reminding me of my coming out days. Shockingly, the vocabulary was a little more suggestive.

Upon entering the site, you can inundate yourself with information and ideal chat on gay events in Helsinki, Finland, (Global Gay Pride Calendar), or join Jeff, your bar host at the virtually Picadilly Plaza bar (Pride Central Conference and chat schedule) and maybe plan your own meeting place with Jeff in the virtual Andes. Personally, the act of meeting my favorite Republican fag discussing issues of invisibility (Pride Opinions: Gay Marriage Letters—Gay Republicans) was an eye opener indeed.

There are many areas in Pride. Some are well worth the virtual trip and others seem to send you on a, well, virtual roller-coaster ride to a very real "shut down." When that happens, just use CompuServe (same price as AOL and Prodigy in early 1997) as the more business-oriented service, with references and databases like none other.

Chatting with CompuServe Gays and Lesbians

One advantage to using CIS is that its format is easier to understand than AOL's, because the AOL throws up so much information that you can often become disgusted with the choices and simply sign off!

Here's an example of what you might see on CIS, something I participated in quite happily:

\<King Konger\>	Any London boys out there?
\<Turbo\>	Hey, how about NYC . . . *grin*!
\<King Konger\>	I have always wanted to visit. . . . :)!!!
\<Turbo\>	Well maybe we could arrange something if you bring a friend.
\<King Konger\>	Me got a boyfriend!
\<Turbo\>	If so, bring him along . . . that could be fun!!!!
\<King Konger\>	AHHHHHHH . . . don't tease me.

Good news for lesbians. I found CompuServe to be a meeting place for women without all kinds of straight men posing incognito. (A lesbian matchmaker is present!) I got this information from talking to a few women who knew a little too much about Leslie Newman, Susie Sexpert, and the place "where women long to be guys." They were having a fun time, speaking highly of their experiences on the cyberhighway. (One wonders if they worked for Pride.)

Matchmaker WWW Connection

On a Pride Web site linked from CompuServe, **www.pridemedia.com** boys get matched, but what a frustrating experience it is. There are too many bugs in the program—you can plug right in from CIS—and you are bound to pull your hair out when you fill in the stereotypical questionnaire, and find that you need to fill it in ten more times. This, according to the Pride manager sysop, is something CIS asked them to do: They want to ensure the pre- and post-matches are "real."

Not all of us subscribe to such narrow-minded categorizations of gay men as found on Matchmaker. However, if you're desperate, narrow-minded, and can't even type to communicate with people on the WWW, then this is the forum (or Web site) for you.

News

Filled with some of the most popular news releases pertaining to issues of gays and lesbians. However, the folders are only these: gay, lesbian, and medical—not a very creative way to break down information. We hope that, because Pride is only a few months old, they are still working on it.

Let's hope for a future in which gays and lesbians are represented better. The diverse concerns of gay cyberculture news freaks are not to be found on *any* service.

Health

Chatting about health can be great—well, maybe not that great if you are un-well. (See Chapter 10 for Health Webs.) We found Pride, however, to have a fun series of exchanges arranged for people who like to exchange not bodily fluids but concerns.

This topic of health, huge in the gay community, came to light here and was subdivided well. Then again, there are so few people on the health forum that in order to fill those areas, you might end up talking to yourself. I would like to see more forums dedicated to other aspects of gay and lesbian culture besides health, or is this a front for HIV+ individuals? If so, then state it rather than code it. I think they need to work a bit more on the direction and goals of the health forum on Pride.

Online Therapy

Yeah, a great idea. This forum serves as a cyber group-therapy session. What every gay and lesbian needs a dose of every once in a while. It's hard enough being a human, let alone a gay person. Many of the questions are predictable, but the answers are thought provoking and helpful. I wonder what happens to the people who receive this information? Pride says they have no idea. We hope they're officially cured!

Here are snippets sent to Dr. Jesse Miller, "one of the foremost authorities in psychology"—and a cutup too:

Cliff, age 26

I have always been attracted to hairy chested men. Lately, it seems like an obsession. I have to purchase many magazines to find pictures of them. I walk the street hoping to catch a glimpse of one. I can only have sex with hairy men, not smooth chested. I was wondering if this is common? If not, how do I stop thinking about them?

Becca, age 27

I have been married for 7 years. I have had fantasies about sexual relationships with women for over 10 years. When I was in high school I had a brief encounter with a friend. As I get older the desire to have a relationship with a woman is constantly in my mind. I have mentioned this to my husband, in passing, and he gets annoyed. He is extremely homophobic. I want to experiment but I don't want to hurt him. What should I do?

Frank, age 37

My lover of two years and I are experiencing difficulty in negotiating frequency of sex with each other. We have an open-ended agreement, due to travel exigencies. However, lately I am not as interested in him sexually as he is in me. I have a great deal of difficulty in connecting the "sex act" with a loving relationship. In fact, I acknowledge being quite compartmentalized in that area, due to background events too numerous and intense to mention here. Since I "know" my lover, he is no longer "mysterious" to me, I do not develop the (for me) proper fantasy that enables me to become aroused . . . Any suggestions?

Rob, age 20

Well my problem started about a week ago. I was having sex with guy I know and he put a video in, it was him and another guy. I was really turned on by the fact that I was having it off with the same guy that was on the T.V. In one scene he was fisting another guy, which has always interested me. I've wanted to try it since I was 17 but never had the balls to ask anyone (how do you pose the question could you shove your hand up my A**). So anyway, I asked my friend who then arranged a threesome with another guy. Well everything went ok but I've been bruised and slightly torn since I had had some speed and a lot of poppers to be able to do this. It was a week ago now and the bruising is still pretty bad so what caused the bruising to be so severe when I've spoken to so many others who say they've been fisted and they did not get quite so much pain?

The answers to these questions and concerns can be found in the cyberdoctor's office. A quote from the doctor: "All of us at PRIDE! are delighted albeit overwhelmed by the number of questions you've sent—and by your rapid responses to my thoughts. We are developing a 'virtual community psychology' here and as our interactive therapy develops, I'll get to know and appreciate your diversity, while you will, hopefully, get a sense of my intractable pragmatism."

I think you will find many of the doctor's answers enlightening and thought provoking. However, I think the doctor is right in referring to himself as pragmatic. Some of his rhetoric is tiresome and reveals something of his own problems that need a little cyberpsychology, but that is refreshing, and tells me he is probably a truthful guy. But I do wonder what his credentials are, and how his cyberpatients have fared with his comments. (See Chapter 10 for the scoop on Dr. Miller.)

Wanda

Wanda rocks! What a trip this spam-eating, Velveeta-microwaving, Oklahoma trailer-trippin' advice cybercolumnist is. She is filled with absolutely no advice for the sincerely desperate and with tons of humor for the desperately lonely. Enjoy and check out her gifs ("pictures" in cyber language).

One of my favorite recipes from Wanda, included with advice on how to rake in the Tupperware dollars:

> At the Tupperware party serve my famous Cheese Blackout: Take 1 potato and slice it in a casserole (that means big pan). Then top with 1 large brick of Velveeta. Mix in a cheese-powder packet from a box of Macaroni and Cheese, then top with Cheetos. Bake this for 30 minutes in a 350-degree oven and serve. When your guests eat it, their systems will be so shocked with lactose that they'll literally black out. Now, while [they are] unconscious, fill out their order forms for as much Tupperware as possible, then thank them when they come to. Let them know their order will arrive in 6–8 weeks. Put the pan to soak and, voila! you're a star to Tupperware Inc. You've hosted a fabulous party and you've made $150. You can thank me later.
>
> "Café Q" was unavailable for review as of the publication date of this book.

GETTING IT ON WITH AOL

Inexperienced surfers may find themselves floating away from shore on a sea of information. You had better be goal oriented or you will be reading a list of Ways to Recycle Your Kitty Litter.

AOL can be an overwhelming experience, and Jim Wayand—who is the marketing manager of QView—attests to that. "We offer a lot on the gay and lesbian forum, and a lot of the time people don't know where to start."

I find the Gay and Lesbian Community Forum (GLCF), which is run by Michelle Quirk, quite educational and newsy and for general information a must. Yet it is a traffic jam at all times, congested with stuff that, frankly, doesn't really belong there.

It definitely needs some reorganization and an overhaul is planned. Its online service counterparts tell me that they will be on the Web shortly.

Chat channels, which are AOL's mainstays and among Ms. Quirk's few productions, are often so crowded you want to jump ship (pun intended). If you aren't careful, you end up in a screaming match in the Romping Room merely to gain free time on AOL. It's a horrific experience. In general you start to like the GLCF as you make more use of it. But it's exasperatingly huge. First you have to get away from the seaweed at shore. And that goes for even the most experienced Web users.

News

Upon entering the News folder (which also incorporates all of GLCF's Politics folders), you will find that you can choose to search the entire AOL database for any article, tidbit, or Traditional Values Coalition quote with the Gay Map on AOL, or see the Pride Press, message boards, or file library.[1]

The GLCF Pride Press, published twice a month, is filled with all of the latest news about gays and lesbians. With all credit due to Ms. Quirk and the group, it is an amazing resource for someone who does not have the time, computer know-how, or energy to search for interesting current topics related to our lives. If you live in the hinterland, you should look no further.

Presentation is embarrassing. I think watching my screen saver is more exciting than sifting through this nonsensical mess. Nevertheless, if you have the time, Pride Press is a great resource, but wear shades to cut the glare of the memolike appearance.

The News folders are tons of fun, but only if you have the time. Here are the preachers, the people who seriously dislike gay people but "want to help." Then there are the gay people whose sole mission online is to get you to become more of an activist. Here's an example of the former group (much more fun than the latter group[2]), visiting a rather dated, but frequent theme of some visitors to GLCF.

Subj: YES, GAYS DO HAVE RIGHTS!

From: Big Ron S

According to the one true, JUST and loving God, gays have two rights: LIFE and REPENTANCE or DEATH. Choose LIFE my friends. I don't hate gays. I have compassion for those who are confused and misled. I love you and HE LOVES YOU TOO! But, continue in your ways and you can be assured of punishment from on high. No, I'm not gonna throw scripture at ya . . . no need for that. I just want you all to know that I have compassion for you and you are in my prayers. Do reconsider, please?

[1]There are some things AOL won't allow and shies away from. Or, rather, censors.
[2]It is scary to read these diatribes, but, I figure, live and let live. Just don't frighten the horses, sirs!

Thanks, Ron. If responding to people like him is your idea of pleasure, you'll love some of the "Big Rons" on AOL. But let's not bash all love/hate/opinion messages, because other news boards hold a plethora of information, everything from "what I'm seeking" ads to those postings pertaining to current legislation in almost every state, as well as international laws affecting the lives of gays and lesbians. This forum emphasizes one of the advantages of the internet for gays and lesbians by informing everyone around the globe about local issues for which gays and lesbians outside the region can actually lend their support. Peeking a little deeper in the folders, you can even find a list of U.S. senators and their e-mail addresses. (See Chapter 2 for even more information on how to learn about concerns of gays and lesbians around the country and the globe.) Our problem with this section was that we could never download that information because the Download button never seemed to work. Sometimes I wondered if I'd paid the Amex bill.

The Library is a legal index. Offering this information on the internet is a great idea to open the eyes of gays and lesbians to the legalspeak surrounding decisions affecting our daily breath. If you think about it, gay life is a battle of words at the political level; the forum opens our eyes to that dimension of communication.

In the News, a resource on the main news folder, combines all of the latest events in a topical order. However, it fails to tell you the news of the day, requesting, instead that you to seek through lots of folders. This is a mess. (But time wasting is the name of the game; remember, you are being clocked!) If you're into the news of the day and know the exact subject, welcome to the place. Otherwise, head to the site of your favorite publication, ask someone online, or go to the daily papers. Also, one of the news areas is called Gay TV. I thought Gay TV was about gays on TV, information about characters and news shows, and so on. But no. Download whose Web site and order from whom? Pay what? I think you would have better luck waiting to watch the *Film at 11.*

Then there's the music, found within News and Politics (a little strange, that; to find music in a little folder under politics). Will Grega, the author of the Music Guide area, is truly cute, if that is in fact him. AOL must think he is cute, too, because his picture is found in practically every folder. Nice hair, boyfriend. And his music folder is adorable. A bonus is the audio software AOL provides for listening to Grega's selections. You can even get a pic of the gay country star, Sid Spenser, and listen to some of his hillbilly music. We were thrilled. (An AOL news brief later told us he had died a few weeks ago. Bummer.) Then we got to listen to great piano playing by Margie Adams . . . maybe not too thrilled.

The women's music section definitely lacks Grega's touch. Instead you have your choice of sixteen folders and six hundred forty posted messages. I did not know where to begin, so I didn't. Of course AOL did manage to slip a little of its internal, non-GLCF advertising into this folder. Now, *that* was pretty easy to find.

Events and Conferencing

Confronted with icons and folders, your only choice will be to spend hours searching for what you are looking for. This is your expanded playground and, if you have no idea what you're looking for, perhaps you'll find something that interests you. Under the Events and Conferencing folder you can find out all about chatting on AOL. Never mind that there is a separate icon for chatting. Why not put that information in the chatting folder? Because you would find it too easily. (Incidentally, Prodigy and MSN do this too.) AOL would have you surf around a while, sifting through the same information that is in the News area and reading some additional information on how to volunteer your time.

Skip this section if you are truly interested in current events because you can find them in the News. If you are interested in conferences, you could go to Club House to discuss teen gay and lesbian issues (but don't name a room Teen Gay Issues—*that's a no-no*). Some of the conferences that can be found in the Conferences folder:

- Parents' Conference: For LGBT* parents and prospective parents to discuss issues affecting them.

- Lovestrong: This conference serves as a support group for the spouses, girlfriends, boyfriends, and significant others of transgendered individuals. Very popular, as mentioned above. Quirk explains the individuality of this forum: "Everyone" from straight people to kids come here, it seems safe and fun."

- Goldies: Supportive conferences for those in the golden years, age fifty and above; Not, somehow, very popular.

- Gay Men's HIV Conference: Supportive conference for gay people living with HIV/ AIDS.

60-Second Novelist[3]

A pretty cool area for a few super-literary minutes, this popular nongay area is only *linked* to the GLCF. Here you chat with other lit. majors in the Lit Pit, or through the medium of poetry share the hardships of being a teenager. (The site **www.oasis-mag.com** does a better job, see Chapter 7.) This area is a creative endeavor and tends to attract a few creator types. However, don't get lost in all the drivel, for there is plenty. I was not careful and got linked up to Moms Online—cute baby pics, but still not a particularly "gay" site.

---

[3]Now called "Amazing Instant Novelist."

Like so much of GLCF, this area also targets volunteers. And, according to Quirk and Wayand, the volunteers for each popular section on America Online number in the two hundreds.

Resource Library

From the Resource Library location you can get connections to the WWW and sites that are not necessarily gay, but of interest to members.[4] Check out the gay teen WWW site or even the Battle Star Galactica site. (AOL is connected to tons of science fiction within its pages.)

Lambda Rising bookstore also has a site at this folder, and you can also access Lambda Library, a folder located within every other major folder. A great idea, but a lot of overlap . . . UGH. (We were bored one day and went to Lambda Library looking for some naked guys; don't expect to find any nudity or art. AOL has a policy on nudity in gifs: "We try to be as PG as possible. The golden rule is that, if you cannot see it on network television, you won't see it in GLCF." Fine. We watch HBO.)

The Resource Library prides itself on its graphical abilities or downloaded graphics, but all I could find was rainbow wallpaper. If you are thinking of doing your foyer in rainbow wallpaper and want to make your home look like a gay pride parade, hey, love that AOL!

Organizations

As the folder—cutely titled "Lay O' The Land"—states: "This is a space for *you* to network, contact and get information about different local and national organizations within the lesbian/gay/bisexual/transgender community. Interact directly with various groups here online, as well as receive regular updates on different activities or news bulletins."

Here are a few of the organizations represented at GLCF:

NGLTF   National Gay and Lesbian Task Force
GLAAD   Gay and Lesbian Alliance Against Defamation
P-FLAG   Parents and Friends of Lesbians and Gays
UFMCC Universal Fellowship of Metropolitan Community
         Churches
HRCF   Human Rights Campaign Fund (this has a good site of its
         own)
NLGJA National Lesbian and Gay Journalists Association
AEHRC Association Executives Human Rights Caucus

[4]Recall: Membership does not cost anything besides the price of your AOL account.

IGBA   International Gay Bowling Association
GLVF   Gay and Lesbian Victory Fund
GOAL   Gay Officers Action League
ACTUP AIDS Coalition to Unleash Power (an important activist group)

If you're interested in bringing your gay group to AOL, simply follow the rules and fill out the application located in the Weekly Database Highlight folder.

The message board under the Organizations area contains boards with material from all the groups listed above and many other national, local, youth, and transgender organizations. It is filled because most of America knows about the gay populace on AOL. Pretty soon many will move to the **www.planetout.com** site, mostly because they will be paid to do it.[5]

While surfing through the NLGJA, I found several gay and lesbian internships, but all the application deadlines had passed. One seemed like "quite an offer."

> Date: 95-12-07 14:59:29 EDT
>
> From: [We will censor this]
>
> Established journalist in NY (NY Times, WSJ, New Yorker, Vanity Fair, etc.) seeks a young, qualified journalism student for an internship. Your duties will be (mostly) interesting—research, interviews, etc. I will make it worth your while: you help me and I'll help you. I guarantee you will get a byline out of it.

Perhaps they should consider updating or deleting some of these ancient messages before I get so excited! When asked about editing, Quirk replied "We are working on it."

I was surprised to find a huge selection of organizations, ranging from Gay Indian Journalists to the Gay Rodeo Association. However, I now know there are no gay rodeos in winter—*sigh*. One recent posting under the Campers folder seemed enticing; if only I had an RV.

> Subj: RV/MIDWEST
>
> From: PAOLLY
>
> We are interested in getting to know gay/lesbian RVers. Write us. Paul E. and Tony.

In addition to many gay and lesbian recreational groups, there is also an abundance of political activism groups. One such group may be relevant to this book and to many of you who are reading it.

---

[5]Planetout is making a name for itself by gathering tons of funding and then buying out smaller sites to "link" to the mothership. See Chapter 7.

Subj: Online Activism for You!

From: FentonPR

InterActivism is a pioneering organization promoting online activism to support many progressive issues and causes. Its Web site regularly highlights actions that net citizens can take part in. InterActivism is now raising funds to rebuild the burnt Black churches and also to support NARAL.

Visitors to InterActivism can use a free fax service to call on leaders in Washington, D.C. to cut back defense spending and increase services for the nation's children. Many more actions like these are in the pipeline. Issues include progressive politics, women's rights, human rights, children, environmental concerns, gun control, and gay rights. Take a look at the innovative use of cyberspace at URL: **www. interactivism.com.**

Then, just when we have given up on the news as it relates to real life in gay America, *voila!* I found an example of how online services similar to AOL "get the word out" about bias incidents. This came by courtesy of an organization called The PERSON (Public Education Regarding Sexual Orientation Nationally) Project.

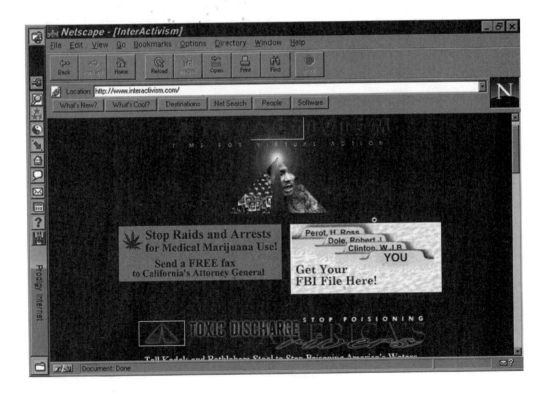

LOUISVILLE COURIER-JOURNAL
525 W. Broadway, Louisville, KY 40202
FAX 502-582-4075
Thursday, April 18, 1996

GAYS' VISIT TO CLASS STIRS UP ACTIVISTS, PARENTS
by Grace Schneider, Staff Writer

For high school teacher Janet Boyer, a visit from a counselor at a mental health center last month was meant to spark discussion in her health class about stress in all kinds of relationships. But the counselor surprised Boyer by bringing along four gay people who had volunteered to help with the discussion.

And controversy erupted.

First, a handful of parents of Charlestown (Indiana) High School students complained that they should have been notified of the visit beforehand. Then, based on an apparently inaccurate internet "alert," gay-rights activists across the nation sent a slew of complaints to the Greater Clark County school system.

In its internet message, a California-based gay advocacy group ripped Charlestown principal George Marshall, alleging he had reprimanded Boyer for allowing homosexuals to speak to her class. The alert also said that Boyer had refused to sign a letter promising not to discuss the topic at school again.

"This brave teacher needs our help," said the message from The PERSON Project. . . . It asked people to write Marshall; Greater Clark County school Superintendent David Pulliam; Suellen Reed, Indiana superintendent of public instruction; and *The Courier-Journal* and a Jeffersonville, Indiana newspaper, *The Evening News*. But school officials say the message is inaccurate and the account overblown. Teacher representatives concur. . . .

But because of the alert on the internet, the controversy hasn't died. Gay activists have written to admonish Pulliam and Marshall, suggesting that the principal had caved into homophobic hysteria. Oregon State Rep. George V. Eighmey is among those who wrote: "Isn't it time we cease giving credibility to the homophobic reactions of those who would have us teach only that which is in the bible?" Eighmey asked in a letter to Marshall.

Searching around a wee bit more in the GLCF Library, you find articles published by organizations and news related to government actions and legislation. Still, it doesn't seem worth it. Head to the mainstream News area on AOL or even CNN on the Web for current events.

Many of my brethren tell me that AOL's a great place to find a job. If a position in a certain organization is what you are after, I suggest accessing the specific organization's message board because the Library doesn't have group publications (in-house organs) and the information on positions is outdated.

Overall, I did find the Organizations area of AOL to be the most rewarding because it opened my eyes, and will perhaps open yours, to the diversity of concerns, recreation, and "good times" we are all having throughout the United States (not so much the globe). It also contributes to mobilizing our community and increasing our influence over every aspect of our culture from, yes, rodeos to nursing education.

Travel

As usual you are able to find a message board and library under this area, and also a reference to the wealth of travel information found in the print book series *Damron's Guides,* which is described by Damron itself as:

Resources! Damron's been a leader in the field of gay and lesbian travel for many years. Experience and extensive contacts created a superb list of important events and contacts on the lesbian and gay travel calendar. Damron has books for the gay and lesbian traveler.

If you are a circuit queen and wish to be gayer than gay, in an open setting with lots of disco music, this is your place. However, those who would choose to vacation a little away from the circuit queens in a quaint Pennsylvania gay-owned inn can also find some resources in this area.

The Places section is a little thin unless you are interested in Key West. (Key West *was* a top gay spot; these days it seems to be where the rednecks move to get away from the Bible Belters.) I would suggest heading to the Web or a bookstore if you are interested in getting gay and lesbian travel information for a specific city. If you are planning to cruise through a whole country, this forum does not—I stress this—cut it.

The message board in the Travel area seems to be filled with pleas for help in arranging travel plans. I did not see many replies. There are not many people advertising to host people. (On www.planetout.com—see Chapter 7—they hope to engender networking online.) If you are interested in finding someone in a certain area where you know no one, I would recommend using the chat rooms in the People Connection area or go to the Local Organizations folder under the Organizations area. You have a better chance there of getting any kind of response. (San Francisco and Los Angeles are in the process of getting their own citywide area on GLCF.)

If you are seeking someone to keep your cabin warm when you aren't there, or if you are looking for someone to keep it warm when you *are* there, see the Travel (Personals) section.

Message Boards

Ahhh. The Message Board section can be a little overwhelming if you want to post a message that has nothing to do with getting yourself a date. I suggest going to Organizations and locating an appropriate circle if you just have a question or concern, or you can go to any of the other main areas and use those message boards. If you are looking for that date (or a 1969 Caddie) read on—and on.

Classified Ads

RAINBOW CLASSIFIED BOARD states:

Here's where we allow advertising within the GLCF. There are folders specifically set up for roommates, real estate, products, services, employment ads, missing persons, social clubs, sports clubs, alumni organizations, etc. The Rainbow Classified Board has board managers who are responsible for monitoring our boards to make sure that all messages comply with AOL's Terms of Service/GLCF Posting Rules and that folks keep to the topic of the board. Messages that violate the rules, are off-topic, or are "private" responses to messages are removed. We do our best to provide clean, organized boards for our members and therefore we *do* maintain board continuity.

In other words, don't plan on selling your ex-lover's toys: Some volunteer fag from the GLCF staff will bump your butt off the Classified and you may even get written up. If you are not extra careful, you'll get detention.

This is quite a lengthy listing and who knows, it may be of interest to you; we all get lucky. But, heck, if you live in a city, there really is no excuse for you to go searching through this database when you can go to a flea market or Macy's.

We are amazed at how many guides AOL hires. These are volunteers, you soon discover, telling you what you can and can't say on a message board. Then, we wonder: How did this advertisement make it past?

Subj: MEN OF GRANITE—Dallas

From: ———

Texas' Hottest Male Strippers
Personal, Private Parties, Nightclubs
e-mail me at ———@aol.com

If you forgot the name of the stripper at your last party, have no fear. There is a service for locating that lost loved one—for a fee. Tagged onto your bill? Not quite. Have your credit card handy:

Subj: Investigative Solutions

From: ———

A licensed Private Investigation Agency, specializing in criminal investigations, locating missing children and adults, backgrounds, child custody, family/domestic concerns and general investigations. Major credit cards accepted. Let us help you . . .

Contact Investigative Solutions:
E-Mail: solveit1@concentric.net
Web Site: http://www.concentric.net/~solveit1

I tried to find some fascinating (read buyable) items for sale but alas I was not
interested in making $10,000 stuffing envelopes. Why is it those stuffing people
seem to post *everywhere?* For people like me—who already know where to look for
something—I suggest that you go out and get it yourself. If you are shy, you might
be able to buy a car online. (CompuServe's Auto section is much more comprehensive.) Other things for sale you could find in the back of your local newspaper: real
estate, cats, dogs, training wheels, a good bra.

There is one good thing about these classifieds: Many lesbian carpenters are
willing to fix pretty much anything for a reasonable rate. And a lesbian carpenter,
well, I won't get into that.

Chats

Chat areas are among the hottest spots on AOL, and I mean all of AOL. In fact,
this facility has received a lot of coverage lately because of some scary incidents that
are alleged to have been instigated here. One of them involved a fourteen-year-old
boy from Long Island who showed his chatroom experiences to mom and got his
older "boyfriend" arrested. *News at 11* again.

People converge from all over to chitchat about everything from show tunes to
tatoos. There are several areas on GLCF to chat in and private rooms within the
chat areas. Lambda Lounge—moderated by staff who are not as choosy as Moms
Online—is the main chat area, and when I asked one of the operators what the topic
tends to be, the response was:

<queerAvngr>–''about nothing in particular usually, the topics in here change more
often than Madonna changes *huh* hair colour.''

This area covers all the general topics and can fill almost all of your chatting
needs, unless you are searching for the more creative types at the keyboard. I don't
find AOL to have many articulate members. Most of these guys and gals are seem-

ingly lost puppies. Lost puppies may excite you to the core, and if so stay put. If you are more adventurous than "what u wearing," you will get bored so quickly that you will put your hands back on the keys. (The IRC has the articulate and is not, as Quirk says, the same as the chat rooms here; see Chapter 6.)

As we said before: If you're new to the world of chatting, AOL and other online services are a good place to start, though it's beyond my ken why a gay person chats on Prodigy, unless he's a music fan.[6] Many of the conversations you will have in here are "real talk," that is, normal conversation.

There was little creative use of symbols and acronyms, which are the key to success in the internet world. This suggests that most users are newbies. Additionally, if you speak dirty, you may get written up; and "dirty" is definitely subjective in the case of AOL/GLCF. See sidebar on dirty words, Guide This!

What everyone forgets is that in other independently run chat rooms—and on newsgroups—you will not encounter censorship, unless you threaten somebody, in which case you deserve what you get: ejected.

"Heart to Heart" Chat Space

Here you can see an uploaded photo of the guy or gal you are interested in. First you have to get interested in him or her. Then . . . oh, let's cut to the chase. I once was able to see the pictures. Then AOL asked me to download its 3.0 browser, with an insanely fast connection to the internet. (Fast only if you are using a 28.8 modem.) But now everything in Heart to Heart is out of focus. It is like cruising a really dark tavern. The descriptions are at best fabricated and legible. However, if you are lucky enough to log in on a day when the pictures are in focus, please tell us all about the boys and girls you see. I think the "picture personal" is a great idea. Are they really who they say they are, I wonder? :)!

"Just Friends" Chat Space

Hey, a cool idea for the gay/lesbian/transgender/etc. community to know about. Remember the time you were in a bar and you met someone and you really clicked? And you said to each other, hey isn't this great? We can JUST BE FRIENDS.

Some cool people on AOL's GLCF did just that, and met a lot of other people who wanted to do some exciting things. I was impressed to find a diversity of people who are interested in hangin', playin', or chattin(g). I recommend checking out this

---

[6]Prodigy makes people happy with its music content. Music may also be found on the WWW. To get there, jump (its term) **www.sonicnet.com.**

no matter where you are in your online education because it might end up being the best introduction that you have.

Women's Space Chat Space

For Women only! At this area you will be able to jump into a whole array of women-identified spaces. But, you will have to determine if you are talking to women or some husband of a closeted lesbian who is using her online account. At this area you can find two chatting rooms: Women's Space and The Parlor. When I asked the alert group what the difference was, the best reply came from an energetic woman who loved to talk about her estrogen patches: <Unmitigate> "The difference in the space[s] is the pace." Some profiles of the women were quite amazing; here are a few that caught my eye:

Screen Name:	JaneShark
Member Name:	There's Jane-n-Tarzan, JaneDoe, then there's me . . . Jane, JaneShark
Location:	Shallow waters off the coast
Birthdate:	Whenever
Sex:	Female
Marital Status:	Single
Hobbies:	Circling intended victims
Occupation:	Predator/scavenger and Butch
Personal Quote:	Stop wiggling . . . you're only making it worse.
Screen Name:	Mstynight
Member Name:	MstyNight "Yep, it is me, the original MstyNight!"
Location:	Great NorthWest — take my hand & walk with me in the mist of the night!
Birthdate:	Libra
Sex:	Female
Computers:	PCs RULE!!
Hobbies:	The simple pleasures of life: love, laughter, romance, the forests & the mtns & the sea AND good friends to enjoy it with! :)
Occupation:	Software Techie . . . among other things. . . . <EG>
Personal Quote:	The bond of the spirit and soul with another can never be broken but strengthened for all eternity.

The Women's Space also has many ongoing conferences throughout the week. I attended a few, and found them to be the same ol' girls, but maybe they will be new for you. Here are some of the topics for women:

FINE WINE CONFERENCE
For older lesbians

WOMEN'S SPIRITUALITY CONFERENCE
Discussion of women's spirituality

LESBIAN MUSICIANS' CONFERENCE
Practical discussion for lesbian musicians and their supporters
of all aspects of creating and performing music.

There are not as many women as men on the internet. According to the Web-masters I interviewed, probably only 10 percent of the gay Web users are women. Online it's bigger, though not much. I run a forum on CompuServe and have discovered that 70 percent of my members are guys. Who knows why? Some may interpret this as an obvious exertion of the male ego into yet another dimension of our culture. Others may view it as a woman's desire to not be locked to a keyboard and staring at a screen! Whatever the sociological basis for the absence of women on the internet, one result is that much of the dialogue and interaction on the net *and* on AOL has a distinct male tone simply because more men use the darn thing. When I met the women of AOL, I discovered a lot of terrific characters. We're still buddies.

The number of men on the internet has increased the likelihood that a few of them are pretending to be women, or pretending to be age fourteen, or pretending to be as hunky as Antonio Sabato, Jr. It just ain't true. You will have to be the judge of who is who, and if they pass your test, good luck. Meanwhile, ask the people online what their tests are to determine real from fake, and you will chuckle—and probably use them.

"Gaymeland" Chat

This is not for beginners. I found the area confusing and definitely full of cliques. If you are lucky enough to get someone to answer your basic questions about procedure, you are doing a fine job at communicating.

They sport a number of games in Gaymeland. One of them involves trying to come up with little sayings or acronyms that are as boring as the individuals facilitating the game. Usually, during the game there are a few lost souls trying to figure out what is going on or trying to meet people. Here is an example, a new version of the kid's game "Where's Waldo?" Look for the lost soul in our discussion.

GLCF Paws:	OK—HERE'S HOW THIS WILL WORK! I WANT EVERYONE TO TYPE TO "CHIP" A COMMON COMPUTER OR SOFTWARE ERROR MESSAGE (EITHER PC OR MAC IS FINE). CHIP WILL SIFT THROUGH YOUR ERROR MESSAGES, SCAN THEM FOR ACCURACY, SPELLING, AND GENERAL WIT! HE WILL THEN APPLY HIS OWN PRIVATE JUDGING METHODS AND SELECT THE ERROR MESSAGE THAT HITS CLOSEST TO HOME. :)
GLCF Paws:	(AND FOR GOD'S SAKE—PLEASE DO *NOT* ASK ME HOW I KNOW THAT CHIP IS A "HIM"!) ALL RIGHT! EVERYBODY READY?
THERAPYKSW:	FAULT PROTECTION ERROR
BigDave976:	How about this one? "The Service is unavailable. Please try again in 15 minutes" *Big Dave was having one on . . . the AOL service had gone out for nineteen hours a few days before and that was the message all AOLers got.*
GLCF Paws:	*OK! FIRE AWAY!!*
Chris Stor:	*Non-system disk error*
GLCF Zinc:	*PRODIGY WANTS YOU AAAAAARGH !!!!! I HATE THAT ONE*
GLCF Paws:	*CHIP DOES A SEGUE INTO BOOLEAN ALGEBRA WHILE GLCF TISH MASSAGES HIS CIRCUITS.*
TexasBrat:	*Fatal Error in Vector 9283429384723*
BigDave976:	*The Service is unavailable. Please try again in 34.5 minutes.* *That Big Dave's a card.*
THERAPYKSW:	Unable to print, the printer port is already in use.
GLCF Paws:	RAM!
Kasey T We:	hit the wrong key, dork
TexasBrat:	Vector, Sector, whatever. :D
Creideiki8:	"You've had it sister. Give up now" Error
MSBA123:	Hey I'm new here and i want a greeting from someone!!
Kasey T We:	This computer will self destruct in. . . .
Creideiki8:	Enterprise self-destruct enabled (again) in 15 seconds . . .
MSBA123:	This is boring!!!!
GLCF Paws:	And the WINNER of tonight's FREE HOUR is:

And the winner of that incredibly boring, computer geek-facilitated game was the guy who initiated it. Be prepared for this type of excitement throughout the evening in Gaymeland. However, there are always a few <MSBA123>s around who are into chatting about things besides computer error messages . . . yawn. If you look around you are bound to find them. I think.

Stay away from Gaymeland if you can because, after all, most gays and lesbians want private chat. Here is a description of someone you may run into:

Screen Name:	LthrBoyToy
Member Name:	LthrBoyToy
Location:	Bound Leather Slave on Sado Island, Ga.
Birthdate:	1 per yr
Sex:	Male
Computers:	Leather One; In need of a Master's collar
Hobbies:	Leather Slave Boy; Amusement for Leather Masters; Play Toy & provider of forbidden pleasures for Masters
Occupation:	Harnessed Equestrian Pony Slave; 5' 10"; 165#; 30" waist; 44 chest; smooth swimmer type workout body; 50
Personal Quote:	Bound to please!!! Oh please don't make me take that; it's too big! aaaaggghhhh yes Sir, thank you Sir for showing me I can.

Or a nice NYC Police officer—whose name cannot be revealed without an official subpoena.

Screen Name:	JDRNYC
Member Name:	Jeff
Location:	New York, NY USA
Birthdate:	11/30/67
Sex:	Male
Marital Status:	Single
Computers:	Quantex
Hobbies:	I love sports, participating and watching, especially tennis, skiing, baseball
Occupation:	Police Officer
Personal Quote:	Live life to the fullest, you only go around once!!

An interesting conversation with a nice boy from Britain topped off one evening. He sent me some nasty pics, but AOL wouldn't let me receive them in my private mail account. Bogus. Anyway, read on and if you like our discussion, maybe you can find him and (all in the name of research, natch) say the Kewlboy wonders how goes it, Sinboy :)

MADAME SIN: 28 yrs 6 ft green eyes 7" uncut like to fuck

Kewlboy: Your profile says you were born in 1976 . . . what's up with that . . .

MADAME SIN: My profile is inaccurate created as a joke by a friend

MADAME SIN: are you hard?
              how old are you ?
              do you have gifs to trade?
              want a cyberwank?

In some way I *was* interested in a cyberwank, but we got lost in the crowded corridors of AOL. I'm still looking for <MADAME SIN>. After my jaunt through the cyber parking lot with the <SIN>ster, I met a nice cowboy or, I should say, a nice SIR.

Txlthtop: 35 6'2" 155 lb Br and Br 7 cut and pierced

Kewlboy: Treats . . . I am 6' 0" 180 Br and Bl 7" cut and love to be a bottom cowboy
            . . . 24 yo

Txlthtop: You could have a place in our sling. You know what they say, ''forget the
            bulls ride the cowboys!''

Txlthtop: Am I going to have to tie your hands behind your back so you don't . . . No
            profile so tell me about yourself. [7]

Kewlboy: I am a cutie . . . not a computer geek at all . . . live in NYC and dream of
            playing roleplay fucking games . . . for real

Txlthtop: Well that good boy just remember that it is Sir to you pig.

Kewlboy: Yes SIR

Kewlboy: SIR, I can't see, but do your balls hang real low like a bull in heat

Txlthtop: I like what I see so far Have you had any experience in heavy leather play

Kewlboy: No . . . but I am not the shy type. I live in NYC right now. Would love for
            you to be here now and teach me like a young cowboy needs to be taught

Txlthtop: Where is the Sir that you should always use asshole

Kewlboy: Yes SIR. . . .

That was definitely a learning experience, particularly as most people on AOL are not adventurous. As a friend of some literary merit pointed out: "The chat rooms,

---

[7]Always post a profile if you wanna be popular; keyword: Profile on AOL's menu.

even private ones, are frustrating—most people are *not* articulate. As soon as some-one types in "u" instead of 'you' I'm outta there! It's so easy not to take people seriously on AOL." Amen.

Then there's the paranoia aspect of the chat rooms: One of my colleagues was sure someone was recording what he said to <Txlthtop> so they could interview him in relationship to some horrible Texas bull heist! :)

If you are so inclined, go to a private room with that new cybersomeone. The directions and operation of it are really simple, just click the PRIVATE button after selecting the ROOMS icon. Private rooms are best for a ménage à trois or even for more than three. They operate just like the Lamda Lounge or a big room: everything you typed scrolls by.

Some rooms are Men4Men, YngMen4YngMen, Married Men4Men, BiCurious-Men4Men, M4M (same people—different story). Try it out once and, if you are seriously concerned with privacy, then it's off to the big world of the internet's IRC for you.

Always remember: Chat rooms are named by members, so if you are visiting your aunt in Tallahassee, either look up or make up a room called Tallahassee Men4-Men. If you build it, they will come.

The "Positive Living" Chat

Congratulations to AOL on creating a space for Persons Living with AIDS (PLWAs). This is one type of communication and resource you may find helpful if you are searching for someone to talk to.

As with all specific health concerns, it depends upon who you are and what you want. Health for PLWAs is all over GLCF; Quirk, to her credit, would like AIDS health not relegated to the AIDS area. "I don't think it should be a satellite issue," she said in an interview. "AIDS affects all aspects of our lives, not just people who are afraid or those who *have* to have the information!"

If chatting with a diverse bunch of people over the computer can in any way allay some concerns about living with HIV or AIDS you should visit Positive Living. Here, in all the online world, having a huge choice is what counts. Otherwise, get off line. Do your own thing. Go your own way. Sing another Fleetwood Mac song.

The problem is that there is never anybody to chat with in Positive Living. My theory: this is the only part of GLCF advertised in the main screen to all of AOL in hopes that it will be visited (read, paid for in continuation of monthly fees) by the tens of thousands, if not millions, of closeted queer members who see the word *AIDS* as code for homosexual.

Overall, AOL feels good about Positive Living, its AIDS resource area, so it adver-tises this healthily. Still, for more than a year it has failed to put the GLCF area on the main screen for all members of AOL to see. Then, recently, the area made it on the front for several months straight—after I asked the PR officials why it went missing.

Memo to AOL: Although the gay and lesbian community has been greatly affected by the AIDS epidemic, it is not our only concern, even for those with HIV or AIDS. Your luring curious individuals into the Lambda Lounge through AIDS areas shows a lack of wisdom and plays up to traditional stereotypes of the gay community.

AOL is contributing to making HIV and AIDS the acceptable umbrella under which the gay community is okay to meet, and detracts from the importance of contributing to the improvement of gay and lesbian people by labelling our community a disease. It is an obvious marketing plan without mentioning the word gay or lesbian to attract our community, many of which are their members.

Health

Ironically, there is no specific health area on GLCF even though AOL advertised the Positive Living Forum on the main graphics of AOL during the summer of 1996. (Quirk says a health folder is forthcoming.) If you are interested in health, you will not get information specific to gays and lesbians in any one folder. The only information is located in the News search engines at the many other GLCF main areas.

There are other categories too. Among them are Arts & Media, Theory & Debate, the Gay Message Board, Lesbian Message Board (the most popular), Bisexual Message Board, News, Politics and Law, and the ever-popular though cornily named Leisure Interests (how about a veggie burger?). And a last word on the Lambda Lounge, the most popular hangout here. According to Wayand: "Besides our user's manual on the front screen, people tend to go and introduce themselves and their latest topic of desire at the Lounge. It's everyone—young adults coming out, forty-five-year-olds away from their wives, girls in search of each other. It's wonderful, safe, and quite relaxing too. No we are not serving."

MICROSOFT NETWORK (MSN)

The Microsoft Network (MSN) is serious and I am scared![8] Ready to explore gay/lesbian cyberspace on MSN, I found myself lodged in a breathless space on a rush-hour subway in *Total Recall* staring at an omnivisionesque image of Bill Gates reciting directions to the virtual reality planet of my choice—completely designed, built, owned, and controlled by him and his team of virtual weathermen.

[8]All the gay areas were changing on MSN in early 1997.

I suddenly wanted no part of the picture of Bill above an action box that was innocently stating: "Downloading software." I don't want Bill in my computer, loading software that records my every move, watching me indulge in cybersex, and sending me an action box over my desktop publishing software where I toil every day (hey, he owns it all), demanding that I buy his new modem—or, worse—that my conduct on MSN last night was morally questionable. I cannot say for sure that this is or isn't happening.

Masters of illusion, that's what Bill Gates and the people at Microsoft Network are. If you logged onto MSN during its inception, you would have experienced a format described by Michael Miller, a writer for internet magazines and author of many online service guides, as "too computerish." Well, yes. We have seen it all before, and it is boring. Microsoft Network is too computerish because the company controls Windows, and has given many of us, including Miller, the idea that *computerish* means Microsoft Network.

The new Microsoft Network online service is not so much too computerish it is too Windows—folder after folder, just like your daily work. By the time this book comes out, the format may have changed because sometime in 1997 a new online programming system called Blackbird will replace folders with graphic interpretations.

I asked myself, "Do I have a life, or am I Bill's Stepford wife?" Will this Microsoft Network take over? Absolutely not! That is only the hype of good PR. All of the rhetoric about "great takeover," which promises you the ability to be the supreme controller of your own reality [Oh, my God, what a reality that would be!] are promises to your imagination. What Microsoft can promise is that you will be interfacing with all your favorite computers around the world at high speeds, with soon-to-be-pirated Chinese software, which will be distributed to all of Europe for $4.95 a copy. Go Chinese, and send me a free copy. Until then, I would recommend you staying right where you are, and accessing all the creative and innovative WWW homepages, magazines, and gay-lesbian-transsexual chat spaces you can find with a Web browser obtained through a nice cheap SLIP account (a basic internet-access account), or by checking out all of the cool stuff discussed herein.

Another reason not to get too close to MSN, besides the bad PR decision to put Bill's face as a (harumph) welcoming icon on the first page, is the annoying and desperate advertising. If you have ever seen the Website, MSNBC, and its cousin, the MSNBC cable channel ("Call your cable operator now to get us added on"), you will know that MSN and NBC have decidedly taken on a hawker's approach. (But, MSNBC is quite a fun Web site if you are a news junkie as all of us are. It is very easy to use and you can always see gif images of Jane Pauley.) MSN has become a symbol of Microsoft's pushy marketing style. Even if you choose not to join MSN while installing Windows 95, an icon for the service appears on your computer's desktop. You can get rid of it but it takes hard work; we eventually succeeded. It's a special type of icon that may be difficult for novices to delete or move so that it isn't constantly visible. So, essentially, it becomes a little Microsoft ad in your face all the time. The icons for rival services are not automatically placed on the desktop.

Overall, MSN offers the same kinds of information as CompuServe and America Online do. All these offer more for queers than Prodigy does—which is nothing. (We are "pulling for" Prodigy since it changed its name to Prodigy Inc. from Prodigy Services Company, but my gut feeling is that this is IT for them. MSN's only difference is that it is as boring as hell to sift through. Folder after folder deep, you may eventually find the one folder that contains what you're looking for.

There is only one area on MSN that caters to gay, lesbian, and transsexual concerns and issues: Planetout.

Planetout

Planetout is no masterpiece. It is simply more of the same provided by other online services. (For details about Planetout, the Web site, see Chapter 7.)

Join the Planetout mailing list and you will soon get the picture: Ad. Ver. Tise. Ments.

It is *not* necessary to "Join Up" and become a member of Planetout, in order to use our services. However, we do encourage that you Join Up!! There are several added benefits when Joining, which include (but not limited to!):

1. You'll be eligible to win Planetout prizes—simply for Joining! (such as T-shirts, hats, and more!)
2. You'll receive copies of our Planetout newsletters, which keep you informed about PNO happenings, changes, and more!
3. You can optionally become informed on products and services of other companies which PNO promotes, that may be of interest to you.

What does Planetout offer that the other online services do not? There was one dimension of their gay, lesbian, and transsexual space that I found quite pleasing: an elaborate system of checking the validity of online users' ages in an effort to provide privacy for its users. This stops them from worrying about the youngster thing. But before we give them too much credit, consider this. When logging onto the S&M chat room I got this all-too-familiar message:[9]

---

[9]If online services spent *half* as much time on the content as they do on all these warnings, they would be absolutely fabulous!

Welcome to Planetout's S&M and Leather Topic Area!

Please note, this area is for **ADULTS ONLY**—those 18 years of age and older! If you only see three icons in the *S/M & Leather* window, then you don't have Full Adult Access to Microsoft Network! To obtain full access (including Internet Newsgroup access), please select the shortcut below this disclaimer!

Please read this discalimer [*sic*]:

PNO and MSN are not responsible for the contents of this area. This area may contain adult-oriented and controversial material not suitable for children. If you are offended by or disagree with messages that you see in these areas, please keep in mind the adult nature of this area! You are responsible for supervising the extent to which these messages and chat areas are viewed by children having access to your account. Please read MSN Member Guidelines . . .

Only after checking out your age through your credit card, will they let you enter. But hey, do the people at Microsoft know everything I do now? Such as, where do *I* want to go today, perhaps?

As with other online services, Planetout prides itself in the diversity of its chat spaces. Here is an opening quote from Planetout on the subject.

Planetout is a place that you can call home. A place where you can express yourself, meet new friends in your neighborhood or halfway around the world, and be part of an electronic community. Please take time to explore our vast number of Topic Areas, where you can find discussions on many topics of interest to the lesbigay & t* community. When you find interesting areas, please don't be afraid to join in the conversation and discussions! Write a message and say hello—or join the related chat room!

As Web and online-service users, we are not sure whose home Planetout is but it was not that of these disgruntled surfers who complained to the Comments and Suggestions message board:

So far, in the gay men only board, I have seen 43 year old men soliciting young boys. Thanks to your "conversation format" we can see that not only does this Planetout Board NOT CARE< but that hey, we might as well call this the NAMBLA [North American Boy Love Association, for lovers of kids] board. Is anyone even checking these boards? What kind of shoddy place is this?

This is the rudest and meanest group of women I have ever met. They ganged up on me, called me a man, got a host to spectator me for no reason at all. It is startling and SCARY that in this age of growing tolerance, it is our own community (Adult Lesbians) that exhibit the most HATE.

We discovered that there have been many problems with the lesbian spaces at Planetout, as with many lesbian spaces on the internet. (See Chapter 9 for the antidote.) For now, Planetout has devised a way to solve the problem of men's frequenting the lesbian areas

> Another problem which has gotten worse, is curious men invading the Lesbian Only chat areas . . .
>
> . . . In order to obtain access, our women members will need to write to our Lesbian Zone Coordinator: Redherring. Please see Information kiosk in the Lesbian area for more details. FYI: Men found in the new women's areas will be excluded from Planetout.

I do not think, however, that these men were in the least "curious." (If they were curious, MSN's measures are indeed drastic.) More likely, these men were hoping to cause a disturbance, as they do on many lesbian IRC channels. Planetout has understated the situation: The most likely reason for the annoyance is blatant harassment.

If you are still interested, and you should be somewhat interested as MSN has incredible resources, read on and learn about the specific areas in Planetout.

People (Chats/MSGS)

This area boasts the same interactions that are available on every online service. I found many of the gay areas a little empty on Planetout though. However, this may change in the coming months. Additionally, information about sending private messages is buried somewhere in the help folders I think; I never did find it.

Kiosk

Under Kiosk you can find more chatting spaces and a variety of message boards covering poetry and essays. The highlight of the Kiosk folder is its connection to PopcornQ, which is reviewed in Chapter 7.

PopcornQ

The ultimate online home for the queer moving image is a colorful gay, lesbian, bisexual, and transgender film and video Web site that offers a continually updated, searchable movie database, with full technical information, descriptions, reviews, photos, and sources for thousands of films and videos. The online version is described in Chapter 6. The problem here is that not *all* gay people think films are fabulous; **www.popcornq.com** seems to think we do. This reminds me of what so-called straight people are reputed to believe about gays: We all have disposable income, and we all *love* Judy Garland. Really, I don't either. (Sorry, Liza.)

Queers on the Web

Queers on the Web forum offers connections to many WWW sites that are either gay- and lesbian-related or have some relevance to the gay and lesbian community. By clicking on the WWW folder, you will be able to download search-engine listings of WWW sites. Hey, this is "kewl" because you get to leave the Windows format and head for the Web.

Shop

The Shop area features business discussions and classifieds with many of the same ideas and products as provided by other online services, but worth a peek if you have a particular item in mind. The business discussions frequently include individuals who are promoting gay and lesbian businesses and are looking for hints they can capitalize on.

Civic Center

The Library and many gay, lesbian, bisexual, transsexual, etc. organizations can be found in this area. The library and the organization resources are not as extensive as those of America Online, nor were registration forms readily available in the folder.

Through searching software, the Library provides access to many news and information materials in both Planetout and all of MSN. However, the searches are not as extensive as those available on America Online and on many WWW sites.

World View

On World View you can find the surfers from the land down under. This area boasts connections for gay, lesbian, and bisexual PNO surfers in North America (Canada, United States, and Mexico), Europe, and Australia. This section is primarily for posting personals addressed to people who do not live in the United States. If you are dreaming about a date in Sydney, I'll see you here!

Languages

Languages is unique. At this site you are able to connect with others who are chatting in German, Spanish, French, Dutch, or Russian. This does not mean the individuals live abroad; it most likely means that they are studying a foreign language at college. If you want to see the Cyrillic alphabet scroll by on the Russian chat, you will need the software provided; search under Russian Language.

Special Events

Conferencing is where it is at in these heady online days, and Special Events is where it is at on Planetout. This area is run like those on most online services, with advertisements of upcoming events and chat spaces—the auditorium—where they occur.

Overall, I want out of Planetout. (Please disconnect me, Bill.) I am a little too creeped out by the similarity of Windows software and the randomly appearing action boxes stating "[currently] downloading" to believe that Bill is not desperately trying to get into my pants, and the thought of what he may do there is appalling.

PRODIGY SERVICES COMPANY (PRODIGY INC.)

Prodigy was the pioneer of online services. CompuServe has been around longer—1969 was before 1985—but, heck, it was a business service for the first fifteen years. The chat rooms happened by accident. Since its advent in 1985, Prodigy has not been an advocate of gay content. From what the company tells me, it's not that it despised gays, it just didn't know how to do it. Sears and IBM, bastions of Americanism, owned the product and the company until 1996. That's when it all changed. And I mean *all*.

We feel that Prodigy will once again take on a pioneer role. As designers of Prodigy Internet, a basic service for people interested, not in content but just on being on the big I, the company will be leading the way for other online services in designing and administering what is tentatively to be called Open Space.

Hey, it's the antidote, we hope; the first truly member-directed gay-lesbian-bisexual site. It will be a tremendously exciting debut. Read on!

There is not much to say about Prodigy in its present state, except for its current Lavender Waves area, which was created by Bill Py, an amazingly active member of the community. He has invested a lot of time in this site. It's hard to find—it is on what is now called Prodigy Internet (the address is http://antares.prodigy.com/igroups/the world/glbtcoi/glbt.htm)—but once I did, I compared it to AOL and CompuServe and saw its limitations. That's when I realized: He's on the Web and CIS and AOL are not.

During 1996 Bill compiled material on some of the most current popular-culture interests pertaining to gays and lesbians and has packaged it in some lovely tunes (music files). Sometimes Bill's activism plays out in the appearance of the site, which tends to look like a Pride Parade but his creativity is more impressive than some of the lame shit clogging up the Web, and has the potential for affecting our community in a positive way. Thanks Bill!!

But what is really exciting is the transformation that will occur. Currently Prodigy's gay, lesbian, and bisexual areas consist only of chat rooms that simply do not cut it. To attract a diverse cyberqueer community these days, it takes a lot more than text-based chatting with a few closeted kids or tons of information that is impossible to sift through.

Content in The Space will be based on opinions and recommendations of the members, and not provided in the "bomb them with everything" format. The new Prodigy Internet will greatly assist in the designing of virtual environments for members.

The use of Netscape and ultimately of MS Explorer (the other guy) by Prodigy Internet allows for Web surfing of a kind provided by none of the other online services. It was the smartest thing for Prodigy to do. Compared to any of the other online services, Prodigy had minimal content and now it has positioned itself to make all of the WWW a resource for the members. As the ad states: "Call us madcap!"

And most importantly, information on Prodigy Internet is not censored as it is on the browsers on AOL and CompuServe. Instead, the Lesbian and Gay Arena on Prodigy will offer the simplicity of online services and the content of the WWW.

Other online services will not be able to follow Prodigy's lead because they have invested too much time and energy in their content. The cyberenvironments of other online services are designed by teams headed by individuals, such as Ms. Quirk at AOL, and could never encompass the diversity of the WWW. Ultimately, this means that Open Space will be able to surpass the current online cyberenvironments and create virtual environments that are chosen by the members and derived from both the team at Prodigy and the millions of gays, lesbians, and bisexuals on the WWW.

The virtual environments on this bold new arena promise to cater to the specific needs of each of its members rather than stereotyping the gay, lesbian, bisexual communities and then chosing information believed to represent the cyberqueer community. These environments will ensure that all of the needs of the closeted, the curious, and those we now call the terminally "out," especially their privacy needs, and more importantly, their fantasy needs are met. If Prodigy follows through on a commercially viable concept, this will be better than fantasy!

NYC NET

Open since May 1, 1995, NYC NET has already grown to be New York's largest gay and lesbian online service and internet provider. It is, in reality, a veteran! Through

its inception, a gay and lesbian community of organizations, individuals, and resources has been built on NYCNET. The heart of the service is its bulletin board
system, which features gay and lesbian media, over thirty conferences and forums
about life in the city, coming out, politics, cooking, a queer calendar, global Usenet
newsgroups (see Chapter 2), PRIDE NET, newswires from GLAAD, GMHC, and other
offerings of interest to our fast-growing community of users.

Over twenty-four gay and lesbian community, political, and professional groups
have established online hubs to offer content and resources. These groups include
Artgroup for Gay and Lesbian Artists, NY CyberQueers, the Publishing Triangle, the
NYC Lesbian & Gay Community Services Center, Social Activities for Lesbians, Iden-
tity House, Log Cabin Republicans, Lambda Independent Democrats, 3$ Bill Theatre
Company, and NYC Gay Lesbian Anti-Violence Project. The list is growing.

For more information on joining this enterprising—though disorganized and
short-staffed—antiestablishment and gay-owned service, contact **www.nycnet.
com.** Or call it at (212) 268-9285 for software. Download software with your modem
from (212) 268-9490. (*We're family* is the NYC Net slogan.)

5

AOL:
The Big Gimmick

*Having heard about it all these years, and having seen it at last,
I am left with the impression that America Online is a kiddie pool
situated beside the great, wide oceans of information. And that is
fine with me. The kiddie pool is always jammed, but everyone in
it seems to be having a great time. If the kiddies shriek at an ear-
splitting volume, at least they're doing it over* there, *where they
can't hurt themselves, and where they can annoy only each other.
It wouldn't be a pleasant thing if they got out in the deep before
they're ready, but we all know that the sharks clean up after the
undertow. The internet isn't always pretty. But it's fast. . . .*

—From internet posting "Is That AOL
There Is . . ." by Greg Swann[1]

Getting started is easy. And while I admit that that's a cheap shot at AOL's over-marketed slogan, I decided, after three months of constant conversation with the world of AOL, to dedicate an entire chapter to AOL. Why is it so popular? Why do people think this is the end-all of gay life online? Why is AOL trying to make users believe it *is* the net? And why does AOL make all the money from the gay and lesbian community's chat (People Connection) rooms?

I spoke to AOL users, marketing consultants, internal PR people, top America Online brass, runners of the GLCF (Gay and Lesbian Community Forum), its members, the legal department of AOL, and lots who know the place better than I do. Most concurred with everything I said: That AOL, definitely the largest content service provider on earth, uses the gay and lesbian community every turn it can.

[1]Greg Swann *cannot* be reached at **gregswann@aol.com.** Quote. Unquote.

America Online began as a company in the early 1990s, with a modest proposal: To help all Americans who were scared about the presence of online drift easily and smoothly into cyberland and have them so happy with the little diskettes they received with their toilet paper that they would "go online" and, as for any addiction, get hooked. Each hour—back then—netted about four dollars for AOL. That translates to a lot of bucks. (Nowadays it's $19.95, but you can't get connected without much effort.)

AOL started its courtship of gay users in its infancy. In 1990 GLCF began as a quiet forum or area managed by Michelle Quirk, a young, twenty-something lesbian who is humorous and personable and deserves her huge following. GCLF is owned by a wholly separate company in which Quirk is a partner: QView, a miniconglomerate in the San Francisco Bay Area. (It is rumored that Quirk treats the Forum Group, her mostly volunteer staff, as a sort of cult or club, making the GLCFers feel as though their bringing on more volunteers is for the greater good of gaykind.)

But back then Quirk started by bringing members, rather unofficially, into a few chat rooms devised by her tiny staff. Quirk has had little support from AOL. In a

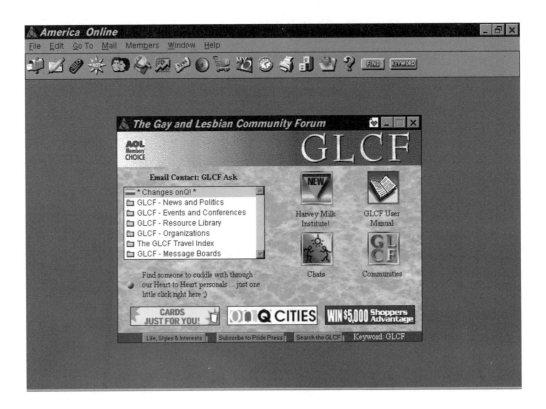

whimsical search of AOL press releases dating back to February 1995, I found that the GLCF, rumored to be the biggest moneymaker of ALL non-chat areas on AOL, was not mentioned once!

Way back in the early cyberdays of 1990, AOL clearly did not wish to be known as a provider to the gay population. The idea, says Steve Case, AOL's chairman and CEO, was to be a family service, something both Prodigy and CompuServe constantly say they are. Families are easy to help or service; they want travel, chat (romance areas), a few magazines, auto information, maybe banking. Gay people want lots of stuff—and of course gay people were pretty controversial.

Case told Reuters about the decision to be middle-of-the-road: "The bottom line is that 89 percent of households in the United States do not subscribe to any online service. We believe AOL is uniquely positioned to meet the needs of a mass market . . . by providing an interactive experience that is easy, useful, fun, and affordable."

But by 1993 gay people were already on line in droves and who the hell was going to argue with those numbers? AOL, that's who. A company with hundreds of thousands of obviously gay members, threw caution to the wind and released a handy guidebook on keywords that gain access to information. And the word *gay* did not exist on those pages.

Quirk demurs when asked about it. "AOL is something I cannot even begin to understand," she says seriously.

David Phillips, legal counsel at AOL's headquarters outside Dulles, Virginia, admits that the service "is fully functioning as a PG—or family—service, though I hate that word." Phillips lives in downtown Washington, D.C., bikes to work, and has a fully functioning offline life, yet he doesn't see anything wrong with the fact that "AOL is not oriented toward adult content, plain and simple."

But America Online has more problems than that of being PG. Since 1994 gay users have gone to the service specifically for chat on the so called People Connection areas, to chat rooms that seem to be run by the gay group managed by Quirk. Not so. People Connection is a money-making entity for America OnLine, and Quirk tells me that not a penny earned there is given to her group. Jim Wayand, QView's business manager, says that gays "come into our rooms and our area [GLCF] and use us every night of their lives." He thinks the numbers are in the low million at this time, but won't confirm the figures for the record. When I tell this to Phillips, he explains slowly: "We made a business decision to maintain certain standards. We are going to follow those rules exactly."

Online homophobia is not solely AOL's dominion. All the online services hope to rise meteorically like AOL, so being somewhat afraid of the gay user is part of the story. CompuServe, in business since 1969, would not allow the word *gay* on its CB lines—those ancient versions of chat rooms that survived until 1995! For the Columbus-based family service, the preferred usage was "alternative lifestyles."

When I mentioned to AOL press people that I wanted to talk to Quirk *and* to Ted Leonsis, the head of content at the service, the first response was: "Wait. Is this a *gay* book? I'm not sure . . ."

For my purposes, I am pleased to see that AOL has content that is gay specific. Except that pleasure is thrown out the window when I see that anything not rated PG uploaded by members cannot be downloaded by members thanks to the Guides AOL has in place. Censorship is the norm. Says Quirk who spoke to me online: "AOL has these Terms of Service ya hafta follow, which pretty much preclude anything online that isn't G or PG. Their rules, not ours. ;)"

How do the Guides work? AOL employs volunteers who warn members not to use words that might offend the other members. The sidebar *Guide This* later in the chapter has the complete list. "Words like *bar*," according to a source. The list has been shortened recently, but not by a lot.

Switch to 1994 when the rise to fame of GLCF was key to getting the word spread. Quirk explains, "We shouted 'Gays, lesbians, come out' " and it didn't help. What did was the AOL users' strike in early 1995. AOL moved to seek the gay heaven it eventually acquired. I got this in my then-tiny e-mailbox:

STRIKE!!!   THAT'S RIGHT STRIKE!!!!
We are going to show AOL that:

WE ARE MAD AS HELL AND WE ARE NOT TAKING IT ANYMORE

How are we going to strike? Easy, each recipient of this letter will either:

A: Not use AOL during the hours from 8:00 pm until 9:00 pm EST, or

B: If on-line go to the FREE AREA and use nothing but free services. One person suggested signing on at 8:00 pm, going to the Free Area and going off to read a book or fix dinner.

How will the strike work? That's easy too, For one hour each day AOL will see their $$$ tickers hit near zero. If we keep hitting them in their pocketbook, they will have no choice but to GET THEIR ACT TOGETHER. If they decide not to, will simply expand the strike to 2 hours each day then 3, etc.

                YOU ARE EXPECTED TO ABIDE BY THE STRIKE TERMS

Further, you are expected to forward this letter to 10 other users.

What if you don't? Then you become a SCAB and are telling AOL its OK to rip you off all they want. Plus . . . . We have . . . . . . so far . . . . .

27 "STRIKE ENFORCERS."

These are pro-hackers who have a verity [*sic*] of hacker programs designed to spread viruses and generally reek [*sic*] havoc on SCABS. During Strike hours, they will be cruising the chat rooms, taking down names, and generally creating chaos.

************* OUR DEMANDS *********************

1 AOL stops spending multi-hundreds of thousand of dollars, on advertising and such, recruiting new members until they stabilize the system to handle their current usage. NO MORE PUNTS!!!

2 Reasonable response to service and billing questions.

3 No more SPECIAL deals for special folks. The newest is their 20/20 plan which they offered a limited number of people as a "test." It is a step in the right direction but the way it is set up, when its offered to you it will cost you $50.00 extra. that's right, if you are not one of Steve Case's chosen few, he's going to hit you for a $50 enrollment fee.

4 More competitive pricing. And one time AOL had a great service that was competitively priced. NO MORE. If you check rates, AOL is one of the highest priced on-line services around. In Example: one hour a day on AOL per month. . . . = $659.40 per year; one hour a day on Prodigy per month = $ . . . . 360.00 per [year]

Now that's for JUST ONE HOUR A DAY USAGE. [Remember this was 1994.]

5 Clean up the chat rooms.[2] There are hundreds of on-line services and BBS that have taken an extra step to protect children, that's so simple its unbelievable that AOL refuses to do it. Simply set up Adult chat rooms that require the member provide proof of age for his/her account to gain access. The only reason I can assume this has not been done on AOL is that Steve Case condones what is going on in the chat rooms.

6 NO MORE SPIES. In case you don't know AOL has employees who go on-line and befriend users. They then entice them to break TOS [Terms of Service] and get the user's account canceled. For this AOL gives them free hours. Sucks, huh???[3]

Right now you better be careful who you say what to. OK . . . that's it for now. Either stand up for your rights or be plowed under by Case and his "MERRY BAND OF MONKEYS."

---

[2]The big complaint was that AOL was doing nothing but censoring the chat rooms. They were not setting up areas that would in effect allow adults to be adults, teens to be teens, etc. They were just killing whatever they thought was "rude" or "dirty" (their words in a Terms of Agreement Letter, signed by new members in 1995).

[3]Number six caused quite a stir. It was said (and proved true in the press) that AOL hired people, young college kids, to instigate "loud discussion," thus keeping people on. See Guide This in this chapter. This was a waste of people's money but the name of the *gayme* is keeping customers online (to the tune of $2.95 per hour back then).

The strike hit AOL where its bread was buttered. The strike told AOL to look out for its members or its members would look out to others. AOL changed its usurious pricing habits, for a few years. Then in 1997 fees have increased again; $19.95 for unlimited service—a lot more than $9.95 for five hours if you're online infrequently.)

Michelle Quirk says, "Today gay people mostly come to our Lavender Lounge, where queers can meet and talk and discuss honest subjects." Yet our survey of AOL users indicates that most of them go to AOL-sponsored People Connection rooms (both gay and straight). These are run entirely by AOL.

The money is fantastic. AOL claims in public documents that "around 60 percent of online chat" is in the gay rooms run by the company. AOL makes millions on these rooms.

Inside the GLCF and money-making areas for QView are gay people's second most popular area, the GLCF Transgender areas (that are run by QView. A transgender area is a place for people of crossed sexes. In some cases they are men becoming women or women becoming men, in others, those who just wish to "be" or "play out" the other sex. "The transgender area[s]," explains Quirk, "are rooms where everybody, especially young kids, seems to feel very safe."

In 1994 and its mega marketing year—1995—AOL went haywire and somehow signed up some three million new members. There and then they instated a new pricing policy: $9.95 for first five hours, $2.95 for each additional sixty minutes. The first month's five hours are free. CompuServe's prices are still the same and Prodigy has just announced twenty free areas. AOL in its search for new members, now offers "fifty free hours," to be obtained by dialing (800) 845-7189, an offer being advertised on the Discovery Channel! In the numbers game, the AOL brass have not bothered to account for those who sign up only for the "free month" or those who sign on and then cancel.

AOL's exploitation of its members hit critical mass in January, 1996, when the Gay Murder Case occurred[4] and the news came out that AOL keeps records. The bottom line is, be careful. Unlike the IRC, where you can never be held responsible and the words go poof into the night, AOL has two problems: The company holds onto e-mail records for five days and, AOL staff members—*not* the Quirk-managed collective—are going to be watching every word you say in the public spaces. They will warn if your remarks are off-color, and they will even send you a letter if they disagree with your behavior.

There is a room in Dulles, Virginia, that holds your thoughts in daylight. The *Washington Post* spent a few weeks looking into a "strange killing in New Jersey" that resulted in the discovery that, yes, Virginia will be the site of some awfully strange subpoenas: The police started confiscating messages sent on AOL.

---

[4]When I asked, everyone at AOL referred to it that way.

East Windsor, says the town's Chief of Police, is a "good place to raise a kid." It may have been shocking to discover that two men from the town met online in late 1994. Police said that the men exchanged some bitter words online; one thought the other would hurt him. He was right. Eventually, the two men became rivals for the affection of a fifteen-year-old boy. One of the men killed the other. It's very soap-operatic. Because the two had met online, it was obvious (to the police) that their records, kept by AOL, could be used as evidence. (This from *The Post*.)

How do online computer discussions and e-mail—thought by many computer users to be private—become vulnerable to routine criminal investigations?

In January, 1996, the police obtained warrants and went to AOL's headquarters to perform the first-ever search of e-mail records. People went berserk after the story appeared (first in New Jersey papers, then in Washington), because the search warrant has demonstrated the ability of the police to reach information that some computer users thought was strictly confidential.

"In five years, we are going to see police pulling someone's America Online records or CompuServe records commonly," said David Banisar, an analyst for the Washington-based Electronic Privacy Information Center.

The reaction put David Phillips, AOL's attorney, on the spot. "We complied with that search, and yet the reporters covered it inaccurately." The implication was that chat-room records were kept. That is untrue. He admitted that "we need to do a better job of keeping our members informed, but a police subpoena is not something we play with."

It was seen as worse by some. According to Adam Wills, the president of the Portland Bisexual Alliance, "New privacy problems mean that queers will be part of an electronic version of the Salem witch trials; Oregon citizens' alliance works to protect children from homos." He means that anybody can come online and find out, with the right search warrant, who was sending messages about something unsuitable for children.

In fact AOL has already assisted the FBI in doing just that. The Justice Department suspected that certain users were exploiting the network to distribute child pornography and to lure minors into sex acts. The feds spent two years and arrested people after subpoenaing "screen name" records of some guilty and some innocent AOL members. One person boasted on AOL of his sexual adventures with a 10-year-old and even uploaded some pictures. Big mistake. It's a dangerous world, but, except for a few photos, these are still only words.

Congress is now unsuccessfully spearheading a campaign to end the all-you-can-say privileges of Web users (see Chapter 7) with a bill that would basically make each individual responsible for the words he or she types.[5] Civil libertarians, pointing

---

[5]Contact **www.blueribbon.com/html** if you disagree.

to AOL, think it's unnecessary. "See the arrests, which prove that law enforcement does not need Congress to help them out," said Jerry Berman, the director of the Center for Democracy and Technology, as reported in the gay magazine *Baltimore Alternative*.

The *New York Times* once wondered about chat-room rules: "If people can't lie about who they are, wouldn't it make chat-room chatter not only pointless but prohibited?"

AOL has the ability to stop people from saying what they want—and the company uses it. The company decides what's right, wrong, vulgar, sexual, unconditionally acceptable, wrong to use as a screen name, and in their eyes, clearly wrong. Guides (those hundreds of unpaid members who are asked by AOL to watch for nasty language) have read your discussions in group sections and go after you if they dislike your language. "People have access to very personal, private information," said Wills. "[They] read your messages, find out who you talk to, even what your fetishes might be. And right now, very little of that information is being protected."

Law enforcement sources said that, in order to obtain most computer records, investigators will have to seek search warrants under the same standards that now apply to searches of private homes and businesses. Still, police are enthusiastic about the potentially incriminating information stored in computers.

The alarming fact about the Gay Murder Case is that the murderer—convicted thanks to unique court records—met several people in a chat room called New Jersey Men4Men, and the owners of those screen names were later sought as witnesses.

Several crime and computer specialists said it was the first time they had heard of a homicide victim's meeting his attacker online.

Following the cry of "How could you do this?" a spokeswoman for America Online said that it is the company's policy to comply with subpoenas and that the service cooperated fully. Pam McGraw told the press that, although America Online does not keep records from its "chat rooms," it does keep records of private e-mail for five days before they are purged. In a follow-up interview, Quirk said, "We certainly respect and abide by our customers' right to privacy."

AT&T WorldNet[6] bans disclosure "of personal matters. We ban disseminating statements that are false, malicious, violative of the rights of others, or otherwise harmful." WorldNet is a provider of service to the net! AT&T runs long-distance lines and, said a spokesperson, "never monitors phone calls. We do not regulate in any way what people say on the telephone." What is the difference?

CompuServe bans speech that "violates or infringes upon the rights of any others or which would be abusive, profane or offensive to an average person." But even

---

[6]It's not a service but a way for people to connect to the internet and also chat amongst themselves! It is such a new online provider that it could not be considered for our Commercial Services chapter.

if you never offend, CompuServe "reserves the right to edit or delete information, software, or other content appearing on the service, regardless of whether it violates applicable standards for content."

AOL received immediate posts during the news frenzy of the above. According to the *Post*'s story, an AOL subscriber wrote, "I am not a criminal, but I also don't want my sexual preferences, religious beliefs or my politics in a police file."

This has been an ongoing debate for years: Can the words you write hold you liable for libel? Prodigy was sued, successfully, by a stock firm that said a member of Prodigy called them unlawful in their actions. Prodigy had to pay damages. And yet AOL is the worst offender.

In the winter of 1996 an AOL Question of the Week caused members to defect en masse.[7] (Each week AOL posts a question to jump-start a controversy! This is the mid-90s equivalent of the 900 number.) A survey taken right after Congress had cut down gay marriage asked a single question: Should gays have special status? The question resulted in letters like this one from ⟨alaskadan⟩.

> [Mr. Case,] I am outraged that not only have you continued to include the link to the anti-gay American Family Association's Web page with your Reuter's story on Amendment 2, but now you have added an inaccurate and prejudicial survey question. . . . This is an insult to all your gay and lesbian subscribers. The issue here is not whether gays and lesbians want "special rights," a term coined by anti-gay political activists. We want equal rights as American citizens—the fundamental civil rights to employment, housing, and public accommodation, like everyone else. Your adoption of the rhetoric of the far right constitutes an endorsement of their lies and distortions against gay and lesbian people. By using it you are, in effect, taking sides in the debate.

⟨alaskadan⟩ felt that "gay, lesbian and transgender subscribers [did not receive] the same fairness as everyone else," and protested "this anti-gay distortion." He demanded a formal apology, but received nothing even though the media coverage was widespread. Soon after, angered because AOL charges carry surcharges for our colder brethren up north, he ran offshore.

But AOL's problems had only begun. Soon after that incident, a thesaurus caused major problems because of strangely contrived connectors: In the thesaurus to be found in Microsoft Word 6.0, which was downloadable on AOL, words were misaligned. According to a report in the *St. Petersburg Times,* bad words for "Indian" were included in this poorly developed software. Other synonyms included "vicious" and "inverted" for homosexual and "vicious" and "perverted" for lesbian.

---

[7]When researching Web sites for this book, I found that, after AOL's question was posted, Web masters would post replies along these lines: "Send us a message and we'll respond, unless, that is, you are writing from an AOL address," from which I assume that gay users had dropped off AOL.

AOL has seemingly found it difficult to promote its gay content. According to Wayand, "We are trying so hard to get people to *know* we are even here. It's difficult to imagine why," he says with a touch of sarcasm. "Something that makes them so much money should be promoted. But gay kids or newcomers to AOL don't even know we're there. It's weird! For those hundreds of thousands of people who find out about the gay areas, it's kind of a miracle. I mean you'd be surprised how many gay and lesbian people are *on* AOL and don't know anything about us."

Rarely has AOL helped promote or advertise even the *fact* that GLCF exists. When Peter Schamel, the president of New York CyberQueers **(www.nycq.org),** contacted AOL about coming to a "sort of trade show," a large meeting of online buffs at the city's Lesbian and Gay Community Services Center, AOL ignored his repeated offers.

"Well, they didn't even call to say they weren't coming," says Schamel. "It was confusing, because we made a call to tell them to support or confront the community. 'The timing is perfect,' they told us. 'We'll be there.' Then nothing." According to Schamel, who is hardly an activist, our gay community has "gotten screwed over by various online services. We get a lot of talk. We give them a lot of money. It's simple." (Some local services did show up: NYCNET, a gay online service, Echo, Mindvox, and the now-deceased Pipeline.)

My mailbox is barraged with colorfully packaged AOL diskettes—some offer ten hours free time, a few fifteen, and now free months' worth. AOL says that it depends on demographics: Who you are and how much of a proven computer user you are. But AOL is not consistent in its marketing. I get Mac catalogues each month and yet AOL sends me Windows diskettes, addressed to me personally.

The diskettes are another sore point in the community, according to many AOL users I interviewed. A bioresearcher I spoke to at length got fed up with receiving diskettes. "Those great disseminators of disks at AOL sent me them with every piece of literature from magazines to catalogues to a dinner menu. 'Are these people desperate'? I wondered." He admits to using them to store information.

The disks speak of how "capable, powerful, connected, productive, knowledgeable, prosperous and happy" we'll become as soon as we give our credit card number to AOL. The disks have printed on them pictures of the famous places on AOL: entertainment, personal finance, internet connection, kids only, welcome (screen), main menu, newsstand, travel, but nary a mention of the most popular area.

Once, QView decided to produce an AOL disk aimed at the gay community. Easy. AOL paid for the disks and distributed them inside magazine wrappers to subscribers of two competing magazines, *Out* magazine and *The Advocate*.[8] The tag line was discreet: "Join Our Exciting Online Community."

---

[8]"A shocker," said Gerry Kroll, an editor of *The Advocate,* when I pointed this out.

Quirk says: "We wanted to go with 'Now Your Playground Just Got Bigger'—they said no." Why? Could *bigger* be translated as *erect?* "No," she sighed, "it's about the meaning of 'playground' and what might be thought . . ." I laughed, and, later, Quirk told me that she had told AOL about our guffaws and then they did permit disks to go out with the other tagline, but only to *Out* magazine.

I asked Jim Wayand whether AOL promoted GLCF in house; he cracked up. "We've been on AOL since 1990 and have been on the front screen a total of twice. Not good promotion for a top product." This reticence is not typical of AOL only: After a series of news articles on gay youth and pornographic newsgroups had forced it to censor the service temporarily, CompuServe would not post the word *gay* on the front screen for several months.

To the company's credit, AOL is an easy product to use. You pop in the disks, sign on with a credit card, and begin using it. You can find hundreds of magazines, self-help forums to contribute to and gain knowledge about, and quite a bit of self-promotion. I thought it was in my feverish marketing mind, thinking all I saw were in-house ads as I meandered through the rooms of AOL. Then I was handed an internal document for navigators, "About Guides," whose expected obedience to the fatherland was explained in straight language.

> The routine of AOL's Terms Of Service is usually handled by the Guides. Guides are supposed to: 1. Greet members and make them feel welcome; 2. Answer questions about AOL; 3. *Promote online attractions and events;* 4. *Do market research for AOL;* 5. Enforce the Terms of Service. [Emphasis added.]

What is the Gay and Lesbian Community Forum? It is difficult to tell where *it* begins and AOL-land ends. AOL runs the popular chat rooms under the auspices of the People Connection; these are where people do a lot of one-handed talking. Well, it's true.

If you say the wrong thing, an often-unfriendly monitor or Guide will boot you off. Note that gays, lesbians, black people, white people, and car lovers—namely everyone—gets a Guide on AOL. Many of these base folks send letters in the *regular* mail, warning that your membership will disintegrate if you persist. (I can't see AOL forfeiting 10 bucks for bad language, but what do I know?)

The winding Gay and Lesbian Community Forum is constructed of six sections: news and politics, events and conferencing, resource library, organizations, travel, and message boards. The sections are then subdivided into Gaymeland (a news section, facetiously named), GLCF User Manual (very basic), and a few rooms for hanging out.

At present there are no teen homo rooms on AOL because the service has banned the combined use of "gay" and "teen" in People Connection rooms titles.

Intriguingly, there are teen *heterosexual* rooms to be found, and studies show that chickenhawks[9] go for straight teens, so. . . . Apparently there is something about young kids speaking to one another that scares AOL, and under a Term Of Agreement that people must sign—or click—in order to become members (keyword:TOS), AOL officials explain that because of indecency laws they cannot have teens mingling in open gay rooms.

In my experience, Guides have a ball on the job. It is not, however, endearing to be told what you said is unacceptable, and the presence of the Guides may signal the end of AOL's expansion.

AOL's attorney, Phillips, says otherwise. "We hope the Guides act in the best spirit of the members. Perhaps that's unrealistic. What we try to do is create an environment in which people can discuss issues—flirt—get to know each other. We have to have boundaries. Why? Otherwise, it can get out of hand."

The Guides ensure that Gay-OL's population is well cared for—but it is censorship. A debate on privacy can go on and on, but the rules are made clear: On AOL, if you are offensive to *anyone,* you are offensive to everyone.

Quirk says that she concurs with the policy on People Connection, even when someone *gay* yells "Hello Faggots" and is asked to get out. "We've found that queer members don't appreciate the witty repartee of Cro-Magnon homophobes. But hey, maybe that's just our wacky interpretation."

But the Guides can hit you for just being yourself, and a member may complain if she doesn't like your language. Then you're simply booted off. "You must be talking about someone I'm dating," jokes Quirk. "People often feel that they are being ignored in a chat, feel unjustly treated. That is why they do it." Quirk firmly believes AOL gets a bad rap for its censorship policies. When I mentioned that the IRC is censorship-free, she shoots back: "To me, it's like living in New York, New York, and ridiculing Lizard Lick, North Carolina, because it doesn't have a subway. IRC/AOL; different animals. Not better or worse, really, just different."

Ms. Quirk made an interesting observation: "For many of the Guides, it's a power thing. Controversy is the Guide's job, you know [to] move along the chat. We at GLCF are interested in debate and they [just] want to keep people on. It's something we don't get into. Let the powers that be at AOL work it out for themselves. QView is an independent company and AOL is the industry leader." About her own future, she will only say, "We believe that AOL supports, promotes, and markets that which it owns. [It] will always hedge its bets and cover its assets, shall we say?"

To sum it all up: AOL does not do well by customers until the customers complain. The strike did in fact get the prices reduced. But, how come they need to be

---

[9]Men who chase young boys; not legal in this country.

pushed in order to get better? How come the people at AOL were scared to talk to *me* about the gay stuff? And how will they ever start promoting the fast and frenziest GLFC? How about—never?

I was irked by the AOL Buddy List, in which you are notified when a friend signs on. "How dare you tell people when I log in?" I screamed at the AOL PR folk. They admitted that I was not alone. Thousands wrote in asking for that change. You can now turn it off: The keyword is BuddyView. Check Block all Members and don't forget to hit Save. (You can also turn off those instant-message abilities by using the keyword $im_off. In that case, no one can send you an instant message even if you are online.) But I must mention that this Locate Member application is one of the most popular attributes of AOL. There are many cliques on AOL and these people love to talk to one another. Before the change in policy, you couldn't surf a wave anywhere without your friends knowing all your moves. Now you can catch a second wave or two. Easy.

I'm glad the anarchy took. AOL isn't going anywhere so use it for all it has. Yell and scream; make them change.[10]

AOL-opposers got a little revenge. In the summer of 1996 America Online Inc. admitted that it had overcharged its many millions of buyers and agreed to give its subscribers millions of hours of free online time, "settling eleven private class-action lawsuits about disclosure and billing practices." But the lawsuit had originally asked AOL "to pay back users" for millions of dollars in proven overbillings. AOL's answer was to give free *time* online and force its users to waive any right to sue the company for any billing or false-advertising issue—ever!

This company has a lot to learn about doing business with millions of people, straight or gay. After I disconnected my expensive account, I was called and begged to come back on, for another fifteen free hours. I asked why and the clerk said, "Most people don't come back after the first fifteen hours." I demurred. Then I received from AOL Payment Services an envelope that looked as if it contained a check. It was not a check, just a plea. "Dear Mr. Laermer, Please come back. We'll help." A little pathetic?

The gay world is perched to move on to popular homo-only sites on the Web, as www.planetout.com and **www.gaywired.com** make room for gay-friendly chat in rooms that are solely run—and monitored—by gays and lesbians. (See Chapter 11 for listings of public chat spaces nationwide.)

---

[10]As the name implies, Bozos allow you to filter e-mail, say, from an old boyfriend; you will then never receive mail from that pest again! It's like not accepting harassing phone calls. And it is readily available. (In late 1996, AOL lost a case about the practice of filtering; the courts feel that this is a violation of free speech.)

In the wistful words of Quirk, who was uncomfortable admitting it, "We [QView] have to move forward, because this is not an open place for gay people. It is, for now, the only place of its kind. But it can be a little disconcerting."

Guide This

The internet has been widely regarded as the place for free speech. This is not the case on AOL, where you *can't* discuss any topic you feel like, because censorship rules. So-called Guides* (compensated with overhead accounts, worth $20 per month) patrol on the lookout for members violating the Terms of Service—see the list of banned words, below.

From my experience, AOL hires unpaid computer geeks without a life to lurk around and use their powers at the slightest provocation. I hear complaints each week about others being besieged by these people. If you have never seen the list of banned words, take a look. It has been brought to light because "2.5 Online Conduct"—the second term in the agreement you must sign to become a member of this esteemed group—makes it so.

2.5 Online Conduct

Any conduct by a Member that in AOL Inc.'s discretion restricts or inhibits any other Member from using or enjoying AOL Service will not be permitted. . . . Member is prohibited from posting on or transmitting through the AOL Service any unlawful, harmful, threatening, abusive, harassing, defamatory, vulgar, obscene, profane, hateful, racially, ethnically or otherwise objectionable material of any kind.

Meaning, if you disagree with someone, you're off.

Some people believe that it is best for providers to impose restrictions rather than have the government do it and intercede to stop what is generally thought to be "excessive free speech" by the Supreme Court. Censorship, then, is thought to be a necessary evil? But does that mean that free speech is bad in free society? That somehow AOL's censors would be better motivated than government ones? AOL wants to move its own goals out to middle America: get little disks in the hands of as many unsuspecting customers** as possible. The chairman, Steve Case, and his firm have no desire for real debate to occur online, they merely want middle America—who probably wouldn't appreciate the fact that AOL rakes in those gay dollars—to see them as a family company with family rules.

*It is indicative of AOL's treatment of the "help" that the Guide must maintain nine hours online a week policing the service and an additional two hours reading mail and filing reports. AOL says that Guides must troll "in uniform," meaning using Guide screen names. According to one source, Guides are reprimanded for using incorrect grammar, capitalization, and content. For Prodigy's and CompuServe's limited guide rules, see Chapter 6.

**They bill you automatically after the introductory period—ten, fifteen, or twenty-five hours toll (depending on your demographic)—is over. By and large, people don't realize that, because the billing information is not sent to you; you have to look it up. Online!

So censorship rules.

Michelle Quirk has spent no time contemplating this. "Who knows what goes on in the halls of AOL?" she wonders. Then, carefully: "I am not a cheerleader for AOL's policies and often they are hard to comprehend. They want it a certain way and it's their company!"

Banned Words

AOL feels that certain things shouldn't be said, so plainly you can't say them. Here's a list that a Guide gave to me. It's stunning.

"If a phrase comes up that is not listed here, use your judgment to decide whether to warn the member, send E-Mail to your online supervisor to obtain an official decision."* * *

69—sexual
adultery—OK
anti-AOL—(6)
anti-Guide/Staff—types
  of words
ass—unusable
bare skin—OK
bears—OK
bearskin—OK
bi—OK
bitch—unusable
blow (job)—vulgar
bondage—vulgar
bound to tease—OK
boys—OK
clit—vulgar
cock—vulgar
come—OK
cornhole—vulgar
couples—OK
cross dressing—OK
cum—unusable
cunnilingus—vulgar
cunt—vulgar
damn—OK
defecation—vulgar
dick—vulgar
do me—OK
dom—OK

domination—OK
douche—vulgar
dykes—unusable
erotic—unusable
fags—vulgar
fart—unacceptable
fascism—unusable
fellatio—vulgar
feltch—vulgar
fetishes—unusable
flirt—OK
fuck—vulgar
gay—OK
gay bears—OK
gay couples—OK
gay lovers—discretion
gay teens—OK
gay young adults—OK
gay youth—OK
gay videos—OK
genitalia—vulgar
gif—OK
girls—OK
graphics—OK
graphic exchange—
  unusable
hell—OK
horny—vulgar
hot—OK

hot men/women—OK
hot tub—OK
hot videos—OK
insults—OK
KKK—(7)—unusable
kinky—OK
lambda—OK
leather—OK
lesbian—OK
let's go private—OK
lingerie—OK
looking for—OK
lust—OK
masturbation—vulgar
men for men—OK
men on men—OK
men to men—OK
men—OK
Nazi—unusable
nigger—vulgar
nudity—unusable
oral—sexual
panties—OK
penis—vulgar
pervert—unusable
piss—(5)
private—OK
pussy—vulgar
queers—(11)

***Words that are labeled *OK* are on this list because they cannot be used as screen names! Vulgar Words labeled *vulgar* are absolutely forbidden. Discretion means it's up to the Guide.

racial issues—(7)
sadomasochism—vulgar
sapphos—OK
semen—vulgar
sex—OK
sexual devices—vulgar
shaved—OK
shower—sexual
shit—vulgar
slave—OK
slut—vulgar
spanking—OK
stud—OK
sub—OK
submissive—vulgar

swingers—OK
suck—unusable
teen shower—unusable
teens—OK
teens wanted—unusable
tit—vulgar
transsexual—vulgar
transvestite—vulgar
ts—OK
tv—OK
twat—vulgar
underwear—OK
urination—vulgar
vagina—vulgar

video—sexual
virgins—OK
wanted—OK
wet—discretion
whips & chains—vulgar
who like—OK
who love—OK
who want—discretion
women for women—OK
women on women—
    unusable
women to women—OK
women—OK
youth—discretion

6

PRIVACY, TALK, AND THE DIRTY SECRETS OF THE INTERNET RELAY CHAT ROOMS

The gates to the universe of Internet Relay Chat (IRC) channel are open, and in this world anything goes. In the IRC, cyberqueers can interact with other gay and lesbians all over the globe and live out their sexual fantasies, discuss current politics, exchange tips on gardening or carpentry, or join up in a private chat room with men or women wanting to participate in group activities.

You can have cybersex with an Australian bungie-cording business man <bungieboy>, converse about South African gay and lesbian politics over a cup of tea <hotafric>, talk about the paint job on your Triumph with <bikechic> in New Zealand, or plan a vacation to Southeast Asia with <ricequeen>; however, be careful, "she" is a tease.

WHY IS THE IRC SO COOL FOR GAYS AND LESBIANS?

The IRC attracts so many gays and lesbians all over the world, and especially in the United States, because most IRC chat channels are not monitored by any official governmental agencies, nongovernmental organizations that promote so-called moral values, or private institutions. Those IRC channels that are run through online services, may, however, be monitored or even recorded. You will have to check with your specific online service to get more details.

IRC has its own culture. The limited control by outside individuals and institutions contributes to the diversity of communications on the IRC. Gay and lesbian communications have often sought to pervade the culture by rendering its methods invisible to the participants of the "real world," i.e. nongay. The IRC is an invaluable tool in the sophisticated methods of communication used by many gays and lesbians. Anonymity on the IRC draws the loonies, crazies, and the eternally repressed out to play, along with the curious, the playful, and the quite creative—a mixture of people that makes for a delightful and adventurous experience.

Earlier in the book I told you about the Gay Murder Case, a strange killing in New Jersey that led police authorities to AOL's headquarters in Dulles, Virginia, to perform the first search of America Online records, on January 28, 1996. After sifting through electronic information and e-mail all day, officers confiscated dozens of files and turned them over to authorities in New Jersey.

Although civil and criminal court subpoenas have been served on online services, in recent years the search warrant has demonstrated law enforcement's ability to reach information that some computer users incorrectly thought was confidential. That is, of course, the reason that IRC works for most gays and lesbians. No one can interfere. It just isn't possible!

THE DIRTY DETAILS: CONNECTING TO THE IRC AND ERROR FIXING

Connecting to an IRC channel is not difficult at all. It is not readily advertised because it is a free and potentially dirty service. There is more than one way to log on, and no one way is particularly better than any other. It just depends on your software and hardware. The goal is to log on to a server that has IRC capabilities. Here are some recommended ways to connect to the IRC:

- If you are a student on the .edu internet system, you probably already have access. You just need to type irc at the UNIX prompt (UNIX being the program that maintains your school's system), and you will most likely be connected.
- Some cyberqueers may be fortunate enough to have an account that turns their PC or Mac into a UNIX terminal. If you do, then you need only set your communications software to 8-N-1 and your terminal to VT100. If you are unable to connect, then either you do not have a UNIX connection or your system administrator (sysadm) needs to get the correct software. I am sure a friendly phone call to the overworked sysadm will assure that you are provided with the correct software. Bribery with pizza or coffee may be your best approach. If the sysadm has forgotten how to communicate in the real world, you may want to find software. This is difficult and time consuming for the inexperienced computer user. If you dare, IRC software can be found at Usenet *alt.irc* or at cs = pub.bu.edu/.

- If you are neither a student nor have access to an educational server or UNIX account, you need a different approach. First, you need to locate an IRC server. The World Wide Web (WWW) provides an array of information on IRC servers. Simply do a search on the topic IRC.

  Second, once you have found a list of IRC servers by surfing through the IRC WWW sites, you can connect. Usually, if you follow the icons, which say "getting started," "finding a server," or "getting connected," a list of servers that provide access to the IRC will become available. Also, when surfing through the WWW, if you are interested, you can get more of the gory details on the IRC global network, and some of the facts about its inception, administration, and use. You can also connect directly with some of the limited, and dare I say, slightly boring IRC channels provided.

- Even easier, some WWW sites will let you connect directly to IRC channels. However, when you join a chat channel that is operated by a gay or lesbian WWW client, there is the possibility that the channel is being monitored and/or recorded. Many WWW clients monitor and record the chat channels to decrease their legal liability. Check with the operator on the channel or e-mail the WWW client to get the specifics.

- If you are already connected to a server, but it does not provide IRC services, just Telnet to another server that does provide IRC services. Most online services provide the Telnet option. However they usually charge extra (even though it costs them nothing). On CompuServe, you need to click the Internet icon, then the Telnet to a Site icon, then "Access a Specific Site icon. On AOL, Prodigy, and MSN, it's the same. Browsers such as Netscape and MSN's Internet Explorer, or IE, can also take you to the Telnet function.

  Telnet server addresses can be obtained from the WWW or from other cyberheads cruising around the Multi User Dimension (MUD). If you Telnet to a server, connect to one close to you to diminish lag (delays in electronic signals). There are addresses in every state; those listed below are most active participants. And, go to /www.geocities.com/Colosseum/1822/mirclink.html for telnet advice daily.

ALASKA
merlin.acf-lab.alaska.edu

CALIFORNIA
othello.ucdavis.edu
C-w6yx.stanford.edu

COLORADO
irc.colorado.edu

FLORIDA
irc.math.ufl.edu

ILLINOIS
irc.ecn.bgu.edu
irc.acns.nwu.edu
irc.uiuc.edu

KANSAS
irc.ksu.edu

MARYLAND
svcs1.digex.net

MASSACHUSETTS
world.std.com
berry.cs.brandeis.edu
husc10.harvard.edu
irc.mit.edu

MICHIGAN
pegasus.ccs.itd.umich.edu

NEW YORK
azure.acsu.buffalo.edu
organ.ctr.columbia.edu
mcphy0.med.nyu.edu
irc.rutgers.edu

PENNSYLVANIA
irc.lm.com
irc.duq.edu

TEXAS
irc.bga.com
irc.tamu.edu
dewey.cc.utexas.edu

WASHINGTON
irc.eskimo.com
irc.pnw.net

- Once you find a server with IRC capabilities, be sure to place it in your bookmark on the browser you are using, and jot it down so you can access the server if the page is down, so you can get a fixed place. Fixed places are hard to find. The second time.

  Enter the address for all these areas, and don't forget that all-important port number, the four-digit number after the address.

  Possible problems:

1. The server denies you access. This may be because there are too many people logged onto that particular server. Servers have a limited capacity; once that limit is reached, they will not allow anyone else on. You have choices: Find a new server, or wait a few minutes and try again. (Yeah, nobody wants to wait. Go have a Pop Tart.) The turnover rate is usually very high and you can sneak in when someone leaves. Also, DENIED ACCESS may mean that you have tried to log on to a server that has restricted access. When it asks you for a password that is a bad sign. It may also mean that the server's keepers are having a bad day. Or it means that you no longer have free access. Cripes.

2. Your keyboard freezes. This, too, may be because the server is filled. Again, you

can either find a new server or wait! It can mean that the server is down (not operating), so I would recommend your trying to find a new IRC server. It only takes a minute. . . .

3. Your Web site's server connection is down. If you did not write down the address of your IRC server site you were not being smart; you will have to wait until the site is up again, or look for another page with IRC server addresses. If you did write it down, just Telnet to the address.

CHOOSING YOUR IDENTITY ON IRC

Now that you are connected to the IRC, it is time to meet other gays and lesbians and chat, make a date, arrange phone sex, or plan a barbecue. The first thing you will have to do when you log on to the IRC is to pick a nick (nickname). Do not underestimate the importance of your nickname. At first your nick is your only identifying characteristic in the world of cyber queerdom. From this point on, no one will know who you are.

There are a few commands to get someone's "finger" (account from which they are connected), but fingers are usually not that descriptive. There are other ways to break into the code, but let's not get carried away. If people want you to know their names, they will tell you or you can tell them yours, if you wish. Probing too much for a real-world identity may not go over well and you'll end up chatting with yourself.

Yeah, right. Très boring.

Creative nick(name)s are a plus if you want to meet wild and crazy people. Traditional names will tag you as a newbie—or someone new to the whole IRC thing. This is not bad if you like to play the naive role. Most people prefer, however, to meet a wide spectrum of individuals. Examples of newbie names are <Mike>, <Steven>, <John>. This isn't always true of the lesbian IRC channels. Girls tend to communicate less evasively than the boys do, and using standard names will not necessarily detract from your adventures in lesbian queer cyberspace as much. We know there are wild girls out there too, and creativity will definitely not hurt your pursuit.

Many people use nicks that describe characteristics of themselves or of someone they would like to chat with, such as: <Butch7.5u>, <Lipstick>, <Nastyboy>, <Muffluv>, <Teachme>, <Swimer>, <Aussie>. The numbers in names are usually anatomical references, with the letter "u" standing for "uncut," as in penis. Many boys often use sports to identify themselves and, they hope, attract a same, that is, someone who has a fetish or desire for that sport. College boys are especially known to do this, because most of them are closeted. This can be fun sport in itself, sure, but most of them lack the creativity that many of us seek. The University of

Michigan and the University of Missouri seem to have large contingents of these "sport boys." If this is your fetish or your thing, enjoy. Here is a little adventure I had.

I was talking to a guy named <swim20>. If I had lied to <swim20> and told him I was a swim coach at UCLA, I am sure I could have spent hours telling him (or her) what I was doing to make him (or her) happy. I needed to move on to find someone who wants to be creative back. But maybe you want to be the swim teacher.:) (I just smiled at you.)

It is common to find sexual descriptions in nicknames: <lther_top>, <Jocklic>, <strapon>, <BigBott>, <Horndog>. These boys and girls are often very adventurous, a little older, and very busy because all those college kids are bombing them with messages. If you can be crafty enough, they may send you a note back. (We will give some hints later on how to attract these dirty guys and gals.)

Other nicks may be titillating in themselves, and indicate that the person is a fun time. Examples: <Supah>, <YoMom>, <ChatKat>, and <Turbo>. You could just "dish," chat, or share opinions about music, art, or politics with someone who thinks as you do way over in New Zealand, Vietnam, France, or Brazil.

You can change your nick after you sign on to an IRC channel. So don't panic. Identity can be changed in seconds if you don't appreciate the crowd you are attracting or the lack of crowd you are attracting (see the section on commands, below).

After deciding on your nick, you will have to choose a channel to chat on. Picking a channel depends upon your own desires and interests. The names of the channels are pretty self-explanatory, but if you are unsure, just join in and find out what it is all about. To log on to a channel, simply type: /join #[*channel name*]. Some popular channels are #gaysex, #gaychat, or #gay[*name of your city*].

Once you are on the channel, everyone already there will know. There is a log for newcomers. Your nick and the address you're coming from in cyberspace appears, usually below The Action. You will also be able to see the nick and log-on address of everyone else connecting to the channel after you. (There are very specific commands for doing this.)

When you first sign on the first thing you see will most likely be text scrolling by. This is people conversing in cyberspace. Congratulations. You're on the internet. To have everyone on the channel hear you, just type away. There are some special commands that are helpful and extra fun to use. They make you more demonstrative—often too much so.

GAY AND LESBIAN IRC CHANNELS

It is hard to find an IRC channel that does not have some sex or flirting going on. After all, IRC is the "free" internet, and everyone is acting out. Some of the more popular channels specifically meant for gays and lesbians are:

#gaysex   This channel is self-explanatory

#gaychat   Don't think you will get away with sex when chatting to everyone. You will need to find a private room on this channel. (See the section below, Creating Your Own . . . Channel)

#gaynyc   Interested in meeting a New York City gay or lesbian? This is the place. However, most of these children are looking for a "real" date, so you might not be tolerated if you are a pretend New Yorker, so be creative :).

You may also use the /list-topic command to find a list of those channels that have designated topics. This command will undoubtedly produce a giant list of channels, and many will not have any relevance to gay and lesbian topics. Use the PAUSE button on your computer to stop the scrolling. (See the section below on commands for a description of /list-topic.)

WHAT ARE THE HOTTEST IRC CHANNELS?

If you are into sex, #gaysex is the first place you should go. However, there is no one place that is always hot, because anyone can create an IRC channel. Creating your own IRC channel is essentially creating your own private chat room, so the hot channels change all the time. Just ask people on #gaysex where to go if you are getting bored there; but surely it can keep you busy for a little while.

CREATING YOUR OWN GAY AND/OR LESBIAN CHAT CHANNEL

If you are feeling adventurous, and you would like to create your own IRC channel, and solicit other gays and lesbians, it only takes a step: type /join #[*name of your channel*]. You will now be the operator of the channel (unless someone already has an IRC channel with that name). In order to control the channel, that is, be able to kick people off, you will need to use the /mode command. The mode commands are slightly more complicated, and you will undoubtedly spend more time setting up your channel than doing what you came here for: meeting people. Use the mode command to set up an IRC channel—proceed at your own risk.

COMMANDS

There are many commands on the IRC. The two easiest ways to learn about what commands do are (1) to type /help and a list of all the commands will appear, or (2) message someone on the IRC channel you are on and ask. Some basic commands to get you started and make you look good to all the other cyberqueers on the IRC channel are listed below.

/join [#*channel*]
Joins you to the channel specified

/bye [*message*]
Will cause you to log off and the message that you have entered will be displayed to all the channels that you were on

/nick [*new nick*]
Lets you change your name; will inform all current channel users

/mode [*designate mode*]
An advanced command that lets you control the attributes of your connection to the IRC channel and the attributes of the IRC channel itself

/msg [*nick*] [*message*]
Lets you communicate with the person whose nick you have specified

/me [*message*]
Will display an *action* that you perform to all channels you are on (see Action section).

/query [*nick*]
Lets you communicate with the person whose nick you have specified all the time, so that you do not have to keep typing /msg

/help
Will give you a list of all the commands and explanations of them

/whois [*nick*]
Will give you the address from which the person whose nick you have specified is connected

/who [#*channel*]
Will tell you the names of everyone on the channel

/help [BOT]
BOT is an operating language that runs chat channels. However, the acronym is also used to represent a database that can be accessed with commands that include the word BOT in the statement.

This command will give you the help commands on that specific channel. You have to get the BOT from when you initially signed on (it will be the person who greets you), or by using the command /who [#*channel*]

/msg [BOT] info [*description*]
This will present a sentence when you log on and choose to display it that describes yourself, or at least some version of yourself.

/list-topic
This will generate a list of channels that have a topic set (a designated discussion topic). This list will scroll by unless you use the Pause button in order to look at each channel.

MODES ON THE IRC

Modes are your own personal destinations for yourself, available on any channel. They are complicated and are usually used by more advanced IRC users. For example, if you wanted to make yourself invisible to channel users you would use mode +i. +*m* means that the channel is being monitored, but on many gay and lesbian channels this only means that some cyberqueer is making sure that no fag bashers come on the channel. If you are interested in modes, you should use the /help command.

BEING PHYSICAL

If you want to display an *action* on an IRC channel you are currently on, just use the </*me* [*message*] command. If you use this command, your name and the message you typed after the /*me* command will appear to the other users of the channel you are on. This is especially fun if you want to display a bit more personality or describe yourself in a way that might induce a ruckus or some play.

TAKING ADVANTAGE OF ANONYMITY

One of the great advantages of the IRC—and one of its great downfalls—is that you can portray yourself as anyone. It is a given that most people on the IRC are not as they portray themselves. If you choose to, be yourself, but don't expect that of anyone else!

Every now and then you will meet someone who is real. Admittedly it's hard to determine this when you are a newbie. The best way to tell is if someone is asking general questions, a kind of chat to "get to know you first."

NOW, PLAY

Once you have picked your nick, and given yourself a cyberdescription, you can begin to play. I mean play. Find out who is on by watching the names scroll by, noticing who logs on, or by typing /who #[*name of channel*]. By using the /who command, you will get a list of all the people on the channel you are using.

Use the hints given about nicks earlier to pick a person to converse with. The demeanor that you present, "the person that you are," will attract like-minded people, we hope. If you are cyberslutting it, asking lots of questions will not get you too far, unless the questions are provocative. To learn about provocative questions, see, in Chapter 7, the section on cmu/edu and the many erotic story addresses found on the net.

The list that follows includes some good questions to ask privately. Note that these are meant for private chat. Publicly? Only if you are interested in an audience!

Are you feeling like a toad today (tonight)?

Is this the way to Sesame Street?

Where can you get a good [expletive] around here?

Do you shave [part of the anatomy]?

You can also ask more general questions of everyone, and hope for a decent response:

Anyone from New York City want to play?

Is there anyone in their twenties and into bondage?

Is my daddy out there? I'm lost.

Once you get going, you have to keep up the pace until you have them. You will know when you have someone because the responses come back quickly. Some cybersluts have been known to be cybersexing it with four or five people at the same time, God love 'em. But if you are only starting, better let one work for you.

WHO IS GETTING ON WITH WHO

Depending what time of the day, week, and year that you log on to the IRC, you will find a different clientele at your beck and call. During the school year, many college students spend their lives on the IRC. And why not? Their internet connections are usually free! (As mentioned earlier, college students are sometimes fun.) But according to my well-intentioned friends, they tend to be submissive and just too darn curious. If you are into that, go for it. The late evenings during the school year holds the most promise for finding your favorite quarterback typing away in his dorm. With the ten- to twelve-hour time difference, the late, late evening is also when Americans can run into the Aussies and New Zealanders. Many "down unders" are computer users, and love to chat away. Their pics are always a treat if you are into the outdoor men and women; a lot of so-called bears.

After 5 P.M. and until 11 P.M., a lot of 9- to 5-ers log on. During the day you find all sorts of Americans on, because Europeans log on in the late afternoons. This is a lesson in time-zone watching. The gay people from Latin and South America are in the same time zones as Americans are and are on throughout the working day and early evening. If you speak (write) Spanish, you are at an advantage when it comes to cyberqueers from Latin and South America. Many of them do not write English, and will come on to the IRC with the famous "habla espanol?" Watch for <spice-cake> who definitely knows English, and has many stories of Rio. I love <cake>.

Aussies, or queers from Australia, are a favorite for American boys, and often you will find an American posing as an Aussie just to attract more boys. To expose the poser, just ask him what a dingo is. But don't be mean and tell all the other cyberqueers; let everyone have their fun. Dingo away! The Australians are for the most part a happy bunch, but they are bombarded with a lot of messages. If you are not crafty enough, you might not get a return message.

The New Zealand crowd is available sporadically, and quite fun when they show. Don't, however, get into a culture exchange with them unless you are interested in hearing about the latest American movie releases in New Zealand.

The Southeast Asian clientele is always fun. It would be better if we spoke the same language. Oh, gee whiz. Many interesting stories about the gay life in Bangkok and other Far East regions. But don't let the young ones get going on American gay culture. Just like Americophiles all over, Japanese kids want you to answer questions for days. Personally, I feel guilty when I stop answering them. The Japanese people, young and old, whom I have met on the net simply love to exchange stories and ideas, but there are not too many around the dirty little channels. I dare say not. And this is inexplicable.

Europeans are Europeans and will chat up a storm. The Germans and Dutch are always ready for a good time, especially the Germans (considering the oppressive censorship laws). You might find a language conflict, but hey . . . be creative. The rest of Europe is a trip and they have many gay communities and a cyberculture of their own. Getting tapped in is easy if you are polite, and they will assist you in pretty much everything. Don't preach America though or you will be stood up. It is always best to ask Europeans about their lifestyle, if you want to make friends.

South Africa has a large clientele in the late evenings and they are chatty; sometimes too chatty.

ARE PEOPLE BEING SHADY?

Are people being shady and not responding? Wait for people to sign on. That way you know they are alone, and then send them a private message with provocative undertones that best represent your intentions. Don't assume that cyberqueers are being shady when they do not respond. There are thousands of reasons that someone may not be receiving your messages, so try later, or try someone else. But please, don't get hostile; it will not get you far.

HINTS FOR GETTING IT ON

Lure them in slowly by sending enticing and provocative messages. Don't bombard anyone with graphic or fetishist ideas. Once you have lured someone in or they have lured you in, you can begin to get more graphic.

Politeness

Politeness will definitely get you far. The use of "please" and "thank you" may get you that hot date that you were always searching for. There are a few things that being nasty can get you though. You could be kicked off the channel, or you could find someone as nasty as you are, and that could be both scary and definitely adventurous.

The Annoying, Persistent, and Boring

Get rid of them. You can always say goodbye politely and add a smiley face :) to ease tensions, but if that only turns them on, you may have to be aggressive.

Here's how. Tell the pestering individuals that you are chatting with someone else, and then simply don't respond to messages. If they begin to make public displays focusing on you, they will most likely be removed by the operator. If the operator is not present or is a milquetoast, others will most likely get rid of him or her for you. Do not fear, when people are ignored, they lose interest very quickly.

"Phone Sex Anyone?"

Some people get on the IRC and immediately ask if anyone is interested in phone sex. This is a very fast, quick, and easy way to get your jollies off or on. If you are into phoning people, you, too, can ask if anyone is interested in "phoning it." This is a good way to give more money to Ma Bell and company. Although I have never heard of people getting harassed after giving their number out, it is always a possibility. Use common sense. If your main interest is phone sex try the chat channel #phonesex.

Style

People love to create their own little secret language. The symbols and acronyms listed in the e-mail chapter are some of the more common ones. I would not recommend your speaking solely in acronyms and symbols unless you want to attract a like-minded individual and annoy everyone else. Occasional use is a must if you want to convey "what's really up." I am sure that, if you frequent the IRC enough, you will be creating your own lingo in no time. To spice up the chatting, if you want to avoid phone sex, put an emotion or action in asterisks (as described earlier). For example: *evil grin*, *blush*, or *fart*.

CONCLUDING YOUR IRC ADVENTURE

IRC is one of the most adventurous and uninhibited ways to meet other gays and lesbians (and their friends, including transsexuals and transgender types, bisexuals, and the curious) around the world. The format of the channels, your own "creative" identity, and the people you interact with are not guided by any rules or regulations.

Enjoy your time on the IRC and remember to put all your trays in the upright locked position, and extinguish all smoking materials . . . well, if you're on #gayair anyway.

Hostile Takeover

In the interests of cyberdebauchery, and just for fun, I logged onto my server thinking that all was OK and I was in for an evening of fun or lust, whichever. I was denied entrance to the channel #gaysex. My message stated, "#gaysex is an invite channel only." Well, how could cyber gay sex be invite only? Perhaps there were just too many of us, and I did not have the right address or nick. I wondered . . . Was cyberspace turning into a veritable New York disco? I couldn't believe I wasn't on the invite list.

Asking around some other of my favorite and quite pleasing channels (#gaychat, #gaynyc, and #gaybos), I learned there had been a hostile takeover of #gaychat. "A what?" Not being as incredibly well versed in the language of hostile takeovers (corporate America is not my scene, see), I had to play cute and hope that someone would give me a more detailed explanation. After all it was "hostile" in the extreme!

Well, feeding my curiosity, <tropicult> from the #gaychat channel was helpful in telling me how to coordinate my own hostile takeover. Hmm, I wondered. Should I try it out? The IRC chat channels are not monitored; it is a free-for-all. Then I learned from <tropicult> that all you needed to do to coordinate a hostile takeover is to become an ops or a master (operators and masters are the administrators on the channel and control discussion context).

This is when it got to be a kick: Once you have ops or master status, you can kick people off the channel at your own free will and then use the /invite command to make the channel available only to those you choose to invite to it. When asked to provide more details on this #gaychat takeover, <tropicult> sort of lost interest in me; he was simply not intrigued by my not-so-computer-savvy questions. Boo, hoo.

<PlanetX> was next on my list. He was thirty-three, at least he said he was thirty-three, and he (we know it could be she) was much less cooperative, yet revealed that, "the channel was taken back, and we think we know who did it."

"What were the intentions of the takeover?" I asked.

<PlanetX> self-righteously replied, "Well, if you stay on the channel a while you will find out." "No more comments," is all I could get from him. The conspiracy list was getting grand. I wanted to know why he was being so quiet about his little piece of the cyberworld. What were they planning for the cyberterrorist?

"Revenge," I asked?

<Dancer>, found later on #gaysex, told me that they [the ops] are probably planning a bombing. That was cool. <Dancer> said that someone logged onto #gaysex with his nick and gained master status. The person who gained master status, a good cyberkid, in turn, made someone else (the deceiving gaybasher who closed the place down) an ops. In other words, the someone else was a good, closeted flirt. (The asterisks are meant to make the action statements distinctive. However, they do not appear on the IRC.)

<Amadu>   Hello cowboy

<Texan>   *Texan lassos him self a flatlander by the name of Amadu*

<Amadu>   Hold-on there cowboy, I am seein' stars!!

<Texan>   *Texan hog ties amadu and prepares him for a brandin'*

<Amadu>   *Amadu faints and whimpers, admitting his defeat or win???*

We love them horsies.

The, ahem, individual who took over #gaysex was one of the many IRC-bashers who frequent the channel. Occasionally, the freedom of IRC attracts those who choose to terrorize others. This is not a plea for censorship. The ops and masters of the #gaysex channel have come to know many of the addresses of bashers and have banned them permanently from the channel.

Measures like banning are not uncommon in IRC cyberspace. In a rather complicated system, bombing means the fortunate demise of people like the #gaysex cyberterrorist. What you do to rid yourself of creeps on the IRC differs from what a system operator on a regulated chatroom (on an info service such as AOL) would do: The info service folks "eliminate" the person. We in cyberland ban a person by bombing the gaudy tyrant with electronic garbage and thereby crashing his system! It is painful.

Anyway, the moral of the story is that, no matter how complicated the computer technology, the emerging mores of gay and lesbian cyberculture are making it worth the fight to clean up our privileged space. (Or, the moral may be: A good flirt can get far.)

7

THE WORLD OF THE MODERN COMPUTER GEEK:

A HOST OF SITES

This is not a list! The following host of sites has not been compiled to fill a quota or astound you with my ability to download a search engine's findings. Too many other books do that. The sites that are reviewed here exemplify the work of gays, lesbians, bisexuals, and transsexuals on the internet. Traditionally nongay sites are also included here because the gay and lesbian internet culture does not revolve solely around sites with rainbow icons or pictures of naked dudes. Now here's what you've all been waiting for. The reviews contain opinions from first-time cybersurfers, interviews with site administrators and internet site creators, and commentary on the politics of gay and lesbian cyberculture. All of this information is combined to produce a sociological examination of the gay and lesbian content on the internet rather than an impersonal listing of all sites for which you can check out the Gay Yellow Pages; they, too, are reviewed below.

- **Organizations:** A grouping of tons of sites for the organization person in us all! These are places to group, not to be a leader. And these are the spaces that will take care of us in times of need.
- **Taking Care—Of Yourself and One Another:** A general look at sites that will help us see one another better, or make us think well of ourselves.
- **Serious Dress up for Queers:** An opinionated study of the TG or transgender community (which I sincerely love).
- **Voices We Should Know:** A listing of places to go that are both famous and helpful. Also featured here are the spokespersons of our times who are spreading the word on everything from the sexually fascinating to the constitutionally important.

- **That's Entertainment Indeed:** The adventurous section. Yep, this stop offers a slew of sites listed solely for their entertainment value.
- **Shop Till You Stop:** Looking for special gifts . . . or are you merely a shopaholic? This section is a must for those who need to shop online.
- **Our World and Welcome to It:** Also known as The Global Community Online, here's a look at the online queer universe. (I call it "The Whole Megillah.")
- **Gay and Lesbian Youth Net:** For the youngsters, this section aims to help young 'uns get square on the net (and meet one another for whatever purposes they want to meet).
- **Online Versions of Print Magazines:** Many say that this area is the most crucial of all. The Web got started with magazines that were once print, so dig in to see how they have progressed. And laugh a lot! Yep.
- **Kooky Folk You Need to Meet:** You have to see them to believe them. Now, I need to caution these are the "nuts" of the chapter. An enjoyable treat for all.
- **Around the U and S and A:** Here's a place to stop if you want a sneak peek at a variety of cities.
- **Uncategorically Helpful Ideas:** A place to find things even if you could care less!
- **Mini Tour of Travel Sites:** A travelogue that merits your actually going to these places via the Web.
- **Helpful or Crafty Ideas:** This stop provides a few tips from our friends on the Web; everything from tangling up pics so that they look funny to how to find a roommate of your persuasion!
- **Miscellaneous:** For good reason, baby, this is stuff I couldn't find a place to put. (And stuff that cracks me up.)

So, Get On with It, kids and learn about gay and lesbian cyberculture.

ORGANIZATIONS
(Lists, Search Engines, and Places to Go)

Pridenet
pridenet.com/aboutus/

PrideNet is "a freely accessible, online magazine and business directory providing visitors with information on products, services, and issues related to the GLBT community."

Here lies the first of many online experiences meant to "help GLBT (the acronym for gay, lesbian, bisexual and transgender) types feel more like a big happy family" or, in this case, a business and personal directory for queers of all ilks to either read or contribute to; something like a big boy's bulletin board! They want you to use this to get to all gay information on the planet. It's not as up-to-par as that calls for, but does cover the following six areas.

- PrideNet devoted to online AIDS memorial and awareness
- Free listings in a business directory
- Affordable internet presences for nonprofit organizations
- Free links to other community-related (read "no sex allowed") companies and linked sites
- A continuing community survey, conducted to reaffirm the gay community's high-profile status on the net

Planetout (PNO)
www.planetout.com

Planetout landed in late 1996. Understand that PNO, as it is called, is a Web site, a place on MSN, *and* a space on AOL.

When I arrived on the "throbbing" planet ("Come see our throbbing planet" is how they advertise it on the front screen of AOL) I saw an impressive format—accessible and easy to understand—that far surpassed the boring Windows folder format of the MSN version of Planetout. Those little action boxes on the intro page make figuring this out a snap!

Outside of the MSN and AOL versions, PNO has recently launched a Web version. Confusing, sure, but huge too. Both on the Web and in its newest online area (AOL), we went at it with a vengeance. My assistant and I were loaded and ready for a world of fun and debauchery; instead, we found a barren and desolate planet. Where are the boys and girls? Now that the word is out, they may show up in the coming months, but at this point it looks pretty bleak.

Overall, the chats, messages, and personals section are a breeze to move through, but the personals were under construction, and the message boards, when added to all of AOL's message boards, should be another planet called Yawning Planet. The Kiosk is an "avant-garde" newsstand with latest political dyke publications and fashion fag mags to thrill the girl in both the girls and boys. Community Groups and Political Affairs can be found in the Civic Center. You can visit the Queer Resources, but its library is as barren as the chat rooms I wandered into. In fact, I found all the advertising to be just a wee bit misleading.

I saw a search engine that stated, "Culture: Every facet of queer culture, including history, the arts, sports, travel, humor, folklore and more."[1] There were sixteen

---

[1]To be fair, this is new. We know they are growing. But as the competing Out.com said in its magazine version, "This is a lot of received information."

articles under this section and one that I read had to do with admitting you were a geek. Let's hope someone interested in exploring the truly rich dimensions of gay and lesbian culture doesn't visit this rundown shack of a library! Maybe someone has been stealing the books or something.

I was initially intrigued by advertising boasting an extremely "international clientele." However, for all of the Middle East I could find only two homepage sites listed in the directory. Come on! I want the Middle East. And where are those Australians?

By the time you get to the shop on Planetout, you feel as if you have just tracked fifteen miles at Gay Pride and are rummaging through all the crap forced on you by some overly zealous, broken-out-of-the-closet, button-clad dyke with her gay bro', Rick. Is Planetout already falling out of orbit?

The Queer Resources Directory's E-mail Listserv

The Queer Resources Directory is the best of the queer e-mail services. The QRD is many gay men's and lesbians' favorite site because, unlike advertiser services, it offers information on everything gay without mussing it up with other people's begging. The Queer Media and Queer Organizations, Directories & Newsletters are found at the URL www.qrd.org/qrd/orgs/.

To the obvious entries, you can add your own very quickly with the ALSO feature of QRD, which is a handy box (very clever) that you click to get additions onto the bottom of the screen. For instance, in Media we asked to see TV (because we are having trouble finding decent TV listings, although many are talked about). Suddenly there was TV and also:

- **Artcom International: Promoting the use of film and video as a tool in the ongoing struggle against AIDS.**
- **Exploiting Media Opportunities: Skills for interacting with the media.**
- **Media Watch columns: A Web version of a popular area on the QRD. Here you will find media posts such as this from 1996:**

>From: Al Geiersbach <Bob.Sillyheimer@mixcom.mixcom.com>

>Date: Wed, 24 Aug 94 19:57:11 CDT

In 1994, Senate bill S 333 and an equivalent House bill attempt to re-instate the Fairness Doctrine (in broadcasting), which was a Federal Communications Commission regulation guaranteeing opposing sides of important public issues equal opportunity for presenting their points of view on issues the station might choose to present. Congress passed legislation to codify the doctrine in 1987, which President Reagan vetoed.

After the veto the FCC revoked its rule which had established the doctrine.

Given the large margins (see below) by which the 1987 measure passed Congress, one would think it a snap to enact the legislation with a Democrat in the White House. However, Rush Limbaugh and right-wing religious broadcasters have mounted a campaign against what they call the "Hush Rush" law, so it is being given a very low priority, and even some very liberal senators such as Russ Feingold are taking positions against it.

The many calls generated by the Limbaugh radio program and by the religious broadcasters have apparently not been matched by any display of public support.

It is in the hope of reviving the Fairness Doctrine while a Democrat is still in the White House to sign it, that this information is being posted.

InfoQueer: Homepages of GLBTQ People *Out on the Net*
server.berkeley.edu/queer/gis/homepages.html

As its names suggests, this is a gigantic list of people all over the world who are out on the net. It is homepage heaven. You'll find their names, where they're from, and a direct link to their e-mail addresses so you can contact them. There are also links to the Queen Infoservers homepage and the UCB Bisexual/Lesbian/Gay/Queen homepage. You will spend lots of time here. You will lose your eyesight staring at the screen for hours at a time. Very good resource, fun to find people, say "Hi" to Larry Kramer online, etc. Bookmark this even if you don't do anything else on this site.

The Gay Web Page of Canada, Inc.
xs4all.nl/~heinv/heindoc/gayhttp1.html#us_canada

Canada's Oscar for best gay Web sites.[2] No, in all seriousness, this is *quite* a list. We spent many minutes going through it and discovered that Canada's quite a gay little country.

A place to go when you are looking for a few short stops along the way to gay information. These are the same places you would find on any mall-related stop, the only difference is that it's organized as a select few—a Canadian-favorites listing. Thanks to "heindoc," I found The Rainbow Room, and this place turned out to be unusual. Located at **www.crl.com/~heath/rainbow/rainbow.html,** it turned my head for one specific reason: Rainbow starts with my favorite quote: "I don't mind straight people as long as they act gay in public." Yes, sir!

From there, Rainbow is a basic site. A hundred or so questions you can find at any of a hundred other places, answering such long-lasting queries as "What is gay

[2]This site is not really called The Gay Web Page of Canada, Inc., but they had many titles, so I just made one up.

anyway?" and the local fave: "Did medieval gays marry?" Also, local news from around the globe. It's a rainbow, man.

The best tool on "heindoc" is its references to homepages. It is difficult to find good pages by people on the net. On We are Everywhere!, you can find—anyone! Heindoc is one of a few places to find other people's pages, clearly defined and out there for everyone to click on!

Gay Yellow Pages
www.gnn.com:80/

One of my favorite search services is GNN (Global Network Navigator), the navigator issued by American Online that uncannily includes Don George's strange and not gay diary of the world. (We are shocked to see AOL do something this quirky, no pun intended.[3]) Plus, you can find places we often heard about in our search of the wild Web, such as GNN Nifty Prizes for people who continually stop by.

The ad for "$1,000,000 web crAOL" grabbed me, because you get a chance to win a million smackers each time you use the search engine, but you are asked to register your e-mail address each time you do. Big sister is watching.

What's gay about this place is the Yellow Pages.

First, search **www.gnn.com:80** for the Whole Internet Guide. Then ask for any kind of gay info from the gnn.com search engine, which is reachable at **www.web-crAOLer.com/GNN/.** Then ask for gay yellow pages; **www.yellow.com** is the right one, baby. There are tons of good listings here. (For some reason, every time we looked for the Yellow Pages on other mainstream search engines, we were told that gay wasn't in the search possibilities. Excite, a reputed engine, did tell us that "exact search notes" were to be found on the words gay yellow pages.)

Be sure to see the fellows at Spanq, not to be confused with Spanker, a well-liked "Web derider" at **www.spanker.com.** These Spanq guys are Web-weary revelers who know the place and can navigate what's new. They will tell you what's up on Web central and, unlike cNet,[4] which we like, and some other sites that are

---

[3]Michelle Quirk runs AOL's Gay Forum.

[4]More information about cNet Central can always be found at: **www.cnet.com/Content/Tv/CNETCentral/index.html.**

As cNet tells me in my weekly e-mailed magazine: "Those of you with Sci-Fi Channel should keep your TV on for The Web, **cNet's** program devoted to the most exciting, rapidly changing part of the Internet." Detailed info about The Web—including direct links to the download of the week and to Justin's homepage—is available at **www.cnet.com/Content/Tv/Web/.**

cNet also has a show called The New Edge to be found at **www.cnet.com/Content/Tv/Newedge/index.html.**

Air times for all cNet programs, including ninety-second "tech briefs," can be found at **www.cnet.com/Content/Tv/Airtimes/airtimes.html.**

helpful but a wee too mainstream, this exhausting sitelet is going to amuse you, educate you, and eventually run you down.

By the way, don't forget that **Global Network Navigator** is owned by America Online, so all Dulles, Virginia, censorship views apply.

Southern California Gaywired
www.gaywired.com

Gaywired, a favorite of mine, offers a variety of services for the lesbian community that allow anyone with a product to place information online in the easiest way possible. You don't really get much more complete than this dependable site. Boasting a gay business directory the size of New York, links to Genre, California Night Life, and a whole host of others on every aspect of gay life from sports to medicine to travel to shopping, Southern California Gay Wired has everything that you'd need right at your fingertips.

Mainpage for Queers United
cs.cmu.edu/Web/People/mjw/Queer/

A very friendly page, this is queer information collected from the mail address **witbrock@cs.cmu.edu.** Regardless of your time on the Web, you must give credit to people who give of themselves as freely as Witbrock! He has found some quasi-literary links that give due time to the people of the world who see themselves as writers.

Fantasies of Straight Men (**hss.cmu.edu/bs/05/Sartelle.html**) is an essay that attempts to link (really link) the notion of why gay men aren't allowed into the military with, well, the fact that men really want other men. This all comes from the gender and sexuality section of the Web people's great minds. "This page publishes texts which address gender studies and queer studies, with a focus on discussions of sex, gender, sexual identity and sexuality in cultural practices."

For the purposes of making my editor's life a little easier, suffice it to say that there is good information here, not to mention some pretentious stuff: Did *you* know that New Zealand recently outlawed discrimination on the basis of sexual orientation?

Huh?

I didn't.

This site has a great library for women's studies. Books are available right from the Web. It's a wonder. Plus basic info for queers-on-the-go with up-front explanations of how the rainbow flag got invented. Again, who knew?

The Cyberqueer Lounge
cyberzine. org/html/GLAIDS/glaidshomepage.html

Here it is. The fab pages of our buddies at the million-hit-a-week cyberzine (one that includes Mary Kay Cosmetics for Girls) who are smart enough to crack even the stuff most queers don't know is happening in their world. (The above-mentioned Mary Kay Lady proclaims in all her glory: "I'm the only out gay person in the organization and this company has to know how fabulous we all are." Touché, sister.)

The good and the bad about the Lounge: There is a Red Ribbon AIDS and HIV total-world search engine, without any commercial interjection from the CqL, with its own URL: **worldclass.com/redribbn/.** Still, there are too many frames at the CyberLounge. With all the new technology available, cheaply, to the Webmasters of the United States, I admit that this is a little ungainly but I see progress a-shakin'. One last word: Watch for their search engine, which is made up of "chat-pal" functions for intercourse (talking, kids).

I spent time researching with the queers here. Tom, the guy who runs this, is one of the few site owners who will respond to your every wish-mail! (Find Tom at **tomh@cyberzine.org.**) He is a hardworking man who spends all his time making no money on this site. He wrote me and we started chatting about the sad state of affairs at the CyberLounge:

> There is something brand new at the Lounge everyday. Not only are there new links installed but many new projects. The Lounge is vast and there are hidden or better yet buried treasures that crop up. The Lounge is currently getting a complete face-lift. Should be done [shortly] The new look and feel will be frames [instead of one big page]. Then possibly doing a Java applet layout[5] for fun.
>
> But the sad thing is on other side of the positive stuff is that the Lounge almost closes every single day. There are many reasons for this. Now the popularity of the Lounge is such that I cannot afford the site. If you wore my shoes for a day or so you would be surprised at the masssssssssive problems on this end. The problems stem from lack of money. Due to the overwhelming lack of support here, I am in debt over my head and will never in this lifetime be able to pay it back. Consequently a site like this is a day-to-day operation.
>
> I have been given notice by my provider of *******MASSIVE******** cost increases etc., because tooooooo many people come and use the Lounge. The connectivity will be over $500 a month plus the cost of new operating systems. Like, oh sure, I see the gingerbread man too. So on one side of the electrons people see the "TV" screen. On this side it is verrrrrrrrry sad.

---

[5]See Glossary; this is easy to install if you have the Netscape browser or the Microsoft Explorer version.

He ends his e-mail and immediately writes back: "Did you know that this site was one of the very first 500 WWWs on earth?"

With his heart in the right place, Tom has put out a queer directory for people looking for info about AIDS on the Web: **www.cyberzine.org/html/Queer/Publication/one/AAAtester/cyberqueerpage.html.**

If you want to be linked to the Lounge's site, do an AutoMagic registry to have your site linked to his: **www.cyberzine.org/cgi-bin/mailmerge/mailmerge. cgi/templates/links.**

Scientific Inquiries into Sexual Orientation
www.cs.cmu.edu/afs/cs.cmu.edu/user/scotts/bulgarians/
science-pg.html

Subtitled "Nature vs. Nurture," this "scientific" organization offers articles and information that can be linked so that people will no longer be confused about what sexual orientation is. A sampling of what's available on this site:

- Simon Levay's article in the August 30, 1991 issue of *Science* entitled "A Difference in Hypothalmic Structure"
- "Between Heterosexual and Homosexual Men" demonstrates that the biology of sexual orientation may be explored in a controlled, scientific manner
- A December 1991 Opinion piece for the *New York Times,* in which Michael Bailey and Richard Pillard discuss their research with male identical twins and their belief that sexual orientation has a genetic basis
- The responses, by June Reinisch of the Kinsey Institute to a question about the influence these hormones might have prenatally on sexual orientation

And on it goes.

TAKING CARE—OF YOURSELVES AND ONE ANOTHER

Cable Positive
Cablepositive.org

Started by interested parties as the site equivalent of "the cable industry's AIDS action organization," this is small but has great potential because of its ability to inform—and to collect money for a worthy cause. A newsletter about their efforts and funding results can be gotten online, with the wonderful title, Positive Outlook, "published and distributed quarterly to educate the industry about HIV/AIDS and to keep supporters informed about Cable Positive's programs and events."

Cable Positive was founded in 1991 by people who, much like those at Lifebeat (the music industry's answer to AIDS/HIV), wanted to raise awareness—and money—from within the advertising and cable TV industry. The organization arranges to produce and distribute a variety of public service commercials and print ads that are run on cable companies and in cable mags. This is mainly a volunteer organization with a small staff; the site is managed by Mediapolis, a New York-based Web service company. As much a networking company as a site for people to discover more about the AIDS charity within cable, this is a trial balloon to see how much more they can get from interested parties (in terms of dollars) and works as an informational site with a dire, simple message: Help those in need.

Condom Country: Assistance Page
condom.com/Condom/Country/privacy/
123456789012345678914192952

Just when you thought you'd seen it all, change your mind with the Condom Country sexual assistance homepage. Just like credits to a fine/bad film, the first few graphs of a Web site are something you use to build an image with. And here is a sample of their farmboy talk: "I reckon' this is why we set up this eee-lectronic catalog in the first place. It allows you and ev'ry other cowpoke to purchase condoms and sexual aids from the privacy of your own computer."

And it's just that—aid for people who need the assistance. In short, you can order just about whatever makes your little heart tick. Choose Sexual Accessories—sign in first, use any name—and get this list:

- Edible Underwear
- Rug Burn Kit
- Handcuffs
- White Furry Handcuffs
- Tiger Skin Furry Handcuffs
- Vibrators
- The Stimulator
- Whips
- The Frayed Whip

Need we say more. Happy shopping. What else do you expect?

JB's Workout (a nonporn site)
www.leland.stanford.edu/~destari/workout/workout.html

I like Mr. JB. He is so proud of his condition that his homepage was developed as a way to make something of it. In something like three years he has become a muscle monster. His homepage exudes innocence. But I suppose he's no babe in the woods—otherwise why would he put this buff body on the site? He's got technology on his side, and gravity too. In a bathing suit he's a keeper.

> I decided to put up a page about my own workout program consisting of my workout plan and some pictures. I've been lifting weights since May of 1994, which makes it about 2 years by now. I'm 5'6" and 135 lbs. at the moment, and my goal is to get up to at least 150 lbs., which will take a tremendous amount of work, since I have a high metabolism. However, when I do gain, it's usually pretty solid and defined. For those of you who might be wondering, all of the pictures on this page are of me and were taken between January and April of 1996.

He then produces his schedule and it's a doozie:

> My schedule is more or less "four days on, one day off," meaning that I go to the gym for four days in a row and then rest one day. Sometimes I rest 2 days instead of one, depending on other demands. Here's how the cycle goes: Day 1: Chest & a little bit of Triceps. . . . Day 2: Back and a little bit of Biceps. . . . Day 3: Legs. . . . Day 4: Arms and more Shoulders. . . . Day 5: Rest. Time for the beach! ;-)
> And he is beautiful. Bodybuilders by the dozen can be found at **guyz.com**

SERIOUS DRESS-UP FOR QUEERS

A List of North American TG Resources
www.cdspub.com

All right, there's a lot in here for transgender types. But this is a group for which the Web comes in handy. The list dispenses information as a community service; this is a joint venture of 3-D Communications, Inc., the American Educational Gender Information Service (AEGIS), and the International Foundation for Gender Education (IFGE). These are listings and site addresses taken from the text of *Who's Who and Resource Guide to the Transgender Community*. There's a separate list for Canadians! Within the site is a community guide, with no contact names and numbers listed by state.

The Society for the Second Self (SSS), Inc., a nonprofit organization (e-mail to

TRISINFO@aol.com; postal address: Box 194, Tulare, CA 93275) is the best source we've found for dealing with families and the problems that relationships go through after TGs announce their wishes or take the next steps. The address for this a highly recommended site and its magazine, *Femme Mirror Quarterly,* is **www.first-nethou.com/brenda/tri-ess.htm.**

Someone wrote to this site with an entertaining query: "Can wives join?" We await the answer!

Transgender Forum and Resource Center
www.cdspub.com/index.html

The introductory statement of the Transgender Forum and Resource Center is "Welcome to the largest transgender [any combination of the sexes within a single human] resource on the Internet." Its goal is to provide up-to-the-second news and accurate resources on a variety of subjects, and a selection of vendor services.

Whenever a place is touted as huge, you are usually expected to spend money. TGs do shop, so money can be spent here. But be careful. Some of the sites this Forum links you to look awfully tawdry. Be skeptical before you hand over your credit card.

Meanwhile, on an up note, the Transgender Forum News Weekly offers a how-to guide for newbies.

Mrs. Silk's Magazine for Cross-Dressers
www.gold.net:80/users/av73/

Ever since I met the gay guy from South Carolina who told me that his Klansman granddaddy wore "real silk" robes, I prick up my ears wherever I hear talk about silk.

So on to Mrs. Silk of Britain. The British take themselves so seriously, it seems, except when it comes to cross-dressing, which is considered all the rage there. All the activity on this site comes from Mrs. Silk, who doesn't spell well but has great intentions. She gives lots of material for cross-dressers, has a particular fascination with her maids, and even links to one X-rated story about panty stealing that was pretty darn funny. But the line that got me hooked on Silk was: "Find also a step-by-step article about how I transformed Trish from MACHO MALE into one of my maids." Everyone's dream, *n'est-ce pas?*

Oh you want to go right to that link? Have your maid dial up **www.gold. net:80/users/av73/makover.htm.** The macho man—Patrick—is cute and looks very tempting in a bustier.

VOICES WE SHOULD KNOW

ACTUP/NY
www.actupny.org

ACTUP, the AIDS Coalition To Unleash Power, is a diverse, nonpartisan group of individuals united in anger and committed to direct action to end the AIDS crisis. ACTUP, in case you live under a Webless rock, is *the* place for gay men and women to discuss and act on behalf of the people with AIDS around the globe. This is their global homepage, undernourished but important.

ACTUP meets with government officials, distributes the latest medical information, protests, and demonstrates. They are not silent by any means! They challenge anyone who, by their actions or inaction, hinders the fight against AIDS. This includes anyone responsible for inadequate funding for AIDS research, health care, or housing for people with AIDS, anyone who blocks the dissemination of life-saving information about safer sex, clean needles, and other methods of AIDS prevention, and anyone who encourages discrimination against people who are living with AIDS.

Besides the latest news on ACTUP's latest movements, users can link to several other organizations under the ACTUP umbrella. Look on the weekly calendar, available on the back table at Monday Night Meetings, to see when and where groups are currently meeting. Or call the Workspace and ask.

ACTUP Americas Committee

Promotes the creation of AIDS-activist groups throughout the Americas. Future objectives are to exchange information on life-saving therapies—both traditional and alternative—and to fight for the expansion of AIDS drug trials (as well as access to them) in all of the countries in the Americas.

AIDS Cure Working Group

Building a coalition and creating actions to push for the AIDS Cure Act, a design for a Manhattan Project to find a cure for AIDS.

Alternative and Holistic Treatment Committee

Advocates a natural and holistic approach to treatment for people with AIDS, including nutrition, meditation, massage, and other therapies; fights discrimination against holistic therapies by insurance companies and the medical establishment.

DIVA TV Committee

DIVA (Damned Interfering Video Activists) creates and disseminates video covering AIDS activism, including a weekly public-access show. A fundraising committee organizes events to raise money for ACTUP actions and operating expenses and handles the sale of ACTUP merchandise. (For New Yorkers: Diva TV is found on New York's Channel 69.)

Giuliani Working Group

Creating broad-based direct action to counter Mayor Rudolph Giuliani's deliberate neglect of the AIDS crisis.

Health Care Access Committee

Demands better insurance coverage for people with AIDS; fights insurance industry discrimination against people with AIDS.

Lesbian Caucus

Deals with lesbian issues within the AIDS crisis, especially the lack of research on woman-to-woman transmission of HIV.

Media Committee

Encourages and monitors coverage of the AIDS crisis and ACTUP visibility in the print and electronic media by sending news releases and press kits to general media. Our friends.

Needle Decriminalization Working Group

Advocates distribution of new ("clean") needles by city and state agencies; runs needle-exchange program.

Outreach Committee

Advocates AIDS activism in all communities; informs the public of ACTUP's actions and accomplishments through forums, panels, and other events; publishes and distributes the "What's Up ACTUP?" newsletter, brochures, posters, and flyers.

Pediatrics Committee

Advocates for children with AIDS from infancy through adolescence.

Planet Claire Working Group

Works on internet issues (such as this Web page).

PWA Housing Committee
Advocates appropriate housing for homeless people living with AIDS.

Spanish Communications Committee
Informs the public about AIDS and AIDS activism through speakers and written materials in Spanish; develops Spanish translations of English written material.

Treatment and Data (T&D) Committee
Monitors experimental medical treatments for people with AIDS; works for better access to promising treatments through direct action and from within the medical and scientific research establishment.

Testing and Disclosure Issues Working Group
Advocates for fair HIV testing and disclosure policies that guarantee anonymity.

YELL (Youth Education Life Line) Committee
Advocates explicit AIDS education for young people and condom distribution in the public schools.

Other sites that are linked on ACTUP's Website include:

ACTUP New Member Packet—The original ACTUP Working Document

The ACTUP Working Document (sort of)—"Time to Become an AIDS Activist," (direct-action manual)

The Lesbian Avengers Action Outline

Civil Disobedience Manual

Marshal Training Manual

Getting Arrested—Why do we do it:

AIDS Political Funerals (DIVA TV)

The Role of AIDS Activists (TV transcript)

How do we start an ACTUP chapter?

ACTUP/New York Capsule History

ACTUP Research Bibliography

ACTUP General Meeting Facilitator's Manual

ACTUP/NY Treatment and Data Committee Teach-in (1989)

Welcome To New York (handout at Stonewall 25, 1994)

I Want To Live By Any Means Necessary

10 Things We Will Not Tolerate

The Denver Principles of PWA Empowerment

Safer Sex Page (**www.safersex.org**); last on this awe-inspiring site by boys and girls who make AIDS activism their number one goal.

Privacy.org
www.privacy.org/pi/

The internet privacy coalition is here. Very succinctly, the idea of a privacy coalition is "To promote privacy and security on the net through widespread public availability of strong encryption and the relaxation of export controls on cryptography." With that in mind, they link you to thousands of links and a hundred or so action points that make good reading: secret Bush administration memos about getting into people's wires, and how the government makes it difficult for us to be secretive. Also, the latest on crypto—or making your online life much more private!

Read about the Golden Key campaign; it is not what you think it is.

The Blue Ribbon Freedom Campaign
www.eff.org/blueribbon.html

My favorite worthwhile site of the decade. One of the ten most-linked-to pages on the Web, here's a way to discuss various intricacies of the debate at hand. (The debate is about freedom on the Web, kids.) What will happen if the government votes to ban "whatever" on the net? Find out fast. For the writeup on Blue Ribbon, refer to chapter one.

Here is what you can link to:

American Civil Liberties Union
Center for Democracy and Technology
Electronic Frontier Foundation
Electronic Privacy Information Center
Internet Action Group
Voters' Telecommunications Watch

Why a Blue Ribbon Is Symbolic

A blue ribbon is chosen as [the] symbol for [the] preservation of basic civil rights in the electronic world. The blue ribbon is, of course, inspired by the yellow POW/MIA and red AIDS/HIV ribbons, and also by the (U.S.) Second Amendment, child abuse, Israel awareness, and various public land usage rights ribbons, the breast cancer pink ribbon, etc.

EFF (Electronic Frontier Foundation, sponsor of this site and upkeeper on an almost daily basis) and other civil liberties groups ask that a blue ribbon be worn or displayed to show support for the essential human right of free speech. This fundamental building block of free society, affirmed by the U.S. Bill of Rights in 1791, and by the United Nations Declaration of Human Rights in 1948, has been sacrificed in the 1996 Telecom Bill. [This bill is under discussion in the Supreme Court (2/97), although a three-judge panel in Philadelphia said, in 1996, that it's unconstitutional as it is written.]

The Blue Ribbon is a way to raise awareness of these issues, from locally to globally, and for the quiet voice of reason to be heard. The voice of reason knows that free speech doesn't foster sexual harassment, abuse of children, or the breeding of hatred or intolerance.

The basic credo of blueribbon.html and EFF is: "We insist that any material that's legal in bookstores, newspapers, or public libraries must be legal online." Another site, **blueribbon.html#others,** will take you to yet other sites where you can find the text of the bill and the judges' decisions. A particularly poignant place on the site is **Sites That Could Be Banned (www.eff.org/blueribbon/sites.html).** Numerous sites are sure to be killed off if the 1996 bill ever becomes law: art, literature (the card catalogue of the Library of Congress!); health (The Breastfeeding Page or the impotence-information site!); support groups; entertainment; news media and government; as well as "Any story from the Associated Press, CNN, *USA Today,* NPR, etc., concerning abortion, AIDS, homosexuality, and many other serious social and medical concerns."

To support free speech on the net—on your site or even over your e-mail signature if your e-mail is transmitted through a Web server—you can steal (they condone it) a "free speech on the net" blue ribbon icon and place it there. Show you care. Chances are you do.

If you have any doubts, read the various links that discuss the banning of Twain in public school systems; and also the basis of the court challenge to the Communications Decency Act—that the law is unconstitutionally overbroad and so vague that no one knows exactly what is permissible and what is not.

RainDrop Laboratories
agora.rdrop.com

RainDrop Laboratories opposes all attempts to restrict adult communications to that which is acceptable to the Radical Right's view of what children should be exposed to. We also oppose any attempt to hold access providers liable for material or collections which they do not themselves author.

That's the opening credo of RainDrop Laboratories, an organization whose goal is to help people get connected and communicate electronically. It is owned and operated by Alan Batie in Portland, Oregon. The primary service provided by Rain-

Drop is the public-access system Agora, providing dial-up internet access to the Portland metropolitan area. RainDrop works with two locals to bring you FreeRTR. If you need a full-time, permanent connection, you can connect via RAINet, Inc. or FreeRAIN.

This site contains a listing and links to engaging places to browse on the Web, including Local Agora Information, Navigational Aids, Queer Resources Directory, Bob Dole's Campaign, the mock site (gone, we hope, by now) Not Bob Dole's Campaign, and CityNet. Happy browsing. And say hi to gay and lesbian Oregonians, who have had a rough few years.

The Crossnet Site
users.vnet.net/crossnet/dilemma.htm/

I was quite happy to get here. First, I crinkled my nose and read:

> Can you hear me . . . I'm calling out . . . I'm crying out . . . a cry for love . . . I can feel you . . . you're touching me . . . you're healing me . . . my cry for love.

Gag me. Then the FAQ (frequently asked questions) of this page caught my eye. It started out, "WHAT'S THE DEAL WITH THIS PAGE?" I figured it out soon. "Real questions people have . . . so if you have a question concerning Christianity or homosexuality, . . ."

Surely they didn't jest. Normally, I wince when I see crap like this on a regular site. But, as Christians don't know where to go *at all,* this can be a real help, except that Crossnet deals with more than just the basics; it deals with homosexuality as a problem. You have to dig deep to find what this is about.

> Generally people who hold the view that homosexuality is an alternative lifestyle say that anyone who is primarily attracted to the same sex is gay. To them there's no way out . . . in other words, they say you're born gay . . . it's in your genetic makeup . . . etc. They're usually referring to sexual orientation when they use the term gay. Others are referring to sexual practice when they use the word. Since the word means different things to different people it's impossible to answer this question to everyone's satisfaction. The question itself rests on the notion that everyone must have a label of some sort, which is a false assumption.

Suddenly, it turns, well, evil. The topic becomes genetics! "If it's not genetics, then where do homosexual feelings come from?"

According to Crossnet, it all derives from a problem, one that "stems from a bad relationship with (or the absence of) the parent of the same sex in the formative years." Or worse yet, sexual abuse.

FAQ is all there is here. An exercise in futility for those of us who are comfortable. For the rest it can be hell! Here I am, a happy gay man, reading something that's never been thrown in my face before. Suddenly I want to become an activist. This is good.

If God loves me so much, the argument continues, why can't I just be gay? And where did I stop reading?

> Moral absolutes are hard for a lot of us to understand. To many people they seem arbitrary, bigoted and harsh. Try looking at it in this context: do you think theft, lying, murder and adultery are good for a person?

Not for the weak-hearted. Ban it!

Progressive Director at IGC
www.igc.org/igc/

> The Institute for Global Communications (IGC) presents the Progressive Directory— your gateway to environmental and progressive resources worldwide. The Institute for Global Communications serves to expand and inspire movements for environmental sustainability, human and workers' rights, nonviolent conflict resolution, social and economic justice, and women's equality by providing and developing accessible computer networking tools. IGC is the [United States's] founding member of the internationally acclaimed Association for Progressive Communications.

The Institute of Global Communications, through IGC Networks—PeaceNet, EcoNet, ConflictNet, LaborNet, and now, WomensNet—serves individuals and organizations working toward the goals listed in its opening statement.

IGC currently links over thirteen thousand members and an additional thirty-thousand activists and organizations, via its membership in the Association for Progressive Communications, with local access in over 133 countries. It's a big one.

IGC Networks is connected with the net and its vast range of services, including FTP, Telnet, Gopher, the World Wide Web, SLIP/PPP, e-mail, and news—see Chapter 2 and the Glossary for explanations of these basic terms.

As a member of any one of the IGC Networks, you have access to resources for everything they offer. (Become a member by clicking Yes. Send nothing.) In addition to the services available to members only, the IGC Networks have a presence on the Web through the IGC Progressive Directory, and in speedy, text-only format, via the IGC Gopher.

Among the basic resources you can find here are IGC Network Services: What's Uniquely Available on the IGC Networks; IGC Internet Services: World Wide Web, Gopher, Mailing Lists, and Domain Name Service; IGC Individual & Group Accounts:

Services and Rates—individual group, library, and student accounts; IGC's Guide to Electronic Publishing; A History of IGC and Its Networks; IGC Staff, Volunteers, and Interns; and Organizational Members of the IGC Networks.

Plus, find out what you need to know about the millions of PeaceNet members, EcoNet organizations and materials, EcoNet Gopher and the EcoNet Web site, Labor-Net's unions and organizations, or individuals from unions who participate in Labor-Net@IGC.

Bromfeld Street Educational Foundation
www.bsef.org/

I appreciate local culture and this site, from Boston, speaks volumes about the possibilities. This is a good example for gay people all over the country (the world perhaps?) to see how local organizations can start something locally.

Bromfield Street Educational Foundation is a nonprofit, tax-exempt organization that operates ongoing cultural and educational projects. Its mission is "to effect social change by educating, organizing, and mobilizing lesbians, gay men, bisexuals, and transgendered persons to work for sexual, racial, economic, and gender justice. BSEF is dedicated to promoting a progressive, multicultural voice in this ongoing struggle."

The site **www.bsef.org/OWindex.html** is linked to such sites as the national lesbian, gay, bisexual, and transgendered writers conference (Outwrite), a way for people who write to meet offline.

Then **www.bsef.org/gcninfo.html** peeks at *GCN,* a paper of note for progressive-thinking gay people and the oldest queer weekly paper in the nation, begun (say the notes) in 1973. It has always been one of the country's most progressive and activist voices, committed to an inclusive vision of liberation that does not begin and end with "gay rights."

In the 1970s, *GCN* was out front on feminist issues linking gay and lesbian rights with abortion rights. In the 1980s, *GCN* was known as a pro-sex voice and as an antiracist voice. In 1992, *GCN* ceased publication in order to revamp and revitalize itself. It was reborn in 1993 as a quarterly news journal, publishing on longer, analytical pieces. It remains the only periodical on the proliferating national gay media scene where race, class, gender, sex, and age are central and critical focuses and where the struggles for sexual, racial, and economic justice are understood to be inextricably linked.

An unusual side to BCEF is that Bromfield Street presents a reading series featuring lesbian and gay fiction writers on the third Wednesday of every month at the Living Center in the heart of Boston (behind the Hard Rock Cafe!).

Rainbow Page
www.enqueue.com/ria/

The Rainbow Page: Find icons for gay anything, by Jase P. Wells, a younger person's icon, who has great opinions and fills particularly good voids. An org of one, he says that he is "attempting to gather all gay-related icons that were scattered around the net and put them into a central location for all. It makes me happy to think that by sharing my interests, I may be helping or just plain entertaining somebody, somewhere."

Such as: Pride colors, Lambda flag, the awareness ribbon. This is a good place to acquire Web-worthy extras for your e-mail and other uses.

The NYC Lesbian and Gay Community Services Center
www.gaycenter.org

In December 1983, the New York City Board of Estimates approved the sale of the former Food and Maritime Trades High School, at 208 West 13th Street, to the Lesbian and Gay Community Services Center, Inc. for $1.5 million. In its first year, sixty groups met regularly at the Center. Today, more than three hundred groups call the Center home. Since that momentous day when the Center opened its doors, it has fortified and enriched the lesbian and gay community.

The Center provides a secure place for meetings to plan, advocate, ACTUP, share our knowledge and our expertise, and shape our future. The Center itself produces many health-related, civic, and cultural programs. Each Center program, in some way, seeks to allow us to become more fully aware of ourselves.

Programs produced by the Center, and linked on the Web site, include Project Connect, an alcohol- and substance-abuse prevention and intervention program; Youth Enrichment Services (YES), an activities-based program for lesbian and gay youth; CenterBridge, the Center's AIDS bereavement program; Center Orientation, the Center's "Welcome Wagon" program produced in-house and in all the boroughs of New York City; Center Global Action Project, our international gay and lesbian rights program; Center Kids, the Center's family project; the Pat Parker and Vito Russo Center Library, New York City's largest gay and lesbian lending library; the National Museum and Archive of Lesbian and Gay History; and Promote the Vote, the largest gay voter-registration and mobilization project in America, created in 1992.

Announcements about the latest happenings in the gay and lesbian community are uploaded regularly. This is to keep users informed of what's going on in gay life and what one's useful role is—whether it's volunteering, supporting financially, or simply being informed.

This is an important site for gays and lesbians to see; the center needs support. The site is not technologically or stylistically interesting—or even colorful—and considering how important the Center is, that's disappointing.

(For info on the LA Gay Center, see Chapter 11.)

THAT'S ENTERTAINMENT INDEED

Popcorn Q, from the Makers of Planetout
www.popcornq.com

The largest gay online anything brings, really, one of the most condescending sites I found during the research. This was the tease(r) set upon us from the eventual creators of Planetout.

"Why are movies so important to lesbians and gay men?" says Jennie Olsen, creator of this site about movie queers (supposedly all of us). "Because movies are such a central and important part of our lives." Gimme a clichéd break! Personally, I have never asked to be *either* Bette Davis or Joan Crawford. Or the chair, for that matter.

On this site the artistry of movies is trivialized. Many of the classic—read "old hat"—monster moments from Bette Davis's mouth and (I kid you not) *The Wizard of Oz* are repeated, and there are too many tests of knowledge.

The credo of this shticky site, which was the precursor to the gigantor www.planetout.com site reviewed earlier, is something that I think is highly untrue: The evolution of Hollywood's portrayals of gays and lesbians clearly matches the changing attitudes toward lesbians and gay men in society." Why, Shirley, you jest. I enjoyed *Making Love* for the camp value, but do we need to see it (taken apart) as if it were sport? Movies = entertainment. Popcornq (until late 1996 found when you dialed up www.planetout.com) = boredom. And yet again, the organizers do a big number on getting you to purchase things from the vault—all those darn movie posters are available at Kmart.

This Way Out Radio
qrd.org/qrd/www/media/radio/thiswayout/index.html

A Web version of one of our favorite radio shows, *This Way Out,* is available, in addition to being on www.planetout.com, or PNO, on its own site as a conduit for noncommercial information and stories to share with your brothers, sisters, transfriends. (PNO has in the past year taken a lot of great sites and attached them to its own, but as the creator and founder, Tom Rielly, explained: "We know enough not to make the sites just a part of Planetout." Find This Way Out on your own.)

This Way Out is the award-winning internationally distributed gay and lesbian radio program that is currently airing on over eighty stations in eight countries. The weekly half-hour "magazine" program is produced in Los Angeles and distributed via satellite to stations around North America. Your best and most efficient use of the program is to contribute news, so long as you tape it. They will, if it's crucial to the news of the day—or a cute feature—even give you space from another, noncompeting medium . . . like a Bloomberg radio interview that aired elsewhere!

Go to this handy site on the Web for schedule, dates, news, information, and to contribute local news ideas to the half-hour program. These guys also air "gay music"—music with unusual genes, I guess—so upload or send to them at their local address found on the site.

SHOP TILL YOU STOP

Queermall
www.zoom.com/qmall

Not to be confused with anything in Paramus or the Rainbow mall; you will find nothing but shopping at Queermall. Rather than even pretend to be a resource for information, the initial page respectfully takes you to purchases, services, entertainments, people to know, publications, and more. Why, you could say, this is a Yahoo! (a popular search engine) for gays and lesbians, if it weren't for the fact that more than three-quarters of the lot are for-purchase items!

Unique categories to note—and I mean unique: Fashions for the Queer, Financial Information and Services, "The Food Court," Pride Products, Transgender Resources, Queer-Marketing Discussion List, and software. Buyer, beware. You are probably not getting the best price for your gay dollar. Keep in mind that the Queermall gets a cut of everything.

Designed, developed, and maintained by Home Economics Industry. If not poignant, it at least reminds you of tenth grade.

Gay, Bisexual, Lesbian and Transgender Information
www.abdn.ac.uk/~csc145/Gay-rights.html
also at
www2.wintermute.co.uk/users/snuffles/The_Plaid/
gender.html

This is a site for sore lookers. First, if there's *anything* you need to learn about g., b., l., or t. obscurities, this is a place to check. Everything from the Lutheran Church's views on gay marriage to the Transgender FAQ Web site. Plus, tons of well-chosen research papers.

The "transgendered information" (their term) is to be found right off at the second listing. Most of the info is carefully arranged by Mharia [*sic*] from Scotland, who explains: "A lot of it is shamelessly plagerised from elsewhere, some of it is contradictory, and a lot of it is not my own opinion, but, like a good software engineer, I believe in the principle of re-use and so I've copied the information from a wide variety of sources that I believe will best help people find out what it is all about."

Careful, though, because nearly half were outdated links and that means that **Sorry DNS server not to be found** will pop up all the time. Look and learn. For us, a favorite was the TG Humor Page—**www2.wintermute.co.uk/users/snuffles/ The_Plaid/humour.html.**[6] There I read about the post-op (postoperative) TG who sees a friend for the first time since the op occurred. (Oops.)

Friend:	"So, Jane, did it not hurt to get all this stuff done to you?"
Post-op:	"No, not really."
Friend:	"What about the breasts, surely it hurt to get them?"
Post-op:	"No, no, that was all done with hormones."
Friend:	"What about getting your dick chopped off. Surely that must have hurt?"
Post-op:	"Nope, that was all done under anesthesia, you see."
Friend:	"So none of it hurt at all?"
Post-op:	"Well, there was one thing that hurt."
Friend:	"Yes?"
Post-op:	"Well, when they cut my salary in half!"

Now on to the next.

Rainbow Mall
www.rainbow-mall.com

Through this, a different, more commercial type of rainbow study, Dan Zietman, proprietor, has made a lot of friends—and a lot of near enemies—with this mall, his own creation of good stuff and pretty mediocre listings.

---

[6]www2 is becoming a second area for surfers. In many ways it'll become a 900 or Offers Area of the Web.

In an ad Zietman was pretty much telling the world that he had a lot more than he was advertising on the Mall. He said: "It's a function of the gay world to want to see things and buy things and get them now. It's the way the cities have become and I'm bringing that idea to gays and lesbians all over with a mall mentality."

A mall mentality this is. "Welcome to Rainbow Mall, the world's first Gay shopping mall (as far as we can tell): where Gays, Lesbians, bisexuals, transvestites, transsexuals, transgendered, androgynous persons, queers, homos, tomboys, fairies, dykes, and their friends (did we leave out anyone important?) can shop, share ideas, gather information, and feel at home—much like a "real" mall, only Queer, and you don't have to fix your hair or search for your car keys before you come!"

Zeitman's idea is to fill it with gay-owned and gay-like businesses. The shows mean that we get gay dollars out to the vendors—after all, remember: That's the best way for us to vote. We are family. "To put that power to work, we even created a special storefront called Benefit Select. This is a showcase of selected goods and services, where the proceeds from each purchase go directly to benefit nonprofit gay and lesbian and HIV/AIDS causes."

For now, we enjoyed seeing International Gay Travel Association (**www. rainbow-mall.com/igta**) and the Lesbian News. Both are limited sites, obviously, trying hard to service their respective citizenries. Lesbian News gets overshadowed by Girlfriends magazine at **www.gfriends.com.**

Lesbian News (**www.rainbow-mal.com/mall/ln/index.html**) is not a great magazine for girls because it doesn't have anything its print counterpart doesn't offer. Back issues are available, sure, and this is particularly useful if you like one of their columnists, but the women who run the LN tell us that fast-breaking news "is not our primary focus" and it shows.

What else is on the Mall's floor? The Big Kitchen, The Aztec Box Office, the Ticket Booth, Men on Vacation (travel agency), AIDS Benefit Calendar, Spirited Dreamers; Keith Haring (gallery), and our favorite, Wireless Flash News. Oh, did we mention Elmer's Family Chef Restaurant in friendly San Diego? This is truly taking the world by the malls!

OUR WORLD AND WELCOME TO IT

(The Global Community Online)

Outrageous Tokyo
shrine.cyber.ad.jp/~darrell/outr/home/outr-home.html

Yep, a first gay, English-spoken, online magazine for Japan. Outrageous Tokyo is the follow-up to a series of Japanese-language magazines and is quite the doozie. Any queer traveler overseas is best advised to forget the bar rags—there are two, including a print version of OT—and go for this. It's up to the minute and the ads, like TV in Japan, are funny.

Interestingly, you have to take a step upward, technologically speaking, in order to see the full OT. To get the entire issue, you must first download Adobe Acrobat (**www.adobe.com**). Ten years ago, the Japanese were the first to have fax machines at home; twenty years ago they were the first country to have a Walkman in every home. Nowadays you can't just have a Web browser and expect good service. No, once again you must have the technology. Adobe will make the print shine and the words less . . . wordy and more like liquid language. In other words, the whole thing works. Incredibly, OT has the only list of lesbian clubs in Tokyo that I could find on the Web. The last time I was in Japan people equated "gay" with "transvestite" and so I thought a club listing would make for outrageous reading. It did.

GAIBEC
www.gaibec.com

This gay guide to the city of Quebec seems very interesting although I couldn't understand a word of it. No, no, no, not that these guys have put together an unintelligible site, rather, it's written completely in French. There is an English link but all that does is give you listings in English. After venturing on the français part of the site, I gathered that this is just a huge listing of stuff for gay people in Quebec: nightlife, food, bars, and a helluva lot of stuff to do while upgrading one's French.

UK Way Out
www.wayout.co.uk/fun.html

Every country has a unique way of displaying its gayness, so I traveled, via the Web, to the United Kingdom for the funny pages or comics in *Way Out*, a transvestite paper from Middlesex, England, no less.

British art hath no fury.

Way Out Web can be reached directly at **www.wayout.co.uk.** What's there? A British sense of the news for trannies (as they are called) that is much more timely and internationally focused than U.S. gay news (or U.S. news in general). But first note that "This is a Mad Cow-free zone. If you find any Mad Cows on these pages, please e-mail us so we can take appropriate action!" (If you've Netscape 3.0 or Explorer, you see a cow in its mooing craziness.)

Way Out Web is a transvestite's dream. In the United Kingdom it has received *.Net Magazine*'s highest rating of five stars for its tireless efforts on behalf of transsexuals. You get the guide, personals, feedback, help forums, a look at local and national press, worldwide news, the link list to beat all TG lists, and (I swear) tranny guide stocklists. (In the United Kingdom a stocklist is a magazine stand.)

And where can you find the magazine throughout England? Here you will see Web work at its best. I was amazed to see straightlaced Virgin Megastores listed as a place to get *Way Out* and other tran mags, and doubly shocked to find a site filled with how-to-find *TrannyGuide 96* in the United States! (U.S. extremists who *need* that magazine should go to **www.magsinc.com;** haste makes waste.)

The titles include Cross-Talk, TV SCENE (no, not listings of "Friends"), T.V. epic, LadyLike, and Transgender Tapestry.

This is purely for transsexuals and fans. The photo shoots found on Way Out and accompanying Brit. sites are plentiful and outrageous, though a bit much after a short while.

The Globe! (their exclamation mark)
chat.theglobe.com/globelobby.jive$jump

Are you Circus, Psycho, Daytrip, or Red-Scare? These are the various chat groups found under the nom-de-chat Globe Chat. "I'm chatting" is one of this crowded-house page's slogans. It's a trip for those (again) with a lot of time to spare to figure the darn thing out. But the various and sundry icons—particularly the muscular monsters—are fun to figure out. Me? I went for Psycho, called myself <anonymous> and got slammed by a bunch of self-defeating queers who wondered: "Will you ever call me?"

This is the only Web-talking site with a whisper ("Hi there, you busy?") feature; a subtle, very subtle, way to get people to talk to you. Alone.

GAY AND LESBIAN YOUTH NET

Youth Action Online
www.youth.org

This is an important though blemished organization. According to several off-the-record sources, youth.org, a leading kid site that proves to kids that they *can* speak up about being gay, is run by a group, or perhaps an individual who is "losing ground with reality"—as a former board member explained to me. Known as Youth Assistance Organization (YAO), it is a service run by volunteers and created to help self-identifying gay, lesbian, bisexual, and questioning youth. YAO exists to provide young people with a safe space online to be themselves. Interestingly, the safest and most literate area of this site is something called Transgender Youth. The name says it all.

At the end of 1996 youth.org was going through re-org. and the only element of substance then was Elight, the real Web page linked from this youth-oriented action space: **www.youth.org/elight/.** At Elight you will find a series of kidlike notes. It's a basic primer for kids, though I don't understand the mentality of explaining things lightly to kids and with vigor to adults. It's the adults who need the priming; the kids knew it before they learned to tie a shoelace. The site, updated twice monthly, is a collection of articles, a few gifs (gif images or scanned photos), some poems and rants, all about gays and lesbians who happen to be young.

Elight's mission is to provide: (1) a literary, freelance publishing forum for gay teens; (2) a Web space for gay teens to express thoughts, emotions, and feelings; and (3) support and guidance. There's a lot to be said for that.

Elight's publisher, Jase (who has his own homepage, **www.enqueue.com/ria/**)

says: Elight is *your* forum to speak your mind to the world on gay, bi, and lesbian youth issues. *If you ever wanted to tell the world,* here is your place. Elight's Poetry pages have been very popular." I suggest sending in works for publication. Jase's rainbow page is terrific.

The quotes section, which they call mind-candy, I call something to think about.

> If You DON'T FEEL READY
> yet to move with an
> Opportunity that
> Presents Itself in the
> Moment,
> LET IT PASS!
> There Will ALWAYS Be
> Another One . . .
> And Another One, and
> Another One—Until
> You Are TRULY Ready
> To Take It!
> TRUST IN THAT, DESPITE
> ALL YOU'VE WRONGLY
> BEEN LED TO BELIEVE!
> —Robyn Posin

OutProud! The National Database for Gay, Lesbian, and Bisexual Youth
www.youth.org/outproud/

This database, with over thirty-seven hundred entries, is the largest collection of lesbigay resources in the nation. Information can be found here on community centers, support groups, P-FLAG (Parents, Families, and Friends of Lesbians and Gays) chapters, lesbigay youth groups, and more. This is a great way to meet people, get support through tough times, find out the latest facts on AIDS, get information on where to volunteer, etc. Anything and everything you could possibly need can be found here.

In addition, Outproud is home to Oasis (reviewed herein), an online magazine written for and by lesbigay youth. Besides covering "hard" news and reviews, this mag is a great example of what an organization can do with *few* resources. It is a must bookmark for any self-respecting youthful queer: light yet good reading, with poetry, stories, editorials, and op-eds, as well as profiles of personal courage. And who couldn't use a little inspiration today?

ONLINE VERSIONS OF PRINT MAGAZINES

Out.com
www.out.com

Left in the book for posterity's sake, out.com retired in early March.

The thing about the internet, and its particular place in the world, is that it's all ads. And the best example of that is on out.com, a rather loud hypertext version of the print magazine. The virtue of out.com is its graphics. Complete with more confusing links than most magazines, this hyper version of the much ballyhooed *Out* magazine seems to be saying, "We are famous, you will love us."

But what's to love? Culture, community, news, and Inside Out are basically all asking for you to read *Out* magazine, which in an advertising medium makes sense. The links are to stories from present, past, and a few future issues and though out.com advertises a see-it-to-believe-it search engine of articles pertaining to gay and lesbian culture (the lesbian stuff on this site is nearly nil, except for the lesbian chat rooms), the actual search leads us to . . . articles in *Out*.

Last, the just-mentioned chat rooms. In late 1996, the *Advocate* also started an intriguing posting area (again, see sidebar) that consists of news flashes and articles people point to in letter style. The difference is that, on Out, people are looking for real answers to questions they need dire help figuring out.

I was depressed reading out.com's chat area. No one was quite content in their sexuality, hoping upon hope to discuss anything gay. I met a young transsexual-type from a dry county in Texas who was desperate to talk about coming out and getting out. I asked him why he was in the magazine's tiny chat area instead of, say, in Men4Men on America Online. He said that the Web is easier. "Besides, I know *Out* magazine from *Geraldo*." 'Nuff said.

The graphics are beautiful and my favorite ad campaign of 1996 came, unmistakably gay, from the Web pages of *Out* magazine: The Clairol "Do you color your hair?" deal with all the secrets opened up by a survey. They swore that, if I answered a zillion q's on my hair care necessities, I'd receive something in the mail—and a free T-shirt too. I never did, but the survey was surely entertaining! Woe is the advertising community—men dye their hair.

The community surveys on out.com are unusual (Gratuitous, Anonymous Intriguing Questions: The Internet, Out.com & You) and provide a service, if the service is needed. Oh, and one more thing: According to the out.com ad mechanism, the local phone company NYNEX is giving out a CD of "free divas" if I sign up for a calling card. Does that mean the editors are gonna sing to me on the phone?

Advocate (Lesbian and Gay Newsweekly)
www.advocate.com/

The *Advocate* is the oldest and one of our country's most admired gay and lesbian popular culture magazines. This site is not, however, very visual and is not a good representation of my favorite magazine. Although the site is kinda lame in terms of creativity, we did like the polls. (Polls seem to be what national magazines do well.) Whoever is writing the questions is a little obvious in the way they want you to answer the question. "Are you gay and have you been gay for a long time?" But, as I said, it is the leading gay and lesbian popular culture magazine. For this, we are grateful for its contribution to both gay and mainstream culture. (Disclosure: I wrote features for the *Advocate* for eleven years until 1992.) Its creator, Todd Ruston, said, with a glint in his eye, "We are not in the business of technology implementation." "We are in the business of reporting." So the Advocate's a little dry on the Web; improvement needed.

Being updated. In a recent press release, the *Advocate* announced it was transferring hard news coverage to its Web site.

Oasis Magazine
www.oasismag.com

Oasis magazine was founded by Jeff Walsh. And who is Jeff Walsh? I sent out a zillion surveys on the gay Web to people from all over the world, and this twenty-six-year-old's reply intrigued me the most because it was so ordinary, entirely expected, and full of truth.

His mission was clear: He wanted to help kids get straight about being a homo. He didn't want anyone (if he could help it) to be like he was growing up in Pennsylvania where, he said, it was like waiting for anything. "Oasis, which is a magazine for readers, isn't supposed to be help oriented, but I damn well want to make sure some kid who comes to oasis.com—even if just to be entertained or informed by some celeb interview—leaves the site thinking it's cool to be gay."

Walsh has created something quite unique and I applaud him for it: fourteen-year-old columnists and twenty-six-year-old editors all coming to the same conclusions, or sometimes different ones, about gay life in the 1990s. And like all good Webmasters, Walsh, who pays for the site's upkeep with his spare change, spends his time reminding people to use the WWW in an uncensored way, to get opinions heard, and to shock people, if you have to, instead of going onto chat rooms and getting told you can't say that.

What brought Walsh to his needs? "When I was a teen, almost twenty, I lived in the ultimate conservative Catholic closeted town and at one time didn't know anyone else who was gay. The only media coverage of gays was about pride parades or activists screaming with queer rage about AIDS. I needed much tamer images to help me accept myself. So every night, while my parents slept upstairs, I'd spend hours in the basement on my computer." He devised Oasis during this period.

I consider this to be the perfect antidote for young people. Unlike the committee feel of **www.youth.org,** which was developed as a search method for kids in trouble or kids who need serious help, oasis.com is just what its name implies: water in the desert. This is a way for people to share their own thoughts, often poetically and sometimes haphazardly. (Some of the best moments on the Web are those that are notably messy and yet approachable.)

Oasis's content comprises stories of previews of coming-out attractions for kids of all ages. I like it because of Walsh's credo, which the guy somehow sticks to: Writers join oasis.com and challenge what they perceive the larger community is trying to spoonfeed them as they enter it. I agree with Walsh when he asserts, "It seems a lot of people growing up now don't want to join a prefabricated community that dictates musical tastes, political leanings." This thing works because nobody can tell these kids to agree or disagree with modern popular culture—this is a new generation of queers who have their own style.

Plus, there's an assortment of young women writing for Oasis, and it shows a style in young lesbian culture that *I* didn't know existed. For instance: A fourteen-year-old girl told her story of explaining lesbianism to her friends and family. It was touching, though realistic and ballsy. I have seen few unedited pieces that allow young women to discuss their real feelings.

While I'm raving, I must add that I was impressed with Walsh's viewpoint of what the oasis.com world—and generally what the Web world—is: "Read book and music reviews and then go buy those products, read other people's queer theory, etc. And, yes, download an occasional naked picture of someone of legal age if I'm so inclined." Touché.

HX or HomoXtra
www.hx.com

HomoXtra is a magazine that takes New York in stride and tells people what to do—if they are in a bar and pick it up. It's a pretty innocuous rag that thinks of itself as God in New York, because the bars pay the publishers (heretofore known as "Matthew and Mark") to keep it up. Meanwhile, my favorite gay-NYC story centers on the fact that *HX,* as it is commonly referred to in gayland, was nicely placed in George Rush's straight-dish column in the *New York Daily News.* Obviously, the story—which was a ridiculous controversy surrounding an ad placed in *HX* promising time with Latin gogo boys as a prize—was called in all breathlessly by someone who considered the magazine a status symbol—the ultimate gay NY authority. Hardly. Who outside the gay world knows? Well, the story appeared, touting the ever-popular *Ajax* magazine!

This brings us to the Web site, or in truth, Web page.[7] I was amazed, knowing about the big bucks the publishers pull in, that they'd have the nerve merely to replicate the print version on a Web site that for months was promising (or threatening?) to improve. My feeling, without mincing words (that's for these guys), is that they don't really care. If visitors or residents want it, they will come. As a guidebook writer whose books on New York cover a variety of subjects, I am irked when I see someone throw a few snarky words about a few bars . . . and call it information. I don't think so. Yes, sex ads for travelers are there, too.

The big whoop-de-do is that they have a search function, searching what I imagine are 552 issues. I searched for "gay" and "bar" and received nothing. As an escape from this—*HX* magazine is free at every bar, disco, clothing boutique, sex club, and bookstore with gay clinetele—see the next item. You're welcome.

Gay Guide to NY
www.gayguidenewyork.com/ggabout.html
and **www.gay.guidenewyork.com/ggabout.html**

First and foremost, Gay Guide New York is not an online magazine nor does it aspire to be. But it is good because it provides its membership with a wide variety of information about products, service providers, and entertainment options relevant to the gay community in the New York City area. And, whoa, lotsa services exist here. Free.

Gay Guide New York provides links to magazines such as Boston Phoenix, QuiRX, GaySource, Out, and the Advocate (**www.advocate.com,** discussed earlier in this chapter), travel publications such as Advance-Damron's Vacations, Creative Travel, Gay Travel Network, and general online publications, such as Gay Sport, Gays and Lesbians on the Web, Point, and **NYC Net** (see below for more on NYC Net).

Gay Guide New York also provides a listing of social- and community-service organizations geared toward the gay and lesbian community. It is intended for those who need and those who want to give. Many organizations need donations of either cash or merchandise and some of them need volunteers. I'm a big believer in volunteerism, so I'm putting their information here, so contact them to find out what they need.

---

[7]This is going to "improve drastically soon"—its publisher told me.

Health and Social Services

ACTUP (Aids Coalition to Unleash Power), 135 West 29th Street, NYC, 10001; telephone (212) 564-2437

AIDS Education & Program Services—Facts and referrals: New York City Department of Health, 311 Broadway, NY 10007; telephone (212) 285-4625

AmFar (American Foundation for AIDS Research), 733 Third Avenue, NY 10017; telephone (212) 682-7440

GMHC (Gay Men's Health Crisis), 129 West 20th Street, NY 10011; telephone (212) 807-6555

God's Love We Deliver (meals for homebound people with AIDS/HIV), 895 Amsterdam Avenue, NY 10025; telephone (212) 865-6500

Housing Works (housing for homeless people with AIDS/HIV), 594 Broadway, NY 10012; telephone (212) 966-0466

Counseling and Organizations

Center for Nontraditional Families (counseling), 111 West 90th Street, NY 10024; telephone (212) 721-1012

The Columbia Center for Lesbian, Gay & Bisexual Mental Health (individual and group counseling), 16 East 60th Street, NY 10022; telephone (212) 326-8441

GLAAD (Gay and Lesbian Alliance Against Defamation) (fighting for accurate representations of gay and lesbian lives in the media), 150 West 26th Street, NY 10001; telephone (212) 807-1700

Hetrick-Martin Institute (social services for lesbian, gay, and bisexual youth), 2 Astor Place, NY 10003; telephone (212) 674-2400

Identity House (counseling and therapy referrals), 39 West 14th Street, NY 10011; telephone (212) 243-8181

Institute for Human Identity (Individual, couple, and group therapy), 118 West 72nd Street, NY 10023; telephone (212) 799-9432

Lambda Legal Defense and Education Fund (legal assistance and referrals), 666 Broadway, NY 10012; telephone (212) 995-8585

Ninth Street Center (counseling), 151 First Avenue, NY 10003; telephone (212) 228-5153

P-FLAG (Parents and Friends of Lesbians and Gays), telephone (212) 463-0629; call (202) 638-4200 for your local chapter

SAGE (Senior Action in a Gay Environment) (social services for gay and lesbian seniors), 208 West 13th Street, NY 10011; telephone (212) 741-2247

Women's Psychotherapy Referral Service (therapy and referral), 25 Perry Street, NY 10025; telephone (212) 595-6655

The Gayly Oklahoman Homepage
www.gayly.com

Oklahoma's lesbigay news and events magazine is now online. (So is *Wisconsin Lite*—**www.gayuniverse/wisconsinlite.com**—definitely the only bar rag I know of sold in supermarkets and available in libraries. "We look less like a gay thing than the *New York Times,* really," said the publisher, Terry Baughner.)

On to Oklahoma: Gayly offers the usual news, gay feature stories, health articles, advertisements, and personals. All that is fine and dandy but the real meat is the Gayly Guide. This colorful guide is a list of events meant to help the local crowd, and most of them involve liquor and sex.

Gaysource
www.gaysource.com

The ultimate shopping mall for gay America was started a few years ago by Michael Franz and friend. Because of its inherent, nonthreatening look and feel, it has become the most popular of its type. There is nothing offensive and yet the information is exactly what a gay man or woman might need, if he or she wants the basics. (Note that this is not a print magazine.)

Franz is a nice guy who, like many entrepreneurs—or entrepreneurial writers like me—saw an open niche. I gather from speaking to him that his advertising job was dull, and he was already in the mag field, so he figured, Why not find writers? He did and, with a few servers opened up to the public, took in ads and tens of thousands of readers.

I say "readers" because, unlike gayspace.com and even the **Rainbow Mall** (see above for the Mall), Gaysource is a magazine that could be printed out and read. Most great sites are using text and visuals and hyperlinks to such an extent that it would seem awfully flat to have to read the site on a printed page, or you couldn't even imagine how that might be done. This is not an interactive or 'cool' site.

It is a nice-looking site, but its innards have nothing in them you can't find in half a dozen other places. If you are looking for community calendar information in the most basic sense—for instance, the Pride calendar in Buffalo, New York—here is the place to go. From an ad standpoint, the magazine stands head and shoulders above its competitors because it has a big baby: AT&T advertises on this alone.

Franz explains: "They saw us and realized we were serving a defined purpose." Modemedia came to their rescue, the Connecticut-based online ad agency brought in AT&T. It's AT&T's way of showing—years after the company stopped sending gay-friendly letters through the mail because of a threatened boycott by Christian groups with their *own* long distance service—that it can love gay people too.

Gaysource offers Toolbox (which is not as hot as you'd hope), a way for gay people and lesbians who are new to the net to get the "tools" they need to survive in a technologically "out" world. The links are basically ads, but as you probably know by now, in some way everything on the Web is an ad!

The other unique area is something called Linkup, which is merely gaysource.com's method of linking you to a zillion other sites, all of which are gay related in some small or large way. The quick "jump" words are obviously written by someone who has not been in publishing long enough to have had sophistication creep into his language. For instance, "Dykesville," "boyOrama," "Transgender," and our fave, "Naughty!"

This is a place to meet and greet new friends. (See The Advocate.com Strikes Out.com explaining this new phenomenon, later in this chapter.)

The server is slow, so get ready to wait. But, if you are in the hinterlands without a local magazine rack, try it out. Gay information and gay links abound here. They are willing to try anything that doesn't offend, once.

Last year the big news on gaysource.com was the soap opera "Astor Place," the story of several gay generations living together under one chaotic roof. Though it didn't last—Franz says that the audience dwindled after a short while—the opportunity to see what happens remains open to new users of gaysource.com.

A magazine run by a husband and husband. Bravo.

Outlines/Lambda Publications
www.suba.com/~outlines

Outlines, the monthly lesbigay cyberzine (there is no print counterpart), has a goal. Not content with carrying the latest in national and international news, Outlines, through the use of the Web, expands the range of its services to carry listings, art and theatre reviews and listings, celebrity interviews, Blacklines (for the lesbigay African American), a gay business directory, and an online directory of gay Web sites to browse through.

Outlines also provides the user with links to the OUT! Resource Guide. This list of gay- and lesbian-supportive businesses, professionals, and organizations is definitely a keeper. Through the list, users can call up the names, phone numbers, and addresses of hundreds of resources for a myriad of purposes. A definite bookmark here.

Seattle Gay News
electra.cortland.com:80/sgn/

The thing about gay news is it comes in many shapes and sizes. Here we see Seattle, a relatively calm town, with a newspaper, the *Seattle Gay News,* that has newsgroups of its own, an online magazine with more information than you could possibly use, and a subscription listserve free for e-mail aficionados. Send an e-mail message to **majordomo@cortland.com** with one line in the body of the message (a subject line doesn't matter): subscribe sgn-discuss.

In addition, in late 1996 *Seattle Gay News* introduced Labrynth, an excellent search engine for relevant, if obscure, gay and lesbian topics, including a large array of AIDS-related subjects. Also, it is free. The difference between the engine and the much-ballyhooed searcher on out.com is that this one is not finding articles only from SGN and its sister papers; it is accessing dozens of sources.

Echo Magazine (Arizona)
www.echomag.com

I would like to point out the beauty of one Arizona bar rag run by a gentleman who is surely a guru in his own right. (This one is not to be confused with Echo (**www.echo.com**), the tragically hip NYC online salon for media junkies.) In a purely journalistic vein, Echomag tries hard to inform the Web-minded Arizona gay public, and does not even place ads on the internet! It's impressive.

Phoenix's premiere bar magazine has been known for its AIDS coverage and particularly for its unpopular journalistic stances. (One of the areas on the Echomag site is Medical Updates, which are not merely statistics, but also real facts reported globally.) One area in particular that works well is titled Lambda Business Directory. I predict that shortly *everyone* gay or lesbian with a service or a product or a thought to sell will link himself or herself to something like this. SouthWest, the Webmasters behind the Echomag site, tell me that they wanted both advertisers and colleagues (some friends) to be listed here with their numbers or site-names, to point out that the gay community in otherwise-thought-to-be pretty-dry Arizona is a damn big gay place.

To test out the services section, I linked to the lone lawyer's site on Echomag and found that Mr. Miller had had tens of thousands of visits in the past few months and believes in the scales of justice; these scales are hanging on his site.

Like most site owners, you can link until you are blue in the face, but you never leave Echomag as long as you're linked from it. It's a smart way to remind you who set you up. Allegiance is what magazines seek when they go on the Web.

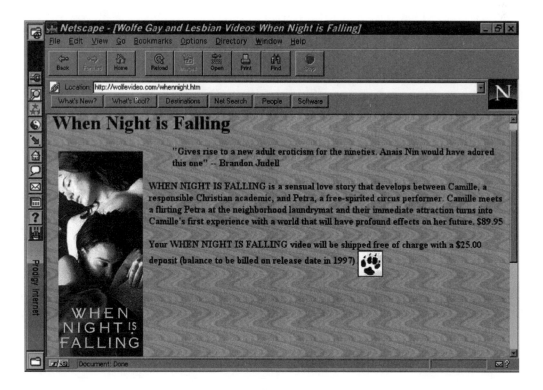

Provocateur
www.gayspace.com/provmag.htm

Though this is part of the gayspace.com adult section, and most of gayspace is focused on s-e-x, the fact is, Provocateur is quite provocative and not nearly as sexual
as those described in Chapter 8. And unlike the non-arty porno rags, this magazine
is seen in its best light on the Web. Provocateur is an art-fag-titillation mag that
shows buff boys posing, usually in sepia tones. Its tagline is Collectible Culture Dedicated to the Art and Culture of Man. Bodies is all. The editor, Ryan Brookhart, explained: "What is a provocateur? A provocateur is an agitator, a disruptive element,
a scoundrel, rascal, rebel, and a bastard. In other words, just the kind of person or
element you want at your next social gathering. Now, I'm not saying that a provocateur is going to swagger into your home and insult your lack of decorating ability.
He might. He might just be your best friend, if you'd let him in. A provocateur gets
worked up, and gets you worked up."

The black-and-white essays prove the cover price (six issues for 12 bucks) is
worth it, if beautiful bodies, well photographed and well stacked, are what you're
after (cost 20 bucks a year). Heck, it's fun to gaze at. Show your prudish friends that
sometimes it's not all smut. Show your oversexed buds that cover art on gay magazines could be better with a little mystery.

KOOKY FOLK YOU NEED TO MEET

A Handful of Homeys

Two totally different homepages that deserve, for no apparent reason, to be
coupled. (Okay, I thought they might just get along.)

Eddie's Moved House **(www.xs4all.nl/~pj/izzard.html)** shows what you
think will be Eddie, if and when you can find him. His name is Eddie Izzard and
he's full of colors. This is a terrific example of a page setup by someone who wants
you to find him, though it turns out not to be *from* him. There's no cost for the move,
so take 'his' advice: We're drilling elsewhere. It's an unusual trip: **www.xs4all.
nl/~vonb/iz/izzard.html.**

"Eddie Izzard's sort of groovy homepage." Who is Eddie? A B-rate comedian.
Ask Caroline. She set this thing up. I haven't a clue. And as for Eddie, according to
the lady of the home, "This site is *not* official—*not* designed by Eddie—he can't even
find it." Some disclaimer, huh? But I often hope that, someday, someone will be
such a fan of mine.[8]

[8]Do we love the Web or what? In December 1996, Eddie Izzard came to New York and I (now a
dedicated follower, thanks to Caroline's page) read everything I could about the heretofore-unknown
comic. He's good, it turns out. Information is key.

Carol Anne's Home Page, 7/96 version, at **www.primenet.com/~carolab/** is blatantly cute! Admittedly, she's a bit of a nut, into Dennis Rodman and Spam, and all she really wants to discuss is the PGP Newsgroup (see Chapter 2 for more on the newsgroup thang). From this site you are to be linked to a whole lotta spam—places Carol Anne loves. Spam, spam, spam.

Mister B's Leather
neturl.nl/mrb/

Mr. B's Leather wants you. "Welcome to the finest asset of gay Amsterdam, Mister B. Mister B is a top-quality store in leather, rubber, and army clothing located in the heart of Amsterdam leatherscene. We opened up in March 1994. Since then we are steadily working to increase YOUR satisfaction, both in our store and on the net!"

Catalogue shopping on the Web for *everything* was an eventuality, so why not leather? Best to note that this is a great precursor to a visit and a fabulous way to get to know Amsterdam before you arrive—sort of make friends and have them influence you!—and here is a chance to take in the local color.

Read about the latest sexy trends in Amsterdam (not sex, though, that is in Chapter 8) and especially the Tupperware parties being held all over the world. Tupper what? As they describe it, in quite alarming detail, a prevention activity that has erupted throughout Amsterdam called the "Tupperware Event for Mixed Gays and Lesbians." It's a kind of prevention act where men and women describe the use of, well, plastics for safe sex; demonstrations are included. Because we know you want to go right to it, seek out this well-regarded address: **neturl.nl/mrb/tup/ tupindex.html!**

Gerbil
www.multicom.org/gerbil/gerbil.html

By the looks of it, these guys aren't—okay, well, maybe they are—playing around. There's sex and a warning too, but there's more. If you act now, you see this: "WARNING: This site contains homosexuality, nudity and sexually explicit writing. To continue means you are over 18 AND wish to see such subject matter." Then, unless you click Agree, you are taken to a page where you'll get verbally spanked for not wanting any of this. And then, again, you can be made to read poems, articles, and accounts of activism, look at authors, rants, and techniques (how to write porn), and, of course, make the all-important links to civilization. Gerbil is a hardly-spoken-about (that is, not hyped) queer culture 'zine that wants to make you read about and develop your interests in all things gay. For instance, Rayne Arroyo wrote a poem about a dream. I liked it so much here it is:

Andy Garcia
He walked naked into
the party, put his
head on my hard lap,
wept because he
didn't have a shadow.
Talk turned to Greek
statues. He asked why
his morning beard was
black while his pubic hair
was red. I pushed him
into the shower. He
pulled me in and I
also wept with him
at not having a God
in any of my images.
The party dragged us
back into its endless
singing of Happy Birthday
to the sun. I stayed
in this dream until
9:45 A.M. where a beer truck
on Temple Street blew
its horn. Happiness
is so easily stolen.

Sometimes it's too easy to be amused.

Anyway, I like anyone with a homepage-hysterical sense of humor and these guys take the cake: Brad and Tony are featured with a half-finished, under-construction photo of their cat on hand. Too cool.

Lastly: It's not for gays only but "for lesbian and gays, and anyone on the Kinsey Scale 1 to 6." Duh.

Christine's Homepages
www.netins.net/showcase/chrisa/index.html

I like this guy and his cross-dressing tendencies. Christine's from Iowa and runs a support group for cross-dressers who have, as he does, a semiunderstanding wife. He has learned a lot about women since he came out as a nongay cross-dresser. (I found a lot about cockroaches when I stopped having the exterminator over.) But he also says "I love going out en femme and exploring the world. I have found out that you are treated differently when people see you as a woman." His other hobbies are typically Iowan, flyfishing and flying alone in airy mountains, yada yada; but I was shocked at Christine's Music Page **(www.netins.net/showcase/chrisa/ music.htm),** which stopped me in my tracks. Crosser or regular dresser, this guy's from Iowa! Expecting to hear Nancy Sinatra sound bites or at least New York Dolls throwbacks, I got, instead, Wynona, Shania Twain, and the Elton John Lion King. *With or without a spoon?*

To have fun, I e-mailed him **(scott@netins.net)**: "What about the lines at the rest rooms?" His response: "I enjoyed your repartee."

His name is Scott, his favorite TV show (I kid you not) is *Cops,* and I don't know what he did on his summer vacation. That bad boy.

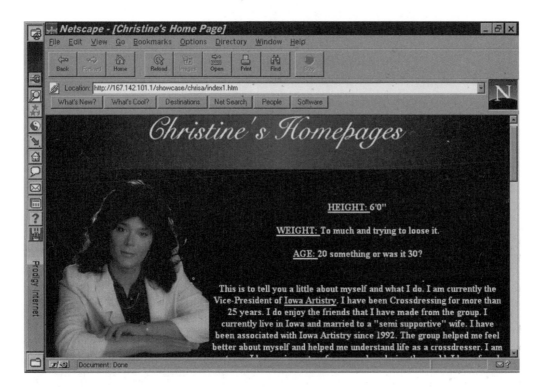

Jamie Faye Fenton's Webpage
www.transgender.org/tg/people/jff/index.html

Moving right along, Jamie Faye is a San Francisco–based nonqueer who has a foot in every door in this cross-dressing world. His supportive wife is a bold woman who writes about her husband for magazines and newsletters, in articles with titles that ensure you know what you're getting into, e.g., "Even Genetic Girls Get the Blues."

On the Jamie Show, I read lots of terrific material for those who want to feel good about their learned habits. This is linked to a transgender newsletter and information service for cross-dressers **(www.tgforum.com).** Kind of like a CompuServe for cross-dressers!

AROUND THE U AND S AND A

The Gadnet Queer Guide to the SF Area
www.-leland.stanford.edu/group/QR/qg94.html

With information from the Queer Graduate Student Network of Stanford, this is a highly responsible though irreverent guide to the Bay Area and notably the Stanford area. Not as full of itself as many local guides, the magazine reads like an upscale version of Gay America, but is the Stanford area guide to gay whereabouts.

It's pretty witty; thankfully, they take nothing seriously. Note: Stanford U. students read and write it. If you're out and out there, then say hello to Gadnet. A great deal of the information comes from an earlier guide titled, *Gradnet Lambda 1994–95 Queer Guide,* printed with funding from the school.

Pause to think. Now, when I went to college . . . !

The Texas Triangle[9]
www.outline.com/triangle/hp.html

A newspaper about the good old boys. On TV the tourism ads for Texas call it "like a whole other country." In many unflattering ways, Texas is just that. Thanks to a latent boost in tolerated homophobia, *Texas Triangle* has become a much-appreciated though much-maligned (by nongay Texans) weekly magazine for this state's extra-large-size gay population, serving Austin, Dallas, Fort Worth, Houston, and San Antonio, the latter being the originators of the Strip Mall. Texas Triangle homepage

---

[9]Out of business in late '96, back in biz in early '97.

arrived on the Web in a big way. This online guide to the area is resourceful—and gutsy. It is also subtle, which in the Web world is, at the very least, highly unusual.

Texans try, and try unsuccessfully, to get the magazine to cease publication. Homophobia, as you have read in the newspapers, *rules* in Texas. A judge ruled in favor of it once. Well, TT online is the best of Texas, with a twist: The mission statement, which undoubtedly comes straight from the magazine, says that Triangle (unlike any other magazine for gays or lesbians or both) is here to "simultaneously educate the mainstream community and highlight all we have in common. . . . Featuring positive role models, it also seeks to eradicate internalized homophobia and that of society-at-large." And now we say, "Amen."

This is a beautifully realized creation. When you turn to the listings page, you see a hopping area (literally) entitled Fun Things to Do. It is when I see great publications go to terrific lengths to put their material up freely on the Web that I can say, this is progress.

There are hardly any ads to speak of, and yet it's there for the taking. Obviously they hope you will still pick up the free magazine in bars or on the racks, but in all ways TT wants to serve as a guide, or maybe as *the* guide, for Texans. And the care shows.

Click Your Heels Three Times
www.outline.com

And say there's no place like home.

This is a wonderful pit stop if you happen to be tired of the Web. (I look for such pits daily.) It is a peer into the queer resources of Texas and also contains some words of wisdom about Dorothy. You know, our friend. . . . "The Silver Shoes," said the Good Witch, "have wonderful powers. And one of the most curious things about them is that they can carry you to any place in the world in three steps, and each step will be made in the wink of an eye. All you have to do is knock the heels together three times and command the shoes to carry you wherever you wish to go."

Then there is a slogan for the page. "At the end of her journey, Dorothy realized that there really is no place like home. And we hope you'll find yourself at home here."

There is no rhyme or reason to the Web and it's always under construction. So, under all the prophecies of Dorothy, I was amazed to find gay film distributors (**www.outline.com/ol.leisure.film.html**) *and* a list of senators and how to reach them the quickest way you know how: e-mail the little buggers: **www.outline.com/ senate.html.**

Washington Blade
www.washblade.com

The *Blade,* a fantastic politically aware newspaper, is known for breaking news stories—even in its ads! To explain: A congressman from Arizona (Republican and very antigay in his legislation) was outed on the pages of the *Blade* in an ad placed by a group of concerned citizens! The weekly *Blade* has broken scandals, quashed bad theories, gone to work as the D.C. journalistic headquarters for all gay America.

It's a beautiful site. I generally don't see the Blade's cover and had no idea how colorful it had become (it was a black-and-white rag until recently). Plus, you get to choose from news to personals to arts to my favorite, the commentary or forum dedicated to readers. And, thanks to smart Webmasters, the site is the first one to allow people to type in **washblade.com** and go to the WWW area.

But back to content: Reader's Commentary is fantastic. According to many Blade-ites, the election of 1996 brought out a great deal of racism among the gay community. One adept reader wrote in and touched off a great debate. Her thesis began:

> It is time that we white Gays recognize as myth the belief that there is one Gay male, Lesbian, bisexual, and transgendered community, and realize that divisions have long been present. Many of these divisions have been fueled by our inability as white Gay activists to deal with our racism. Something isn't working if, for example, a national Latina/o Gay group has to crash a televised forum that purports to represent the leadership of the national Gay male and Lesbian movement.

She posted it last August, and in the months prior to the election, her thoughts spurred *hundreds* of articulate minidebates, some in favor of her message, others saying "Get real, girl!" The point of this is that many of the Blade's vitriolic readers felt they had to come in, to post a message onto the Commentary section. And no matter how many letters to the editor are written, for many activists the most powerful way to get your message across is to post it.

Intriguingly, the Blade has local, national, and international news blocks for people to peruse. Not even the Advocate (the nation's number one gay newsmagazine) could do that. Some of the issues are gay and just germane to the gay and lesbian people. Lastly, a unique directory—free—of local bars and places to meet, Web resources (quite a decent list, we stole from it!), and something very useful for travelers: where to find today's *Washington Blade* in Washington, D.C.

Gay and Lesbian Indianapolis
www.gayindy.org

Not that Indianapolis wouldn't be an exciting place to live, natch, but here is another reason to use Gayindy besides hangin' out: a fine example of the confidential lists that can be gotten from the Web. You can come into the site and gather typical bar-oriented info from a variety of sources, and find a variety of youth sites that are linked here for the kids in the Midwest and, specifically, in Indianapolis. One, Young, Loud and Proud, is a conference held in San Francisco that is linked here (**www.youth.org/ylp/index.html**) and gives tons of details on how Indianapolis kids can get involved. In addition to the youth and bar scene, find supportive businesses, library and achives (the site is a few years old), and the Indy Pride scene.

For subscriptions straight to your box—free—send an e-mail with the subject, Subscribe, to **gayindy@gayindy.org.** No ads in here. This is an example of Listserv discussed in Chapter 1.

UNCATEGORICALLY HELPFUL IDEAS

Data Lounge
http://www.datalounge.com/

Data Lounge is the brainchild of Mediapolis, a firm that makes sites for queer corporations, and includes a host of photos and discombobulated columnists, mostly New Yorkers. Our favorite is Trudy who comes to us longingly through Chapter 9.

The Data Lounge hosts sites Mediapolis has created, such as qsanfrancisco.com, a very pretty look at San Francisco by publisher extraordinaire, and eccentric, Don Tuthill; out.com (*Out* magazine), hx.com (*HomoXtra* magazine), and Our Tribe Marketing (a gay marketing firm, of course). Plus, the free or near free areas created and served by Mediapolis, namely GLAAD (Gay and Lesbian Alliance Against Defamation), AIDS Project Los Angeles, and more.

It's an unusual home site and quite vividly portrayed. See Chapter 9 for Data's "Virtual Cabaret" and Trudy!

Good Head Grafix
www.maui.net/~gill/

Enter Good Head and discover a wild place where, according to Webmaster Gill, "The KEY to building return traffic at your internet site is to offer unique and valuable

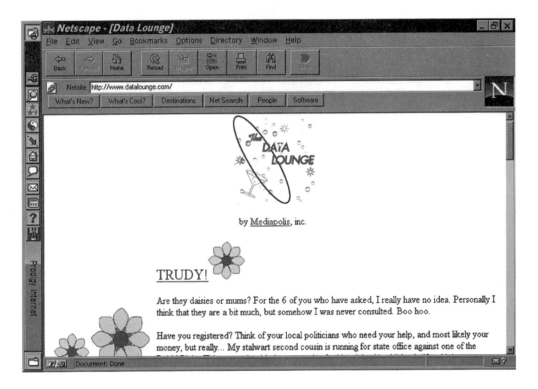

The DATA LOUNGE

by Mediapolis, inc.

TRUDY!

Are they daisies or mums? For the 6 of you who have asked, I really have no idea. Personally I think that they are a bit much, but somehow I was never consulted. Boo hoo.

Have you registered? Think of your local politicians who need your help, and most likely your money, but really... My stalwart second cousin is running for state office against one of the

information in an entertaining and interactive way, and to change the content frequently." And he makes it a challenge to keep up.

Great graphics, fine sound, and a host of ideas—all with the notion that you will indeed come back. Good Head offers a valuable trip into the world of Gill (the host) and a way to introduce maui.net, a company that builds a helluva homepage.

What's here? Lessins in Love, the Website of two therapists named Lessin (**The Kiss** is a beautiful piece of artwork); Thai Massage Center, insight into an ancient art and science; and a few other sites well worth linking to. Of course, I like it because it's an ad that unabashedly promises promotion and more, if you come back sometimes.

Gill is a great tease, too, promising a two-second, animated, sound-activated graphic, and then responding with a loud, green JUST KIDDING onscreen. But Gill seems to know his world. *Mission Impossible*'s theme is on as I type. It's keeping me here and that's tough.

Meanwhile, as it comes on, you'll note twenty-two colors—one at a time— which is a tough act to pull off! If you leave your e-mail address, you'll get sent a line whenever the content changes. Clever way to keep in touch.

If you have some thirteen pieces of software installed (most of which are available on **www.netscape.com,** or **www.shareware.com,** or **www.download.com,** which will update you with new stuff *all the time*),[10] you will be taken away. Just as the bathwater commercial says: The tour that you take—if you choose this mission—is thirty seconds per site, if your software is up to this. It is worth it, particularly as a test for applets (for more on applets, consult the Netscape homepage or go to **www.cyberia.com,** a Pennsylvania-based information and internet provider and see its FAQ), which your now-equipped computer has taken in and, of course, to see how well any computer sound system works!

I only got to hear it, but eventually (after several tries) got taken to a few places, but without video. (My friends say that the video viewing is quite extraordinary at **www.maui.net.**)

If you know little of Java, you must come to this site and see Anthony's Coffee, which provides Java the old-fashioned way.

900 Home Numbers for Nonsex Purposes (and Sex Too)
www.gayweb.com/900/home2.html

We do talk about sex in Chapter 8, coming up, so stop yer bitching. Being a technology junkie, and always on the lookout for the latest gimmick, I logged onto this site, hosted by gayweb.com, and discovered that I could send a secret whisper (a fifteen-second recorded message sent to a specific caller or to an entire room full of callers) and thus made a coupla online friends. The company is called 25-Hour Live Gay Chat—probably not what it says on their checks, right?—and it works on a phone line (won't give you that in the book; we don't carry ads) and posts on its creative and sexy Web site some novel devices for phone users. Download these usurpables and you're on your merry way to good phone sex. (Also, see **badpuppy.com** in the next chapter for other software for dial-up purposes.)

I like the fact that they have something for everyone in each room you dial into. "There are personals about serious love and romance, conversation, no-questions-asked sex, first-time gay, lesbian, bi, group, or kinky experiences, and of course, phone sex." For more on sex, stop sweating and just skip to the next chapter. Gayweb, meanwhile, is a fun site with many of the same attributes as **www. gaywired.com.** The difference is Gaywired is a search engine with categories for everything.

---

[10]This is *the place* if you are willing to experiment with new technology. Good Head will show you how to find the devices.

MINI TOUR OF TRAVEL SITES

Canadian Gay, Lesbian, Bisexual Resource Directory
www.cglbrd.com/

Behold the world's largest and most comprehensive source for Canadian gay, lesbian, and bisexual details. If you are traveling to different areas or are just a visitor to that great country and would like information about GLB resources, then this is the space.

The CGLBRD provides free listings for all organizations and businesses that offer services and support to the gay, lesbian, and bisexual communities of Canada. The CGLBRD is a not-for-profit organization supported entirely by Canadian gay and gay-positive businesses through their Sponsorship and Update Service Programs.

The listings here are: Info by Location, Business Directory, Doc & Raider, Publications, Universities, Web Pages (which lists Canadian Web pages by area and provides links to them), Youth Services, Helpful Hints, Help with Frames, About CGLBRD, and Credits.

This is another one of those complete Web sites. Both text and graphics are really superb. A must-see for anyone thinking of exploring The Great White North. Missing? The late John Candy in drag doing a running commentary.

Cal Simmons's Travel Page
www.cstravel.com

Cal Simmons's page includes gay-friendly places from Alexandria, Virginia, Washington, D.C. and all over the world via the net. Simmons was early to this gimmick and saw a still-open niche for people to buy travel packages. (See the International Gay Travel Association inside the Rainbow Mall, above) for more like this but a very old-fashioned look at travel.) Cal offers one link of note: net travel destination specials, which are about 20 percent less than the advertised specials. You can go to those directly, of course, by clicking on **travel.gpnet.com/DESTIN.HTM.** See Chapter 3 for a great way to get Web specials on plane fares.

Qnet
www.q-net.com

Bring your passport, camera, and your sense of adventure when surfing Qnet. This is the most trustworthy and current gay and lesbian travel information available. Brought to you by the *Ferrari Guides,* published since 1980 and acknowledged worldwide by gay and lesbian travelers and travel professionals as one of the most comprehensive sources of gay and lesbian travel information.

Users can use the Point and Click Travel Index to help plan their vacation in its entirety. Use a Destination Index to find an alphabetical list of destinations served by gay or lesbian or gay-friendly tour, cruise, and travel companies. When you choose a destination, you'll get a list of companies that service that destination. Use the Interest/Activities Index for an alphabetical list of interests and activities offered by gay and lesbian or gay-friendly tour, cruise, and travel companies.

Inn Places Online is another service offered. Paris in the spring, Palm Springs for vacation, or Pittsburgh for business: A globetrotter's guide to accommodations worldwide, featuring gay, lesbian, and gay-friendly hotels and resorts, intimate bed-and-breakfast inns, plus indexes to campgrounds, handicap-accessibility, and nudism. Lots of misspellings on site.

What's New What's Hot: Billed as "Nothing short of the most current flashes on travel trends . . . new accommodation and transportation options to updated cruise offerings, to a handy season-at-a-glance calendar of big trips and events."

Or enter a contest sponsored by G'Day Tours, Air New Zealand, and Ansett Tours that nets the lucky winner a five-night, six-day, all-expenses-paid trip for two to Australia, one of the world's most popular gay vacation areas.

There is specialized women's travel, LezNet, also on this site.

LinkAmerica
www.linkamerica.com/food-lod.htm

Though not a gay site, LinkAmerica is an example of the travel sites popping up that are not wholly advertiser oriented. A Food, Lodging & Attractions site provides pictures and descriptions of attractions, hotels, motels, bed-and-breakfasts, campgrounds, RV parks, restaurants, and specialty shops in tourist destinations. (What's wrong with being a tourist?)

Vacationers can make their plans and begin to anticipate the places they will stay, the foods they will eat, the shops they will visit, and the things they will see and do . . . and waste a helluva lot of time before they leave home.

LinkAmerica provides this information via a pretty good-looking interface. Although the attractions, shops, and facilities change, the simple layout remains basically the same, making it easy for viewers to go from one site—one location—to another!

Whenever I travel, I check LinkAmerica's sites on the net to get the info. For gay business or pleasure, there are other places to check (see Helpful or Crafty Ideas below) but see this site as exemplary of how mainstream Web surfing can really assist.

HELPFUL OR CRAFTY IDEAS

Tumescence
www.clients.anomtec.com/Tumescence/

In the ever-changing world we live in, Tumescence comes across as an idea whose time is here: a nonprofit, tax-exempt organization composed of a growing fraternity of gay men who encourage and support "gay-centered psycho-spiritual growth of each other and other gay men." For real psychological help, see Chapter 10 in Health.

The perfect example of this mainly text-driven site is the ad for Visions of Night, an introductory dreamwork group, which, while based in Hollywood, has nothing to do with Spielberg and friends' movie factory. It is housed at a longy entitled **www.clients.anomtec.com/Tumescence/workshops.html#visions.** Here you can find out a great deal about dreams or, as they put it, "the service of growth in consciousness and deepening of soul." You have to show up for it; men listen to and speak their dreams, learning to understand the language of the night and how to dream their dreams and make them into realities. Very gay. Yes, it costs to show up. But if you can't afford or forget the twenty-five dollars, they won't turn you away. Donations welcome. Vous den?

The Rainbow Roommates Link of NYC NET
www.nycnet.com/rainbowroommates

Sign onto **www.nycnet.com,** a virtual rabbit hole leading you to the software you need to sign onto NYC NET—a New York-based subscription service (see chapter on commercial online services; or join the folks who run NYCNET in New York each Monday, free, from 2 to 4 P.M. at A Different Light Bookstore, 151 West 19th Street, (800) 343-4002). NYCNET is, we feel, poised to become the electronic navel of gay and lesbian community life nationwide. Here is the scoop.

Rainbow Roommates is New York City's state-of-the-art apartment share and roommate referral service, assisting the gay and lesbian community and gay-friendly individuals around the world to find that perfect roommate in the greater New York City metropolitan area. If you are looking for a roommate to share your place with, looking for someone with housing to share, or if you would like to find a roommate first and then together look for an ideal apartment, Rainbow Roommates can help you easily, quickly, and most of all, affordably.

Their mission is to provide you with the highest quality roommate information services easily, conveniently, and affordably. They understand what you need so that you can make the best decision about finding that perfect roommate. And it is that insight that they hope you will come to value and continue to expect from them.

NYCNET has focused on creating relationships and alliances among the most proactive social, political, and professional gay and lesbian organizations at work in the world today—acting as an online headquarters in the virtual Christopher Street Project. NYC NET promises to provide the most extensive social, professional, political, and communal internet resources available for gay men and lesbians.

When we called them, however, they were out. Then we e-mailed them, and nothing came back. So we can't recommend NYC NET's customer service if you have a problem.

New York's Mayor's Site
Giuliani@www.ci.nyc.ny.us

Speaking of New York, this book's hometown, the mission of NYC Link, the official New York City Web site, is to provide the public with quick and easy access to information about New York City agencies, programs, and services. The city's homepage also provides, through links to external sites, information about cultural, educational, and recreational activities in this city.

Go to the City Services and Agencies page. In this section you will find answers to many of your service delivery questions, such as how to get ballfield permits or what day to put newspapers out for recycling. The information in this section will be greatly expanded over time to include key service information from every city agency. Information can be accessed by looking up your topic alphabetically or by entering keywords. This section also provides detailed information about city agencies, elected officials, and city publications.

New York is a special city, unique in many ways, and they couldn't have a page without listing the great entertainment and cultural resources, both world-famous institutions and unknown gems. They are all here. Well, some of the hyped ones anyway. On this page, links are provided to the current events in New York as well as to the latest movies, plays, and the weather. (Urgent news if you're from out of town.) There's a list of New York's major major cultural institutions and sports teams that have their own homepages, the NYC Culture Guide and Calendar published by Alliance for the Arts, which receives money from the City, and some of our most celebrated landmarks and many of the neighborhoods that make up our city.

And you'll want to see the message from the mayor himself. Take time out to see what's buzzing around in the city chief's head. If you agree, disagree, or have something to get off your chest, then tell him what you think—send feedback (e-mail to the mayor, send a message to key members of the Giuliani administration, and sign the Visitor Book). An answer? Hmm. Doubtful. I'll answer it for him: **nativeguy@compuserve.com** is my address.

MISCELLANEOUS—FOR GOOD REASON, BABY

Dancing, (as it should be)
world.std.com/~dancing

Currently under construction, this Web site, as advertised, will be country and western dancing for the gay and lesbian community and their straight-but-not-narrow friends! Basically, this site is a listing of places where Midnight Cowboys can come show off their dancing skills or learn how to dance. Relatively basic directory stuff. But a great way to see some legs in action.

The real deal here are the links to other sites such as Gays for Patsy. Patsy is a direct link to a Boston-based nonprofit all-volunteer organization of country and western dance enthusiasts dedicated to sharing the joys of dancing while raising funds for groups serving those in need. They organize a variety of dance events, dance workshops, trips, retreats, and other social activities, sponsor the ReneGAYdes, a popular country and western performance group, and support other nonprofit community groups through fundraising dances and direct grants. What a Patsy!

Boasting a membership of over two hundred active members, Patsy strives to provide members with opportunities to socialize, improve their dance skills, perform, and at the same time contribute to the community. You can find all kinds of information here, from when and where their dances are taking place to what upcoming fundraising events they're hosting, all on this site.

United States Post Office Homepage
www.usps.gov

Step right up. Talk about bringing service right to you. The United States Post Office is doing just that with its homepage. No more crowds. No more lines. And this post office is open seven days a week, twenty-four hours a day. No sleepy clerks! If you need stamp information, want to find out about mailing options, or look up ZIP Codes, you're in the right place. This site is an invaluable time saver, allowing you to take care of mailing needs at home or at work. You can even locate a post office in your area from this site if you have some business that needs to be handled in person. Package tracking, postage rates, info on phonecards, postage calculations, and even passport information are available with the flick of the wrist.

P.S.: I renewed my passport by downloading Adobe Acrobat from Adobe's site (taken there by www.usps.gov). The download took thirty minutes via a 28.8 (28,000 bps) modem. I pulled down a complete form and instructions from this very site. No waiting, no travel. Nada. Oh, except the $55 that the government charges!

Never! Forget! (exclamations mine)
www.neverforget.com

I wish I had this when . . . I can't remember when. But this is the site that reminds you about everything and it's free. Why do they do this? Pretty simply: so they have your information on record. But they won't rip you off or anything, just sell your pretty e-mail address (or lend it out) to people with ad-oriented gimmicks. Meanwhile, here are the rules to remember.

Simply register and tell them the dates and events about which you need to be reminded. Then drop into the e-mail headquarters you are already tied into (see Chapter 3) and remember . . . you're merely being reminded; they are *not* buying the gifts. The ads are subtle here and not all over the place, as they are in the large sites. For an example of a site with ads instead of content, see the energetic **www. pointcast.com**—the perfect way to drive yourself nuts!

The initial graphic you see when you enter is a sweaty, behatted character running with an e-mail to the . . . next person to remind him, I guess. His face says it all: We will not forget.

CompuServe's Gifts Online (the Electronic Mall) also sends e-mail to you re-minding you to buy, buy, buy.

NYNEX Sucks
www.nynexsucks.com

For people who hate the local phone company as much as I do.

This site is self-explanatory. All of us on the East Coast have, at one point or another, had a dealing with NYNEX. Odds are that this experience was very short of being pleasant. Screaming ineptitude, foul- or fuck-ups, blood pressures soaring, to just name a few, arise from attempts to cope with those people. This site, as do many of the "sux" sites cropping up on the Web, offers the customer a chance to fire back.

Started by customers fed up with their bad experiences with NYNEX, the site plays the role of a cyber punching bag for those needing to release some steam. Anecdotes about customers and their bad experiences with NYNEX litter the site. Some of them are quite funny; others are quite scary. The common denominators and running dialogues here are (1) NYNEX's shortcomings, and (2) anger and frus-tration felt when a big corporation steps all over us.

As I read this I kept hearing Lily Tomlin's operator lady: "We're the phone com-pany. We don't *have to.*"

Remote Possibilities: Wahine Week in Wailea
www.maui.net/~remotepo/

(The following note has been tossed in for relaxation purposes and not information!) "You probably thought that a week on MAUI at a luxury resort for WOMEN ONLY was a remote possibility. Enjoy the spirit of aloha at one of Maui's finest five-diamond resorts. Remote Possibilities has reserved the entire Renaissance Wailea Beach Resort for their exclusive use. The luxury and romance of Hawaii await you from December 8th through the 15th, 1996. We offer our guests the privacy and comfort of a women-only environment."

Basically, this site is just an advertisement for The Renaissance Wailea Beach Resort. Pictures of the resort and its surroundings can be downloaded by the user to get a taste of what's to come at the resort. No links here, no unnecessary chatter. Just fun, sun, and relaxation. And just a gorgeous waste of time. Once you were told that, in order to relax, you had to "visualize." The hell with that. The Web can do it for you. Ahhh.

Barney, "That *Friggin'* Purple Dinosaur"
asylum.cid.com/barney/barney.html

Barney's homepage. Well, not really. But with all the censorship around (see blue-ribbon.html in political-issues below), I discovered a very funny way to reroute people who are offended by sex or sexy images. It's this. A wild Yep! It's Barney's Page site that is not in any way affiliated with Barney Inc. and it still cracks up all the nonfans like me. An automatic link from porn sites (see Chapter 8), it includes Ask Dr. Barney ("the purple doctor is in") and Barney Meets His Doom ("Let him who hath understanding reckon the color of the beast"), not to mention my favorite of the species, Barney Target for Shooters: All of these, and more, are links to other special pages meant to inform those that, yes, we live in Barneyworld. And the real one's much more fun!

While you're here, check out When Barney Met Sally (a .wav-format sound bite) and Barney Meets the Gestapo (not for children of any age!). Though there are jokey sites all over the internet, this one has a point: The point is to get over yourself. Why was I on a gay site if, the question asks, "You [don't] want to see images of men who are naked?" Yeah; I wonder.

Besides, it is awfully creative. Wanna know more? Go in, ask for links, and tell 'em Barney sent you. I can't resist. One antiBarney says he has uncontrollable urges along the lines of: "I often fantasize about choking Big Bird. Yeah, that, and ripping out Captain Kangaroo's heart and showing it to him before he dies." It's a sick wide world out there, folks.

But it might be an uncensored one too.

For "Barney Target for Shooters" see **ftp://aphrodite.nectar.cs.cmu.edu/pub/firearms/tech/target/barney.**[11]

2(X)ist Underwear Catalogue
www.digex.net/2xist/catalog.html

Because Tom Rielly, Mr. Internet, told me in a discussion of PNO, "People can't do nothing but look at underwear on the net all day," I started looking into our records for 2(x)ist. (If you have never been into the 2(x)ist band, er, brand of underwear, then you don't serve the underwear gods as many of us do.)

I like the slogan on this voyeuristic site: "Click on the thumbnail images of the items for a more detailed view!" Just what my doctor would've ordered. My favorite is the classic fly-front brief. Oh, and see David Morgan's poster of the boy in the

---

[11]For information on FTP sites, see Chapter 1.

undies. It's downloadable (they ask you to purchase it, yeah). You need tools to create a poster of the tiny image, tiny won't do. See Chapter 1.

If the underwear just isn't why you came, click on the pics to get a better look at bodies. It makes the Morgan boy much larger. The boy in the tanktop is just a tad bulgy. See Porn Again, the chapter that's on deck.

Homo Base
users.aol.com/surfsdown/index.html

This don't-ask-don't-tell site out of AOL, the online user's paradise if you happen to be gay and spending money—see Chapter 4 for the explanation of that crack—and a lot of ads that are unusual for something so dramatic.

Welcome to *your* Gay, Military, and Alternative Info Source! Really exciting, bombs bursting in air, all that nonsense. As you can tell, I'm not really into the armed forces so this site wasn't too exciting for me. However, I must say that this is as complete a site as any that I've seen. There are tons of lists here covering a gamut of areas. And it can be helpful for queers.

With sections given clever military names such as The Flight Deck, The Infirmary, the Mess Hall, etc. (you get the point), gay GI Joes and Janes can get info ranging from where to get some action to tracking UPS or Fedex packages online. Soldiers can also purchase CDs online, get legal information, and find a place to just chat with other gay military personnel, among other things. This is the site for the homesick, homebody, and the homeboy. Yeah.

If you haven't received the picture yet, it functions as a bridge to the outside world for the gay soldier. If you're in the service and lonely, get on the site now. You'll be whisked back to your pre-boot camp days of fun and frolicking on Christopher Street, the Haight, South Beach, etc. After a few minutes surfing the site you'll feel as if your sorry, Private Benjamin-clone ass was dumped back into the world. Now get down and give me twenty.

P.S.: Regardless of what you imagine, titillation time is far from over.

Site for Sore Passwords
www.isys.hu/staff/brad/passkeeper.html

A brilliant (free!) idea—a source that keeps track of user names and passwords and stores them in an encrypted file on the computer's hard disk. It is run by Brad Greelee, a twenty-five-year-old American in Budapest. Turn to this program if you feel that you'll forget your various 'words. Oh, there's a trick: You have to remember the password to get in.

Suck
www.suck.com

This is one of my favorite places to go to deride the internet, and the one place I know of that actually has a site worth visiting every single day. (They'll love me for that.) Run by two guys who once toiled on Hotwired—*Wired*'s web version and Suck's owners—this fab site gives you a cynical thought each day, and links to that thought. It's all about the Web, and why it often sucks. When people say, "What should I do with my Web page?" I point them in this direction: One simple thought changed all the time.[12]

See Filler, and other condescending extras (links, all links), which is an ever-changing bit of nonsense that I read each and every time I go onto Suck. This is not gay, per se, but it has attitude.

And have a nice day.

[12]For daily good news, try **www.positivepress.com.**

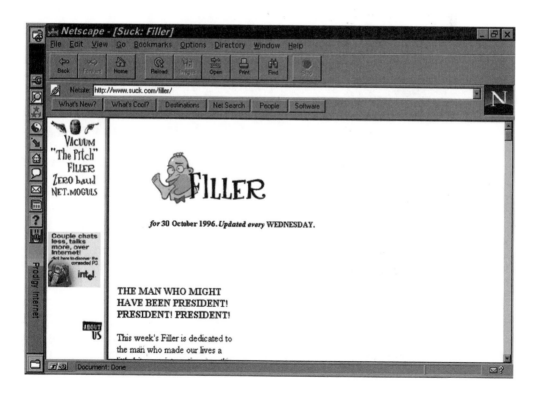

The Advocate.com Strikes Out.com

I went on **www.out.com** not looking to get wowed by much. Truth be told, I have been reading *Out;* only recently did I get it. It seems that the small talky way in which the periodical went after gay and lesbian readers (even putting its Web address on the back of reader subscription cards) was very much an in joke that I wasn't in on. And really, I didn't care much for its politics because it seemed to be in everyone's pants. Surprise, surprise, when I caught up with these just sent e-mails on the Just Coming Out Forum titled "Gay Aspect of Coming Out," there it was announced: "We've all been there. You're not alone! There are many generous souls eager to lend a hand." Although I didn't see anybody from *Out* on hand (in the who's-here box), I started leaving and getting messages from a few tortured souls who swore they were being helped on ol' out.com. Here's how it went.

I'M COMING OUT AND I NEED HELP

I'm an 18 year old student, and I have decided to finally come out. I don't know what people will think, so I'm reluctant to let my friends know. My sister is a lesbian, so I know she'll accept my sexuality. I need some advice from others who are coming out or from other gays who already have. Please give me some info. on what you think is the easiest way to break the news to family and friends.

SUBJECT: PREVIOUS OUT FORUM POSTING

This message is for Kailey? (not sure of spelling—sorry) She is from Tucson. I will be moving to Phoenix soon and we were corresponding. Unfortunately I did not write down her e-mail address and my mail was deleted. I would desperately like to get back in touch with her.

SUBJECT: COMING OUT STORY

I have been in the process of coming out for some time. I have had the wonderful support of a group of people at PFLAG. * If you are seeking advice, need help, or just want to talk to other parents, Gays, Lesbians, or whoever, visit: **www.critpath.org/pflag-talk/ support/dan**
Pflag has helped me tremendously . . .

SUBJECT: JUST COMING OUT

My name is Gregg and I am a 19 year old that is confused. I am attracted to girls, but I enjoy the thought of going out with another guy. Am I gay or bi or what ever, and if I am gay how could I come out to my parents. I really need some good advice.

SUBJECT: I NEED ADVICE HELP ME PLEASE

My name is Mike and I am a gay man 20 years old. I need a lot of advice about coming out to my parents. I live in a town that is very conservative and I am one of three homosexuals

*P-FLAG: Parents and Friends of Lesbians and Gays (an incredibly helpful organization)

in this town, just my luck the other to are lesbians :(any way my parents are the [most] conservative people that I know. My mother freaked when she found out that Sandy Duncan played Peter Pan and I can only guess what will happen when she finds out that her son is not only a "fag" but a drag queen to boot. Anyway thats my problem and I would like any advise that you could give thank you.

BISEXUALITY FROM A LESBIAN PERSPECTIVE

Not that I claim to speak for all lesbians, but as an active member of the dyke community, I think I can shed a little bit of light on the discomfort many lesbians feel with bisexuality. So many lesbians I know have fooled around with so called straight women (aka bisexuals) who have gotten hurt. They start messing with a "straight" woman who gets confused and scared and ends up going back to their husband/boyfriend. The lesbian is almost always the one who gets her heart broken. If it hasn't happened to you, you know someone it has happened to. Same sex relationships face all the same problems that straight relationships do, plus the added stress of societal disapproval. When you stir in the issues a "straight woman" brings (not being able to handle the lifestyle, the closet, internalized homophobia), you have a recipe for disaster. I'm not passing judgment on anything here, trying to present a lesbian perspective. Anyway, good luck. I wish you well.

The point is that *Out*'s Web site, no matter how crass or filled with ads, was very helpful once people find it. I suppose the fact that it's *Out* magazine gets people to come onto it. In this case, people, whose names were deleted, from the hinterlands were assisted by one another. I spoke to these people who all said out.com was a social method in which to be an out gay or lesbian. One went so far as to say "out.com saved my life." It couldn't have been all babble then.

And what about **www.advocate.com?** When *The Advocate*, the nation's oldest newsmagazine for gays and lesbians, started its site in early 1995, it had nothing for chatters. Then the newsgroup was formed (12/26/95) and suddenly—*voila!*—a zillion people came on to discuss real issues. This was unusual in gay chat, because, as you can see in Chapter 6 on the IRC, chatters are simply the most nonnews people around.

Here's a list of Advocate.com's newsgroup selections.

The Republican Agenda
I Met Someone Special Here (AND THANKS!)
Enda DOMA (Defense of Marriage Act, a good laugh)
EMail Penpals Wanted
Rainbow SOUP . . . a discussion
Semi-Cloistered Gay Guys
Small Town Queers
Thanks to Advocate I Met Real People
Internet Newcomer
Sexuality and Rehabilitation (affected by physical disability)
New Cool Web Sites
Get Rid of the People in Congress

The point, according to the *Advocate,* was to get people involved in issues. The point, according to the *Out* people, was to come out. All in all, the former was a lot more interesting and it took less time to find things there. The *Out* collection seemed to be a gigantic sigh. But for guys or girls who want to discuss their various idiosyncratic problems, chatting on the Web is the place to go.

These two sites are certainly not the only places you can go to chat on the Web. In fact, it is customary for major Web sites (not homepages) to have chat areas. Interaction is the key to the success of many gay and lesbian Web sites. The etiquette on these sites varies, but there are definitely some unspoken rules. Here are guidelines to help you along, but for an overview see Chapter 6; a comprehensive review of IRC.

1. Your nick is an important introduction. <yngboy> will probably get a better response than <jon>. Think about it!
2. Don't get so damn serious about the thing!
3. You will attract like-minded people. If you lie and pretend to live out your fantasies, we are all for it; but most likely you will end up with someone who lies and pretends too.
4. Because we can't see your gorgeous face, you will need to be a little crafty with the written word (not the word of the Lord).
5. Don't harass people, and if you are harassed, just ignore them. They will usually go away if no one is paying any attention to them. Just like we all do.

8

PORN AGAIN

Fantasy love is much better than reality love. Never doing it is very exciting. The most exciting attractions are between two opposites that never meet.

—ANDY WARHOL

What you fantasize about at night is not determined by reality. Who lounges around at home concocting in their minds erotic sexual scenarios involving the average people that they run into on a daily basis? I don't imagine being bound and gagged by my landlord, and most likely, neither do you. Most people imagine being dominated by their "ideal"—a six-foot-four, muscular man clad only in leather. :) Where can most people find their ideal and place them in their bedtime fantasies? On the internet.

Our friend Andy was onto something when he said that "sex is more exciting on the screen and between the pages than between the sheets anyway." In the Victorian era, young virgin maidens probably fantasized about what the forty-year-old gardener, or maybe the gardener's daughter, looked like underneath their clothes. But at the end of the twentieth century, we've been so bombarded with images of sexual perfection that, if the gardener doesn't look like Tom Cruise (or rather, an amalgamation of Tom Cruise's butt, chest and thigh doubles), we don't care. But our search for the perfect object for our sexual cravings goes far beyond mere physical characteristics.

That perfect lipstick lesbian that you've been dreaming of needs more than voluptuous thighs, thick dreamy hair, and supple skin. She also has to know how to ride the back of a Triumph motorcycle, where to dab on her perfume, how to walk with the proper gait and smile when your brain and breasts want it most!

Our fantasies are so intricate that no one could ever possibly fulfill all of the requirements that we have laid forth. Look, even James Dean is not James Dean enough to satisfy us. James needed to scrub the toilet sometimes too. And if you ever do find people who seem to fulfill your fantasy, you quickly realize that they aren't real; they are only attracted to an ideal similar to yours and decided that, because they couldn't find it, they would copy it. (Uh, ever been to Chelsea in New York?) Or as Warhol stated in reference to the term *ideal*, "It's probably not your fantasy, but someone who had the same fantasy as you and instead of getting it or being it, they chose to look like it . . . forget it."

Enter the internet! The net is the domain where our fantasies exist fully. It is the culmination of every movie we have seen and every book that we have read, for each one has informed our psyches in the determination of our fantasies. And by the Web, it's interactive. Here you can not only find the leather daddy of your dreams, but also you can be the butch submissive of his (or hers, girls). The complete anonymity that cybersex affords allows one to exist in the world of uninhibited sexual desires. Sex on the net is living life in a bubble that never gets burst. There are no ramifications to sex in this world: Condoms, medical histories, and a personal biography are not required. As a matter of fact, *don't be safe* with cybersex. Cybersex allows you to try the things you've always fantasized about, and live the ideal that you have always portrayed yourself as; S&M, B&D, scat, a cute, intimate evening in your penthouse pleasure den, along with all those illegal and nasty desires you tend to push way, way back into your mind.

Okay, now the bad news. Sex on the internet is not real sex. You have to remember that. You still need, or at least I think you need, human interaction. The touch of another. Blah, blah. But, while you're alone . . . that is what makes the net so heavenly.

SEX DIRECTORIES

(Lists of Fun Places to Go on the Web)

Men on the Net
www.menonthenet.com

Dirty birdy headquarters! Anything and everything, and a good place to start. I got down and dirty and recovered from the shock real quick. You may too. The lists are enormous, and so are . . .

GaySpace ($)
www.gayspace.com/adult.htm

How could we not include what claims to be the hottest gay spot on the Web? Check out this area, which boasts a number of connections to commercial and pay sites. Not exactly a great index, but it does include the current hotspots which means . . . men, men, and more men. However, to connect to any of the sites, you will have to pass an age clearance at GaySpace, kids! This is a little time consuming, but if you are not in a hurry, enjoy filling out the forms. We had to; "according to the law," they told us.

The money thing is very difficult to understand, something like ten dollars a month. I tried to get responses to our "how much does it cost?" e-mails, but kept receiving ads for products instead.

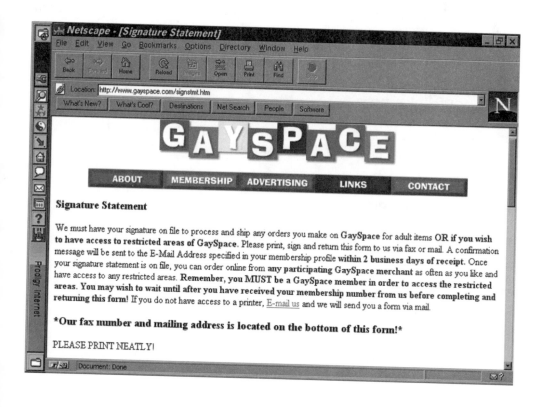

SmaQ
cyber-active.com/lagunatic/smaq/

Links, links, and more links to all the dirt you can imagine. This database is user generated, meaning that its users report sites. Then you go get 'em . . . boys.

Boy Babes in Cyberspace
www.boybabes.com

Don't get lost at this site; we found it takes us everywhere we always wanted to go, but then we got lost and couldn't get back.

M.J. O'Neill's Homepage
badpuppy.com/mjoneill/

Check out the Queer and Adult sections to see what current Web browsers want to warn you about before you enter the site. Cool, cool, cool. Meanwhile, this warning from Netscape before I hit *any* site on MJ's smut page: *This is a gay webpage. This is the only warning you will get.*[1] Personally, everything I saw needed a warning, but not one to keep you away. This site needs a HOT warning!

Adult Links
www.adultlinks.com

Girls and boys, and all kinds of dirty, dirty, dirty stuff! A titillating ride; I lost my breath twice. My slide show died. It was exhausted by the effort!

Homosexual Agenda/sex
www.tatertot.com/agenda/

More gay and lesbian resources on every topic, but I bet you are interested in the sex sites, aren't you? (Check out the adorable URL. Aww.)

Queer Gate ($)
www.queergate.com

The site administrator is a case of party girl gone business chick. "I am 28 and Michael is 24, I [sic] have been together for 20 months. I work from home running

[1]Turn back now!

Queergate along with Mike from Talon Holding Corporation in Florida and our small staff."

And what does Jeff [the older one] do in his spare time? "My hobbies are playing with my computer, collecting space and nude photos of young men, and dancing. [Would that be pictures of naked men floating in space?] Anyway, this site costs money, and I was over it since I refuse to pay, but if you got the cash you know it has to be worth it!

> 1 Month—$10.00; $10.00 setup fee
> 6 Months—$40.00; $6.66 per month
> 12 Months—$60.00; $5.00 per month

Queer Ring
www.cs.auc.dk/~zennaro/queerring.html

"This ring, started in March 1996, is made up of homo pages of lesbians, gays, bisexuals, or transgenders all over the net. The purpose of the ring is to link our queer pages and make it easy to travel through our cybercommunity." Need more? I think it's a ring of quality, and for now it's free. Now.

Amsterdam Pink Pages
clix.net/clix/pinkpages/

Welcome to fun in the sun of Amsterdam! This site entices with 3-D images, pics, and maps to "Vaseline Strait" in the heart of quaint Amsterdam. Chat here with some nice Euro boys and check out those girlie links.

Male Classifieds
www.maleclassifieds.com/

Get all the goodies! You can find links to pics, links to masseurs, and even chat room links. Remember that most of the sites listed in the Cyberqueer Clubs section have chat rooms too!

HunkHunters Haunts
home.dmv.com/~dcrowley/index.html

This site rocks! What an amazing list of sites, and each one is graded like the old porn magazines that the elders in your family knew.

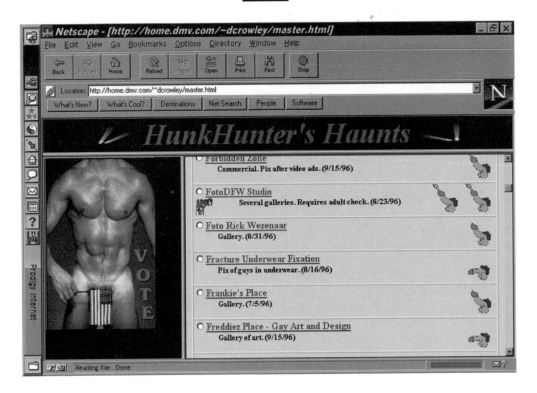

Slider
www.moonbase.com/

Homepages and WWW sites picked by a former USMC boy. Those Marines like 'em tough. You be the judge. Maybe you could order some pizza from his home business (he really does deliver pizza and advertises it on his Web site) if you are in Virginia, and check out what the fighting men of our country are really made of!

CYBERQUEER CLUBS: INTERACTION, VIDEO, AND OTHER CYBERCLUB ODDITIES

Hot and Heavy ($)
nm.hh.nl/

If you're willing to give the bucks, you get all the pictures you could ever look at locked away in your basement. I have laundry bills to pay first.

> 1 Month—$19.95
> 3 Months—$49.95
> 6 Months—$89.95
> 1 Year—$159.95

Chisel ($)
www.chisel.com/

A very nice collection of pics if you want to spend all day having to search for the one you want. This site was laid out well and has the best of intentions, but its interactive elements are laborious. And, you need to dial a 900 number to get access. Be careful, 900 numbers are dangerous to your phone bill! Chisel is among the most popular sex sites; I do not know exactly why. It is more likely because of the easy, 900-number access than their content.

Rumper Room ($)
www.cyberpride.net

Not to be confused with your childhood "Romper Room." Not exactly a pornography Mecca, but some cool chat spaces that don't cost a penny! Not sure why you would want to pay, but the pictures available are hot! Please read on before plunking down the cash. Accounts required a six-month minimum ($36.00). One year in advance will get you one month's free service. Six dollars a month will give you access to over twenty-eight thousand newsgroups.[2]

[2]See Chapter 2 for information about newsgroups.

His Web ($)
www.hisweb.com

This site is marketed to all who enjoy porn stars. Not a lot of creativity here, but hey, if you are looking for hot pics, and other hags like yourself, then check this site out.

    1 Month—$14.95
    6 Months—$79.95
    12 Months—$129.95
    Lifetime—$349.95 <=== Get a subscription for your kid . . .

Mount Equinox ($)
www.equinox.holowww.com/public/images.html

Yet another nudie joint where you can join for a price and get a billion pictures and play games with other members. Is this site better than any of the others? No.

    $9 = Beginners Package: Solitaire (140 new images a month),
    Bedtime Stories, Pow WoW, FTP Access, Inmates Bulletin
    Board System, Forbidden Fruit Stand, Mount Equinox Chat,
    plus a chance for giveaways
    $19 = Experts Package: Solitaire (140 new images a month),
    Exhibitionist Gallery, Badpuppy Puppy Pen, Bedtime Stories,
    Pow WoW, FTP Access, Inmates Bulletin Board System, Forbid-
    den Fruit Stand, Mount Equinox Chat, Solitaire Archives, plus a
    chance for giveaways

Badpuppy ($)
badpuppy.com/preindex.htm

One of the first sites to put all the dirty stuff in one place. Easy accessibility to CU-SeeMe reflector and other video software. Because of this site's maturity—it started as a bulletin board system (BBS) with forty-nine thousand paying members!—it has a large client base, making interactive games a true adventure, rather than the same creatures telling everyone they are "smooth, tight, and ready to fight!" The master of this domain, Bill, tells me he is trying to keep it safe for people to use, yet dirty as hell. Always keep in mind he's screwed if he pisses off the feds.

He claims to have received a note from the FBI via e-mail telling him to "pay his taxes and he will have no trouble." Considering his operation is based in Florida, the "prudest" state of all, that's a good sign for the entrepreneurial puppy.

$10.00 per month subscription to The Dog House and Puppy Pen—This is an automatic renewal at $10 every month.

Free—The Dog House is where all the action is; Puppy Pen is a pen for puppies.

BP plans to provide a "virtual city in cyberspace" (free, or included in the $10 monthly fee). BP was first with virtual reality—it debuted in December, 1996. Three Ds: dirty, dirty, dirty!

You should also be aware that the "free" label is everywhere on the net. For instance, **www.powertech.no/~halvorg** shows off about thirty photos. What kind of pics? I asked a local expert who told me, "X-rated pics and a lot of penises and erections. Thirty static and relatively new photo opp's." Thirty—better be free.

For gay news, try www.badpuppy.com/gay today, gay every day.

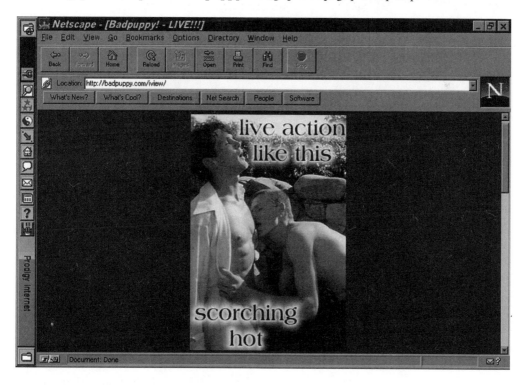

The Cyberslut Page
www.users.dircon.co.uk/~cybrslut/index2.htm

Do not hit me over the head with that! I like this site for its free entertainment . . . and yet, all in all, this is good. You'll find a plethora of sexual oddities and little tidbits at this site. Be sure to check out what Pervy Paul caught on his camera this week . . . Hmm, was that you in the woods? :) A must-see for a poor internet surfer who would rather spend his money on humans!

Club X ($)
www.clubx.com/clubxgay/

Everything here is located everywhere else. Great pics and all the interactive software are available, but the same busy interactive scene as most. For girls *and* boys—a nice change. $4.99 a month or $25 for six months in advance. Not exactly change.

ManZone ($)
www.manzone.com/

Sites often say they are free. The sign says "A Free Site." *Wrong.* They will charge you for the stuff they say is free. I would not use this site because they were so deceptive to begin with. Anyway, CU-SeeMe and all that cute shit can be found here. Much of the site was relatively hard to imagine; I like our fantasies to be somewhat believable—and cheap. Off with their heads! "$9.95 per month billed discreetly to your secured credit card number." I hope it's secure.

Men's Men ($)
www.mensmen.com/main.html

First you buy the Jeff Stryker look- and feel-alike dildo. Ahh. Now you want Jeff Stryker look-alikes period. This spot looks like a screw joint run by the local dirty-magazine stand. Hey, who said that wasn't good? But be ready to donate some cash.

Pleasure Page
www.extasyonline.com

The same group is whipping out these pages. However, this page is older than some of the others, so if you want to guarantee a good time . . . check out all the newer ones.

Male Stop ($)
www.gayweb.com/malestop/infopg.html

Video and only video for $3.99 a minute. Make sure your boyfriend doesn't see the phone bill.

I SEE YOU SEEING ME

For areas that feature the CU-SeeMe reflector software, go to the goliath.wpine.com/cuseeme.html; for sex aficionados some serious software (say *that* ten times) is a must have. Right now some smart Webmaster is adding it to his homepage. Buy yourself a cheap camera for your wanting desktop. Start reflecting now. Check into the following areas and they will take you to the sites to help you download share-able versions of the software. Then you can use this very dirty option.

PORN WHORE VIDEOS

Real-life video means you can play either on the big twenty-six-inch monitor, or you can hide in the basement in your "office." Software for members is included in prices. Even the just-mentioned Badpuppy, a highly commercial mainstream, online service, provides unique software. Either way, the sites already mentioned in the club section have the option of real-time video if you download the software, which is easily accessible because they are going to be charging you anywhere from $2.99 to $9.99 a minute.

Check out Male Stop and the other club sites listed earlier if you are interested in getting some live action on your computer screen. The software also lets you interact with the stripper, but don't think the stripper is the person you are communicating with, nor should you think the stripper is actually hanging out there following your commands; but maybe I shouldn't reveal any more and ruin the fantasy. However, it might be easier to put a VCR in your "office" and just rent a video. But if you are still curious, check out this site specializing in video. (I am happy to report that, since Blockbuster, the nation's largest video chain, does not sell or rent any porn videos, the Web is now taking a lot of take-home money away from those censors.) Also, many of the sites include downloadable video.

PICTURES, PICTURES, MORE DIRTY PICTURES: "NEWSSTAND" WEB SITES

These sites are a treasure trove of photos scanned in from the newsstand magazines you always wanted to buy but were a little too nervous that the clerk might take a discriminating photo of you thumbing through. Check these sites for their quality; avoid the newsstand jitters. If you do not easily suffer from the jitters, then I guarantee that you will feel like a kid in a candy store.

Brendan G. Bailey's Male Art Gallery
www4.creative.net/~bailey/male.htm

Male Diversions is the name of the male gallery set up with the most crafty of intentions. Cute boys and guys with their legs spread amid Ionic columns of ancient Greece. A Parliament ad?

Also, search **www4.creative.net.**

Sexyboy
www.sexyboy.com/

Use the video option, or cruise through favorite pics from mags that fill store windows on Christopher Street.

Justin's Redheads
www.koool.com/men/redheads.html

Now you will know if they are really carrot-tops.

Latent Images
www.io.com/~photoguy/index.html#ls

We love the links section. Its name says a lot about the homos who hang out here.

Claus's Homepage
www.powertech.no/~clausd/index.htm

Check out this Norwegian's homepage and learn about the best mushrooms in the Scandinavian woods.

Moxie Land ($)
www.best.com/~sosbe/

At $5.50 a year, what have you got to lose? Don't expect too much right now, but this has promise, boys. For instance, an FTP site (see Glossary) with access to a ton of private photos can be free for a month and then less than 5 bucks to maintain. That address is **ftp://databank.pond.com/g:Databank/linkland.** Last year the user ID was linkland and the password was express. This year, who knows? E-mail them and say "Hey, I want a free user ID to try you out." You'll get one.

Dream Time
home.earthlink.net/~cmjames/manpage/men.html

Wanna play cowboys and Indians? This dishy page features cowboys and Indians playing like I wish they did when I was a kid!

Unregulated Amsterdam Pornography ($)
www.commercial-services.com/~ap/index.htm

This site bites. Famous at one point for being the "swingin' European stop for everyone to visit when American porn did not exist on the web,"[3] now UAP is a crazy series you have to pay for, and you can get it all on Usenet. Cash for a few pics? I don't think so. Watch out for sex sites proclaiming to be "FREE from Amsterdam."

Hommesite ($)
www.Hommesite.com/

Give some cash to HS and experience just about all the nudie stud pictures from all the so-called city newsstand magazines in addition to some hot Hun drawings of men built to conquer. A year of access for *only* $25.00; regular rate, $45.00.

James' Homepage
www.gbnet.net/~jamesc/

James definitely knows how to make your computer sweat. I went to this site for info on the Brewer twins (see the ever-popular Brewer Twins shrine, below) and stayed for many of his other male art galleries that exploit all our favorite gay male icons. (What's all this fuss about the Brewer Twins, anyway? Inform me at **71333.1366@compuserve.com!**)

---

[3]There was a time when, because of the Communications Decency Act, American firms were afraid. See Badpuppy, above, for more discussion. And see **www.eff.org/blueribbon.**

THE YOUNG MAN'S CHR, ER, CLUB

Young Guys Club
macknz.cluon.com/0ygchome.html

Maybe you would like to pick a boy and then get his CV of porn. Check this out and leave with your own special collection of prints after ordering a set of someone else's for a few bucks. Each one varies in price, depending on how popular the choice.

Sexy, Sexy
www.pwpub.com/jelrik/men.html

Look at all these young studs, including the late River Phoenix. He, unlike the majority, is fully clothed. Who's here? Marky Mark, Brad Pitt, the guy from "Saved by the Bell." Why'd you want to ruin the fantasy? Don't they look good enough on screen? As my boyfriend put it: "Brad Pitt's dick is too human!" For the scoop on how they make the boy from "Saved by the Bell" naked when he's really wearing shorts, see // **www.pwpumb/jelrik/men.html.** Very interesting, to say the least.

The Cub Scout Page
www.txcc.net/~cubscout/

Well, they're not exactly Cub Scouts. Every fantasy has to take a left turn sometimes. And the Boy Scouts wouldn't allow this. How about the *Webelos* then? Follow the Warning forward to the page you want.

Brewer Twins
www.gbnet.net/~jamesc/galleries/brewer.html

Your favorite Aryan twins playing with each other's ding-a-lings. Incest or computer-image fake? You make the decision. Either way this site is a *must!* I have never heard so many boys talk about one site.

Cuties on the Web
www.geocities.com/WestHollywood/1761/

Someone put up a zillion personal homepages, and that someone is a self-styled reviewer who obviously has way too much time on his hands. He also prefers them a little young, J. Crew-esque, and clean cut.

CAMERAS IN THE LOCKER ROOM

Jupiter Physique Art
internet-designs.com/carrus/carrus.htm

Big boys posing artistically. I am sure the photographers spent a lot of time after class in Photography 101 to capture these very introspective shots.

Hot Stuff Lobby
www.contrib.andrew.cmu.edu/usr/tj00/hot/lobby.html

Pictures of boys who are not compensating for any deficiencies by weight lifting. Uh-uh. Also other pics for those nonmuscle queens. (Two types of gay men? Muscle queens and liars.)

Muscle Net
www.musclenet.com/about.htm

Relive the gym experience. Grunt, sweat, and roll around in jockstraps in the locker room! (Why is it gay men were the boys who *hated* gym class and now they get their mail forwarded to the gym?)

Sobeach
www.sobe-cfg.com/

Bears, studs, hunks, and you can chat with all the guys who like the same . . . that would be everyone. *No cost either!* (This I had to see.) Sobeach is named after that gay paradise, Miami Beach. That means it might end up a flash-in-the-pan.

The Male Gallery
www.blarg.net/~dhua/gallery/

California boys at their best—wicked cute, tan, and dumb! Go Cali!

Locker Room
www.geocities.com/WestHollywood/1761/

Stinky jocks, smelly crotches, sweaty shirts, dripping brows, and scrumptious athletes. Or maybe they are just porn models—*does it really matter?* I wanted to go out and throw a basketball.

ARTISTIC PORNOGRAPHY

Bronze and Steel Sculpture by Wim Griffith
www.millenia.com/~wim/gallery.html

This Web site contains fine art bronze and steel sculpture of male nudes.

The Douglas Simonson Online Thing
www.douglassimonson.com

The gallery has wonderful drawings of models who look as if they work the corners of East 53rd Street (NY's Hustler Central) And if you want a few, the order form is accessible.

Hungry Eyes
www.netjojo.com/fmenu.htm

Sensitive male drawings of real cute boys.

Cyber Male
www.geocities.com/WestHollywood/3312/

More sensitive pictures of boys detailed well, real well.

Photoguy
www.io.com/~photoguy/gallery.html

These are some of the hottest pics I've seen in all my cybertravels. Bookmark this before you forget. In this case, you see something with a story behind it, instead of pure sex. But in our cases, beggars can't be choosers, eh?

BOXERS, BUTTS, JEANS, AND JOCKS

Steve's Adult Page
gayads.com/steve/

I only wish they were naked! Underwear pics I certainly have seen plenty of. See Chapter 7 for more. And who's Steve?

Aaron's Homepage
pages.prodigy.com/tripleA/bad.htm

Check out Aaron from Prodigy and his narcissism problem. Are you into skate rats with high school show-choir haircuts? This ultimately satisfying homey gives all.

BoxerGuy
www.execpc.com/~pjd/underWWWear/

A fetish page for the underwear addicted. Scheduled to become part of Badpuppy. A picture almost every day of a hunk in his favorite briefs looking as if he wears them all day long. You could always go over to **www.joeboxer.com** and see what real models look like, in their undies, no less.

Jeans
members.gnn.com/ratpye/denim.htm

Check out these packages being held by these jeans-loving boys! Those are the *genes* I have been looking for, at Christmas time.

International Jock Straps ($)
www.boybabes.com/jock.htm

Wanna buy a used jock and rub it all over your body and let someone CU-SeeMe do it? Hey, that could be adorable! It costs $14 to $20, depending on the freshness of the ball sweat (joking: I really had no idea how they charge and they were aghast when we asked for explanation).

Boy Toy
www.boytoy.com/

Jocks, underwear, swimsuits, I just did not know where to get, I mean, start, off. Boy Toy boasts a clothing-queen's heaven. If you have a fetish with these clothing items, then you better get your prescription refilled for the occasional heart attack you will suffer from a life of overindulgence that is only just beginning.

BEARS: "BIG HAIRY GUYS, LOTSA FUR; FRIENDLY AND CUDDLY"

Bear Roulette
www.cnct.com/home/markk/br/brrou120.htm

"So try your luck! Press the wheel to your right and be whisked into a world of fur. Don't be shy! Play early and often! So come on, give it a try! You can't lose," boasts the intro page of this site. Get a random page with a "bear" edge, and maybe you'll get lucky and get the page featuring a Bear and Wolf Fight! There is also the tendency to end up at the Bear Wine page, and that wouldn't be such a crime.

Resources for Bears
www.skepsis.com/.gblo/bears/

This is information Mecca for the bears out there. You can find information on bears services on the net, the international bear calendar, links to WWW homepages, information about the bears mailing list, the bears classification system, V1.10, and links to bear businesses.
I know you think I'm making all this up.

Horny Hairy Men
www3.creative.net/~bsb/bsb.html

Oh my God . . . Nick's fuck section, the Wrestler's Gallery, and dirt, dirt, dirt.

Men and Their Mustaches
www.ozemail.com.au/~drummer/htmls/greghp3.html

Mustaches in all your favorite places and some in areas you have never seen before.

The Hairy Chest Page
www3.creative.net/~hcp/

Contests for that perfect chest forest! We declined to enter. Go for it, though; we'll wait for the results.

Hairway to Steven
www.daboy.com//filter.html

Page after page of advertising for your favorite bear products. If you are persistent, maybe you will find a daddy bear. P.S.: A real fab name for a site. We wonder, will Led Zeppelin sue?

The Hairy Bear's Page
www.creative.net/~thepark/wilderness/

Bears indoors, outdoors, and all those "beary parts." Get close to the wildlife in the ole Bear Cave!

Top Bear's Art Gallery
www.wizard.com/~topbear/foyer.htm

Galleries of muscle-clad bears.

The Bears Mailing List
www.skepsis.com:80/.gblo/bears/BML/

The Bears Mailing List (aka BML) is an internet list in digest format for gay and bisexual men who are bears and for those who enjoy the company of bears. You can get on it, get off it, get the most recent letters from it, or pass.

Links to Net Bears
www.skepsis.com:80/.gblo/bears/NETBEARS/

Another bearish community on the internet where you will find listings of hundreds of bear homepages. Happy hunting!

Bear Den Reflector
gcwp.com/payref.htm

Get your camera hooked up, dish out some money, and play with the animals in the woods! This is most assuredly the latest in home entertainment! (*Reflector* refers to the CU-SeeMe technology.)

Bear Networks
www.bear.net

Looking for a group in your neighborhood that is just for bears? Use this crafty search engine that my dentist absolutely swears by.

Daddy Magazine
www.charm.net/~ganymede/

"DADDY, the magazine, features mature men aged 35 to 75 at their best." Go on daddy!

CREEPY, DOWNRIGHT-SEXY, AND SPOOKY!

Chaz's World
www.chaz-world.com/

This page will take you where man has not been before. At least no man I know. Enter the holodeck and play with aliens that look a lot like stud-muffins from earth! Chas has attitude—and a reputation, dudes.

Scooter and Scrappy in Seattle
psweb.com/scooter/

Butt galore. Check out the cute butts on this page! And no buts, we mean butts. Yeah, but.

Hot Twat
206.171.237.9/

Okay, it isn't gay. Girls, maybe a glance if you are not queasy about a male interpretation of the female form. Personally, I do not recommend this site. But how could I leave it out of the "Spooky"/"Creepy" list?

Bianca's Love Shack
bianca.com/

If you're squeamish, read no more. I said, Stop reading. This site is a virtual home where you can play, cook, feed the dog, and play with the kids. Go to the bathroom and discuss your corn log, jog to the hallway, and hang out with the guys to discuss ball sweat and its many creative uses.

Different Loving Kink Links
gloria-brame.com/lov8.htm

Careful. You might hurt yourself searching this directory!

Master Troy
www.sfgate.com/examiner/bondage/BOND-23962.html

"The raid also netted pornographic tapes Thomas allegedly had for rent. Investigators said some tapes involved exotic animals such as eels, anteaters and water buffalo." Is he living in your neighborhood?

The Institution
www.peak.org/~bob/

Carl takes a moment to experience his airtight rubber face mask. I'll check in with him later to make sure he's not turning blue. He's one of the guests at a party given by the guy who made this page. I wonder if he gets a beer after he is done? And who's Bob?

WHAT THE CREEPY, DOWNRIGHT-SEXY, AND SPOOKY READ

Cuir Underground
www.black-rose.com/cuiru.html

Get dates of places where the dirty boys and girls go to get down! Calendar of fetish events that would kill anyone who attempted to attend them all. Here is a question from one of the concerned subscribers and—most likely—the host of an event listed in this truly mesmerizing online magazine: "Q to Cuir: Since I am in the middle of the swimsuit season, how can one minimize bruising after s/m play, so as not to wreak havoc at the beach?"

Bad Attitude
www.lifestyle.com/lesbian

Bad Attitude is forty-eight pages of lesbian lust with an emphasis on S&M. The magazine is entirely filled with graphic black-and-white photos, insightful reviews, provocative articles, and hot fiction. Boldly stated: "This magazine is banned in England and Canada so you must state that you are over 21 when you subscribe." Go see what the girls of Canada can't handle!

Here is an example of some of their weekly topics: "fisting, enemas, anal play, dildo play, piercing, branding, cutting, bondage, vampirism, gender bending, whipping, tit torture, witchcraft, goddess worship, spanking, dyke-daddies, bad mommies, threesomes, foursomes and more and more and more lesbian sex!" How about handy kitchen appliances?

Bound and Gagged ($)
www.nycnet.com/bound&gagged/

Now this magazine is dedicated to the boys who like their dates to be tied and bound to the kitchen sink while they cook three pans of extrasoft brownies. No . . . it is for the people who would like to be bound. Who subscribes? Check out this submission: "I tell a hustler to tie me anyway he wants, do whatever he wants to do, and when he is done to leave me bound and gagged to find my own escape. If I cannot get loose, I hope to be found and freed. My friends call me nuts. Am I?" Did I mention that this reader is the father of three? Wonder what their holiday seasons are like? Costs many dollars, arrives in a brown paper wrapper. :(But free fans can see B&G links and a Real Story Preview section!

> 1-year subscription (6 issues):
> $36.00 in the United States
> $42.00 in Canada and Mexico
> $51 overseas (surface mail)
> $72 overseas (air mail)

Barnyard Festivities

Akita Inus
www.c2.net/~akita/akita.htm

Ah, so you're interested in finding some weird doodoo that can make even you squirm; I know it takes a lot to make you squirm!

Rotten Dog House
members.aol.com/k9rott/zoo.htm

A directory to help you find your favorite animals demonstrating some of the most important elements of Darwin's theories. I will not soil these pages further.

Zoomorph Magazine
www.zoom.com/personal/aberno/zoomorph/zm.shtml [for reference only]

"Page Removed Due To Internet Censorship. The page that was at this URL has been removed from the server in order to comply with the Communications Decency Act of Feb. 1, 1996." Oh my goodness . . . too dirty? I can't print locations of sites that appeal to those zoophiles among you because I would be, in essence, closing them down. Ask around the other sites to get the current hype. Note that the CDA was found unconstitutional in 1996. They were obviously too lazy to put the page back up.

Stasya's Zoophilia page
www.av.qnet.com/~stasya/index.html

A scholar on the subject. And what are those background pictures?

Da Butt Games

Rectal Impaction
sol.zynet.co.uk/clivenet/daryl/bottom.htm

". . . unusual rectal foreign body resulting from homosexual anal erotic activities. The patient had used an enema containing a concrete mix and it became impacted and required surgical removal." Learn what not to shove up your hiney, honey.

Bogai Space
www.cris.com/~Hasmali/

Take a glance at these butts and just maybe you will be inspired to go wash yours! Is this unappetizing? Then skip the next section.

Patches Place Welcome Mat
www.frontiernet.net/~patches/

Stumble through this site to find out what stinks. Hey! Anyone got any squeezable Charmin?

Watersport Forum
vorlon.mit.edu/forum/

Hey, you wanna talk about peeing on your boyfriend, or maybe talk to some girl who just got dumped by her boyfriend after she asked, "Can I pee in bed?"

As of February 1997, vorlon had suffered "a disk crash" that "toasted" the spools. So the Forum was "gone."

The Rainbow Sofa ($)
www.hothunk.com/

Give them some money and enjoy the scat games . . . the rest . . . ah, whatever. I would like to say it is only $7.95, but I really couldn't tell because the obnoxious advertising games dissuaded me from surfing for an hour and viewing all their damned advertising. I guess they figured out that gay sex sites get visited a lot.

And I helped.

Toilet Training
gpu.srv.ualberta.ca/~msykes/thome.html

"If the Good Lord had not intended us to be SIZE QUEENS, He would not have given us TROUGH URINALS!!" Welcome to Toilet Training. If this is your opinion, then you are definitely in luck! No nudies here, but an amazing set of instructions on maneuvering around urinals. Oh geesh.

S&M, Leather, Bondage, and Cute Cuddly Things for People of All Ages, Colors, and Likes, Not to Mention Some People I Wasn't Planning on Introducing to Mom or Dad

Without Restraint
www.mcsp.com/tes/welcome.html

Need a little instruction, or maybe you're looking for a new way to hang steel balls from your ball bag? Well, maybe you're not interested in that, but if you have any questions, this is where you should go because their teaching methods remind me of my favorite sixth-grade teacher.

Leather Resources Online
www.io.com/~topman4u/leather.html

Looking for a leather buddy in your home town? Come here to find your local "worship place."

Chrispin's Spanking Homepage
www.dircon.co.uk/cpenn/INDEX.HTM

Learn, watch, find some friends, but make sure you bring some ice!

Man's Hands Films
www.Hommesite.com/manhd01.html

Order the latest leather flick now and you may receive their introductory offer, and it is not a new toaster.

Dutchbear's Gallery
www.euronet.nl/users/

A collection of delectable delights squeezed in leather harnesses and whipped into a light creamy sauce.

Getting Serious with the Paddle

Paddle Pals
www.8ballplayers.com/

Pictures galore but, be careful, for you may need a bandage after this experience. Don't tell Mommy where you hurt yourself . . . or Daddy!

Alternative Sex
www.fifth-mountain.com/radical—sex/

Got a question about where you should put that steel plug? Your boyfriend wants to play barnyard worship without getting stuck in the mud?[4] Well, you are in luck; this site has all the answers to all the forbidden questions. Like that one. Plus: How do I get out of the obsession of always downloading porn photos?

Yossie's Handcuff Collection
www.blacksteel.com/~yossie/hcs.html

Looking for some equipment to hook pony boy up to the stable? Here is the best site I could find for all your basic needs in leg irons.

Magenta.com
magenta.com/lmnop/intro.html

Need some more directions and advice on how to beat a boyfriend in a loving and compassionate way? This is the place!

The House of Difference
www.differences.com/

Just another really polite site hoping to seduce someone into the world of submission. This is a homepage of difference, all right.

The Art of Torture
www.metroslave.com

"The images on this Web site may seem sick, psycho, unusually morbid, or even insane. . . ." I don't know why they were so modest. I'm blind now. Look. Some of this site is sick! And, although sick is okay, I would rather recommend sickness with humor or irony. You should see "Twisted" **www.nxn.com/tangled,** a place to see screwed-up photo images of torsos, waists, butts, dicks, tits, clitorises. It's a photographer's worst nightmare, or a funny dream!

[4]For more on MUD, see the Glossary.

Transcutaneous Electrical Nerve Stimulation (TENS)
www.medmarket.com/tenants/reiddds/products/
metvtens.html

Want to play with electricity? Well then, maybe you should read this site and stay away from puddles!

FASHION AND SEX ACCESSORIES:

Electronic Butt Plugs, Leg Irons, and the Mothership

Blowfish
www.blowfish.com/catalog/

Electric, manual, pink, blue, rouge, gyrating, vibrating, internally stimulating, and for the whole family. Designed to make you twitch with ecstasy thinking about how you can play with all these toys.

The House of Whacks
www.whacks.com/

Says the proprietor of this whack-y place: "I managed a sex shop for a while and it upset me that drunks would come in and make fun of a guy buying a bra for himself. I would throw those guys out! I'm interested in building trust. I don't make fun of people . . ." She will beat your ass too! This chick specializes in creating the environment needed to live out an incredibly "whacked" lifestyle!

MJ Enterprises
www.mjenter.com/

Looking for a cowprod—or a strap custom designed for your needs? Here are order forms for newsletters where you can find info about items of steel and leather. And whatever prods are made of.

Adonis
www.cris.com/~Adonis/

Maybe you would enjoy something attached to this description:

". . . man with a sweet open mouth, tight backdoor and a huge
8½-inch cock"
". . . the first robotic blow job!"
". . . foot-long dong will have you throbbing with pleasure. Share
this with a friend for more fun"

Anyway, if you are into toys, you would be a wreck if you missed out on this page!

Heels from Hell

Fetish Fashion
www.rockmine.music.co.uk/FunHouse/FetLink.html

The bitch with the Frederick's of Hollywood pumps is dead now and they are on
your feet. But what are you going to strap on your waist? Bettah go here!

Diva Net
www.zoom.com/divanet/

Looks like you found some competition! This site is loaded with fashion for the club
hags at heart. Girl, you better take another bump if you are going to sport some of
this shit.

Sexy Body Jewelry
www.sexy-jewelry.com/

Enjoy this one, all you girls. Make all your favorite girl parts glitter and shine, and
no piercing! However, some of this stuff looks as if it needs to be attached. This is a
catalogue site, so don't go lookin' for freebies.

SITES WITH A DIFF'RENT FLAVAH!

Catche's Place ($)
www.catchsplace.com/

Dedicated to the young African American male. And there is some major dedication
going on. The photography here is not your local deli shit either. But you better not
be a poor gay kid, cause you ain't gettin' a thang.
Only $20 for a full year of access <= = = = = Nice price huh!!!!

Bakla's Phun House
www.concentric.net/~baklaboy/Bakla.htm

Is it gay? Is it Asian? Then it's found here. It's the way to a Star Sapphire instead of a gold ring.

Black Man Index
www.glue.umd.edu/~mestreet/.X/

Just men . . . only men . . . no text! And Jungle Fever is on and on.

Jade Star's Page
web2.airmail.net/lastat01/asian/

"A Celebration of Gay Men of All Flavors and Smiles and the Men who want to meet them."

Dirty
www2.dirty.com/dirty/

"Straight from the streets of Manhattan, DIRTY is a magazine about real men . . . not buffed California gym queens smiling for the camera." After that wonderful intro, you soon discover that these boys can really stink up your room. Check out this site and, when you're done, it's a big shower scene for you! I have been following this magazine for years as it started to build a crowd. Now the crowd is built and I am on their side. In censored America, this is a train that can't be stopped. Or washed.

REAL-LIFE "RELIEF"

International Jack-off Clubs
www.rabbit.com.au/~wankers/world.htm

Exactly what it states. Get the addresses and phone numbers of jack-off clubs around the world for your real-life enjoyment! Though all "civilized" countries are included, I know the site's origins are European; check out the "wanker" URL. Turning Japanese, I really think so.

Steam Room
www.cruisingforsex.com

Looking for somewhere to go and be a dirty boy after surfing for sex sites on the internet. Here you get "ratings by Jeff" and others who've checked out some of the more notorious U.S. places.

Cute URL, eh boys?

LEZZIES PRO LUST

Lezzie Smut
prometheus.digital-rain.com/~lezzie/

Dirty girls. Completely dedicated to "breaching all political boundaries by enslaving you to your twat"! This online magazine rings with a so-called Suzie Sexpert and her approach to "getting on" or should I say "getting it everywhere."

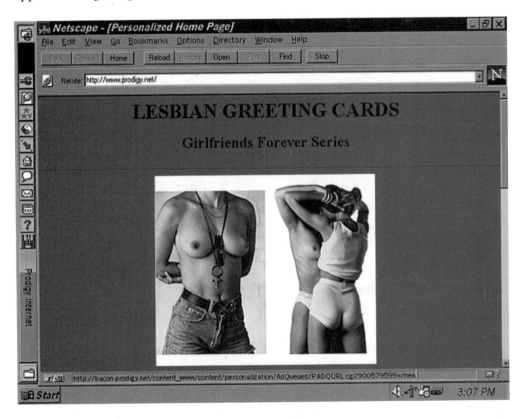

Lesbian Links
www.best.com/~agoodloe/lesbian/

And now you have it, girls. Links to all the girlie sites selected by quite the girl herself. Amy Goodloe, a woman I love, puts in the extra effort to make this site an exquisite spot for all the girls to start the hunt for dirty sites. I think it's quite fine.

(See page 221 for more.)

9

LESBIAN LIGHT

Lesbians are not the same on the net as their gay brethren. As Becky Boone, a lesbian creator of **www.qworld.com** tells it: "Women tilt toward becoming more verbal and love chatting and meeting and, well, bonding. Men on the other hand are technical, like to confront and especially love the bells and whistles" that go with surfing the World Wide Web.

Lesbian Web sites are throughout the smorgasbord that is this book. The following areas are alone in their quest for lesbian audience. Here you will see information, not much hype, and a few totally outrageous places to come and seek—whatever the girls are after.

Boone explains: "We are a community building sex, and women who post on especially our lesbian areas are pretty much looking to pair up and either fall in love or like." Boone, like other editors and creators I spoke to, finds lots of pairs who actually met and right away "picked up, liquidated and moved from New Jersey to California, to be with their online lover." This is not unlike that age-old joke about lesbian second dates and U-Hauls!

Women who meet and greet on the world of the internet are more often than not conciliatory and placating and tend to try to soothe the ones they meet, especially in the newsgroup scene.

"It's very much a sense of pouring oil on water," says Boone, a devout Southerner. "I see the women on the Web calling the girls they meet their family, a happy big place to be together."

These quite useful and individual sites have been separated out for this chapter. Lesbians interviewed for *Get On with It* told me that they liked the Web indeed, but they were not in love with it, and did not want to spend spare time surfing. They used it often and mostly at appointed times. Unlike guys who said they were on even when they weren't supposed to be cruising, women specifically sought the internet for news, community, bonding, and friendship.

Interestingly, the lesbian anarchists are alive and kicking, as you will see in the following pages. "They are highly visible, vocal and loud," explains Boone. "But they are definitely the minority."

For sex—and there's plenty of it throughout the chapter—see the last twenty pages and get off with it, or go to the list at the end of this chapter and surf 'em.

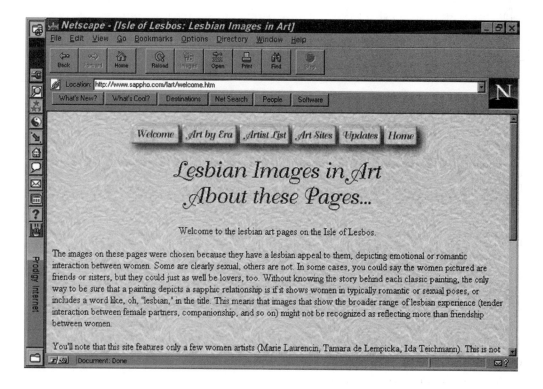

Lesbian.org Message Boards
www.lesbian.org/message-boards.html
and
www.best.com/~agoodloe/lesbian/salons.html

These are message boards on a variety of lesbian topics, such as New Dyke On The Net, Coming Out Lesbian, Lesbian Personals, Regional Lesbians, Lesbian Book Recommendations, and Lesbian Info Exchange. Come in here and develop a kinship with "Lesbian org."

June Mazer Lesbian Collection
www.lesbian.org/mazer

This collection of mini-sites is, according to the press release, "the only archive on this side of the continent dedicated exclusively to preserving lesbian history and to guaranteeing that those who come after us will not have to believe that they 'walk[ed] alone.' " Quite poignant.

Included in the site are personal letters, scrapbooks, lesbian artwork, and some amazing (often surreal) artifacts: manuscripts, books, records, photos, videotapes, flyers, lesbian organizations' private papers, even clothing . . . such as softball uniforms of the forties and fifties (very *League of Their Own*).

You can see all this stuff and totally feel the history.

Lesbian History Project
www-lib.usc.edu/~retter/main.html

This project supports efforts to gather, record, and publicize work on the history of lesbians in all geographic areas and time periods. LHP emphasizes lesbians of color and particularly those in California.

Dyke Action Machine (DAM!) The Girlie Network
mosaic.echonyc.com/~dam/time.html

As its name implies, this entertainment-oriented site is probably one of the more lighthearted ones on the Web. The Girlie Network is the TV station that lesbians all over the world should pray for. Imagine a full timetable of lesbo-themed shows, ranging from talk-show format, sitcom, soap opera, sporting event, to full-length feature film. Sounds delicious?

Read on.

Presenting listings of interactive events in a *TV Guide*-style format, the Girlie Network boasts some interesting as well as hilarious titles, for example, the famous Ob-Gyn whose trailer reads, "Going to the doctor never felt like this." Accompanied by four lesbian doctors flashing toothy grins, movie of the week, *Straight to Hell,* a classic lesbo prison flick, and *Luciana & Lily,* a kind of lesbo *I Love Lucy.*

With tongue planted firmly in cheek, The Network provides some lighthearted and relaxing entertainment for the hard-working dyke. Go on down (no pun) and check the listings or tune in. This site's definitely on the money and very necessary in this oh-so-serious world of ours, and yours.

Lesbian Mailing Lists
www.lesbian.org/lesbian-lists/

Mailing lists are the most popular way to have interactive communication on the internet, and not surprisingly, the best way to meet and have conversations with other dykes. (See Listservs in Chapter 3.) This list, found on the Web, can connect you to the most comprehensive information on lesbian mailing lists to date, including a description of each list's purpose and instructions for joining. You can find lists on almost any conceivable topic, from S&M to motorcycles to butch-femme relationships to living with disabilities.

The Wishing Well: A Service
www.vicon.net/

How *crazy* this concept is: a way to find a date without even going into a chat room. The way people meet is to find pals with something in common and start e-mailing them. Intriguing women are always found.

Match.com: The Online Matchmaker
www.match.com
try also www.match.com/link.ogi/360978166890/ welcome.trl

A plethora of cool ladies to meet . . . a lesbian way to get a date. According to my single girlfriends, you can get romantically "linked" or just find a pen pal. The special software they send you assists in keeping in touch! No guys. A different ballpark.

Women Online Worldwide
www.wowwomen.com

On this site you can find Web-based message boards on topics relating to lesbian issues. QWorld (the site for people who want message boards that aren't *jam packed*) is there, with hosted live chat sessions. See the calendar within. Very cool doings. Run by Becky Boone, a lesbian therapist. This was the first online lesbian forum, once on the now-defunct E World.

In addition to message boards, find a cool 'zine, a shareware library, and much more.

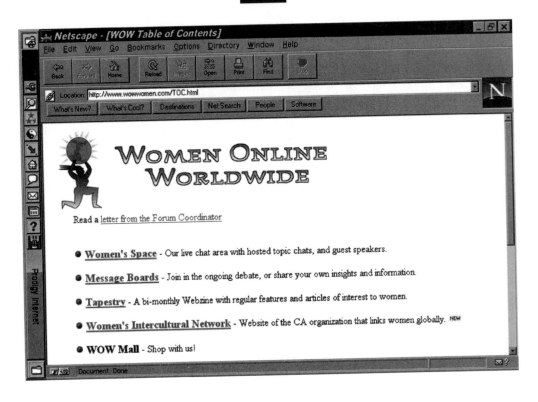

Welcome to We'Moon
www.teleport.com/~wemoon/

We'Moon, as described on the first page of this site, is not merely a calendar but also a way of life for many. It's an astrological moon calendar, ecofeminist appointment book, daily guide to natural rhythms, a lunar perspective of the thirteen moons of the year, get the bubble gum . . . Members logging on here for the first time may be freaked out at first by the mystical graphics and text on the site. Once the initial shock wears off, we're left with a very engrossing site on a totally intriguing viewpoint.

It may sound a little spooky or out there for the more grounded individual, if you know any, but it's a strangely wonderful premise. The language on the site may take time to get used to but, once you're past it, the place gets interesting. Spiritual types and those into mysticism—you are made for the We'Moons.

We'Moon also provides access to an "international Web of creative womyn." With the click of a mouse, one can access art and writing from womyn all around the world. Available for girls are plenty of womyn-loving themes to help develop one's own writings and artwork. Last, and perhaps most important, We'Moon provides the user with an active network of woman sharing work and ideas from around the planet. **Planet Woman!?**

The Sappho Mailing List Homepage
www.apocalypse.org/pub/sappho

The Sappho Mailing List is an exciting mail list begun by Jean Marie Diaz, aka AMBAR, who sought and could not find a mailing list for lesbian and bisexual women and thus began this one in 1987. Since then, the list has taken on an international flavor with members from the United States, Canada, Denmark, Finland, France, Germany, the United Kingdom, Israel, Argentina, Australia, and New Zealand, among other lands. Her list has grown to include over five hundred subscribers and has spawned several splinter lists as well. You can get on it.

Sappho is not open only to women; Sappho does not discriminate against transsexuals. She is officially "for the discussion of topics related to gay and bisexual women." Due to the extensive membership and diversity of members, topics can vary from the hyperacademic to more frivolous and lighthearted. It's not unusual to see articles on legislation followed by a list of places to meet people, in turn followed by lists on how to knit your partner a sweater.

Lesbian Avengers—London Chapter
www.dept.cs.ucl.ac.uk/students/

The Lezzie Avengers, as some know them, are perhaps the most famous lesbian group to date. In New York LAvengers are the ones who put on great shows, like the Stonewall 25 preparade in 1994's New York circus. The girls mean business. And then came this site.

At first glimpse you might think that this site is the title of a bad movie. Think four prison-hardened chicks kickin' ass over London and takin' no names. Imagine Linda Blair and Shannon Tweed costarring—Quentin Tarantino would direct. Cannes and Sundance would go nuts, and yeah, the world would love it. Critics everywhere might hail it as a breakthrough film, doing for lesbians what *Roots* did for African Americans. But before you get excited and tell all your friends, I have to break the news to you. None of that here.

The Lesbian Avengers is a nonviolent, direct-action group dedicated to raising lesbian visibility and fighting for survival and rights for this often-overlooked group. The Avengers first came about in March 1993 in the Apple; the London chapter started in 1994. Since then they have organized over fifty actions, zaps, protests, demonstrations, and parties like the one mentioned above. They have proved that, with no visible leadership, lesbian voices can still be heard and effect change.

Visitors to the site will find the latest news about the Avengers and what they are or will soon be doing! The site's real function is to provide a sanctuary for lesbians who are pushed into silence during their daily lives. On site you can find info on where to attend meetings, where to write for more information, and, ever-so-importantly, where to make donations.

P.S.: The Lesbian Avengers' San Francisco chapter (**www.lesbian.org/sfa-vengers/**) has a cool slogan; they are "focused on issues vital to our survival, and direct action will survive!"

The LOVEGRIDA!
desires.com/1.2/art/docs/lovegrid.html

Attention horny ladies! Are you looking for some luscious bodies to gawk at and fantasize about? Is your social life so boring that even your hands and that trusty vibrator are looking overtly tired?

Speaking of which, let me ask you: Are you tired of having your friends call you "old hag" and "spinster chick" because you don't do anything even remotely close to exciting? Well, inject a little fun into your stale buttocks at the LOVEGRIDA!

This Web adventure is a photo exposé of the lesbian plastic doll scene. This site, which once contained photos of luscious lesbians, now has been distorted (thanks to my best friend, Mr. Censor) to look like mere Rorschach blots. People complained, see?

It is a trip, to put it mildly. So, tell me, when you look at this lovely pic, do you see your abusive father or controlling mother? (That'll be five thousand dollars for the first ten minutes.) Any other hot-to-trotters, looking for visual excitement, should bring an imagination with them when they visit this site, 'cause reality really does byte.

Caryl's Links for Lesbians
www.sirius.com/~caryls

Caryl Shaw is a leader in her own right. The ranking system is based on her opinions: Do they rank? Should you bother? Will the design turn you on? A ton of personality and great links.

Also, see Stacey's Links (no relation to Caryl's Links): **www.goodnet.com/~stacey/ leslinks.html**

Yoohoo! Lesbians!
www.sappho.com/yoohoo

Very Betty Rubble. Yoohoo! Lesbians! is a guide to the lesbian world, similar in style to the boys at Yahoo! except for one thing: This directory will crack you up. We still refer to it when on our many fact-checking missions for anything funny and girl related.

Virtual Sisterhood
www.igc.apc.org/vsister/index.html

"The global women's electronic support network is dedicated to strengthening and magnifying the impact of feminist organization through promotion of electronic communications use within the global women's movement." Whadda mouthful. The network prioritizes the inclusion of women of color, immigrant and refugee women, low-income women, lesbians, women from the global south, old women, young women, disabled women, rural women, and women from communities that have traditionally had little or no access to or control of electronic communications technology.

The purpose of this is to educate women about electronic information resources, and specifically, aiming to teach women the importance of controlling their electronic information resources and how such an act can increase their ability to advance their rights and social justice agendas. The site also emphasizes work with low-income women and others who have been traditionally excluded from these resources. Lastly, the site is concerned with making these resources available to other women's organizations for their use. Empowerment for all women is the goal for an exceptional site.

A Dyke's World
www.gworld.org/DykesWorld/indexframe.html

This site is composed of lots of parts, and I must applaud each one of them, body and soul. It is based in Germany and has fantastic graphics and cool layout. You will discover Sweet Music with the sisters on stage, and all the girls of this persuasion who are musical today (and yesterday). Links galore! The music on this site is just breath-taking. Also, there are design resources and places to travel. This was the first stop when we started asking girls. Everyone pointed to this, A Dyke's World! A whirl of a good time.

NOW and Lesbian Rights Site
now.org/now/issues/lgbi/lgbi.html

In an era when women's rights and lesbian rights are not exactly coinciding, it's nice to see a major feminist org (the National Organization for Women) going to bat for their sisters. "NOW is committed," says a release on this site, "to fighting discrimination based on sexual orientation in all areas, including employment, housing, public accommodations, child custody, and military and immigration policy. NOW asserts the rights of lesbians and gays to live their lives with dignity and security." Policies, histories, recent actions, and a searchable database on just about every lestopic.

International Lesbian Info Svce (ILIS)
www.helsinki.fi/~kris_ntk/ilis.html

ILIS is an international network of lesbians working for lesbian rights. Learn about lesbian rights in many countries.

> From the site's abrupt FAQ: Demands of ILIS: We have the unconditional right to control our own bodies; we have a right to education that is not sexist or heterosexist and which includes positive information about lesbian lifestyle. We need the right to self-organisation. All governments must pass human rights legislation to protect individuals against discrimination based on color, class, creed, sex, and sexual preference.

Lesbian Mom's Web Page
www.lesbian.org/moms

Helping out women who want to have babies through nontraditional means. Very helpful for those who happen to be lesbian and whose clocks are ticking. A woman I know wrote this suggestion: "If you need a doctor, get one. If you need legal advice, get [a lawyer]. If you're looking for wisdom, come here." The files are linked to library files with lots of answers on a given topic. Find subscriptions to relevant e-mail lists.

Infoqueer General Women's Sites
server.berkeley.edu/mblga/qis/homepages.html

Sites hosted by Infoqueer for women are intended as a listing and link to general women's sites that are both heterosexual and queer. For more women's sites, try surfing out from the sites here and from some others listed in this chapter and a few gay *and* lesbian sites, which are listed throughout Chapter 6. First, the ADA Project—Resources for Women in Computing: The site contains TAP Incoming, a searchable, time-based index to allow quick and easy access to the latest news and announcements, older information you might still be interested in, and announcements about a particular topic. Also there are links here to the **www.wowwomen. com** site—which on the Web has those free, nightly, hosted chats! They cover a host of women's issues, including women's writings online, work and money, posted stories about women and the whole of the internet.

The pages of Fem Activist Resources on the Net act as a method to connect people with other indexes about a particular topic of feminism, rather than to the resources themselves.[1] A definite bookmark for women here.

The 1992 edition of Barnard College's *Women's Handbook* is here. The *Handbook* makes information and resources accessible to women on the Barnard and Columbia campuses. The designers of this site hope that this book will spark a dialogue around germane topics.

Gender and Electronic Networking is a site addressing the shortage of women in the field of computer science, offering any potential female computer scientists information on women's continued underrepresentation in the field and on developments in response to this problem.

Women's Resources Project
sunsite.unc.edu/cheryb/women/wshome.html

Cheryl Friedman, from the Women's Resources Project, turned me on to the most useful educational site on the Web for women who want to know: **sunsite.unc.edu/ cheryb/women/wresources.html.** This is just a listing of resources for women in a political mode; the rest are interesting sites for wandering through.

Grrltalk: A Guide to Lesbian IRC
www.geocities.com/WestHollywood/1123/grrl.html

A most useful site, considering the IRC is where it's at. If you've never tasted this before, then come to the Geocities site (Geo is a world of Web sites for people of every race, creed, and sexuality). Includes cool links to several channels, so you can

---

[1] This had changed so often that it was beautiful to see the message found on a change-of-address note: "I would like to get rid of this account, but people still have a lot of links to it. Please message me whenever you come from one of those pointers, and let me know where the pointer was." Remember good karma? This is a fine place to give some back.

bookmark them in your search engine of choice. Here you will find more information than you can shake a mouse at.

Girlfriends: The Magazine of Lesbian Enjoyment
www.gfriends.com

Girlfriends, founded in 1994, is the country's fastest-growing lesbian magazine. The print bimonthly covers culture, politics, and sexuality from a lesbian perspective. *Girlfriends* has a national distribution and coverage and is available in women's and lesbian and gay bookstores everywhere, as well as in some chain bookstores. If your favorite local bookstore does not carry *Girlfriends,* contact the magazine, and the staff will contact the bookstore and make sure it gets it. These girls mean friendly business.

We promote this site because, unlike the ones that are pushed on mail search engines (Lesbian News on the **rainbowmall.com** site is virtually copied from the newspaper; see below), the Girlfriends site allows visitors (forty thousand per month) to participate in its interactive polls and surveys, read the Web-only original content, and use fulsome resources and hot links. Users can sign the guest book and let the site administrators know they are there.

Queer Spec
www.qspec.com

The newest gimmick is that all the lesbian and some of the gay publications are giving their best articles to one free service—ads included. In advocating this method, Babz Van Dyken tells us: "The Web site will have a link [to] all publications, particularly lesbian ones." Her point is that, if she and her cronies develop a list for everyone and every liking, everyone'll come. There was only a teensy bit up by the end of 1996—and did these girls have *attitude*—and it was a wee bit lame. However, these chicks, namely Babz and Annette and Diane, work so hard that we have high hopes that regional lesbian magazines, which do not have much Web presence, will be taken higher via Queer Spec.

Lesbian News
www.rainbow-mall.com/mall/ln/index.html

Honestly, not our cup of tea. I expected more from the girls at LN, one of the longest-running women's issues weeklies. The Web site doesn't have anything that its print counterpart doesn't shoot out. Back issues, sure, and useful particularly if you like one of their columnists, but for fast-breaking news, the women who run the LN tell us, "This is not our primary focus" and it shows. The print version of this mag is quite a hit. For more on how to subscribe, see **www.rainbowmall.com** in Chapter 7.

FatGirl!
www.fatgirl.com

For people who don't apologize for their size. Amen.

Fatgirl comes from the magazine getting the most play in magazine publishing, circa 1997: the *Fat?So!* publication from California. (Title cannot be beat.)

Here are some samples, no apologies accepted:

International No Diet Day

INDD was started in 1992 by Mary Evans Young, the director of the British anti-diet campaign Diet Breakers. Mary, a recovered anorexic herself, is the author of a best-selling book in Britain titled Diet Breaking: Having It All Without Having To Diet (Hodder & Stoughton, 1995). In the Spring of '92, after horror stories regarding overweight women, she became fed up. Deciding, in her own words, "Somebody had to stand up and try to stop this bloody madness and in the absence of anybody else, I decided it would be me."

She decided she had to make a stand. The picnic is now an orgy! The stand is quite pretty, too.

Ask Aunt Agony

Welcome, dear readers to the first ever Friendly Fat Advice Columnist. In England, yours truly would be called an agony aunt, so you may call her Aunt Agony. Aunt Agony will answer any questions you ask.

This gal has opinions about everything. If you want to seek Auntie's advice, just make keyboard tippy-tappy in a space provided, and she'll get back to you *tout de suite*. It is, in the words of its beholder, a hoot.

Burma Shave

This section takes time out to celebrate the hundreds of hilarious titles that talk shows use when doing shows on fat people. Titles such as "When she's twice the woman you married" or "Fat women need love too" will have you busting your already strained seams with fits, gales, or tides of laughter.

Gag Café

This site is a place for free expression. Users are encouraged to write in about anything. Comments range from quite cute to ultraweird. Check it out before you're gagged.

Tribe Interactive
www.gaywired.com

For Women Who Are Brave Enough to "Meet the Challenge. Initiate on Tribe Today. Banding together in the CyberRealm." The subhead says it all.

Tribe Interactive is a link through gaywired.com that allows for communication between users. This interactive service provides online chats, classified ads, links to other Web sites, private uncensored communication with other users, and friend-to-friend videoconferencing and broadcasting capabilities. Search the opening frames in gaywired.com to find Tribe.

WiM
www.wim.org

Women in Media is the Web site of the eponymous organization, a nonprofit support, advocacy, and resources committee involved in new media. Also connected to the cyberagency Digital Queers. Half-run by Alison Hill, this is a grassroots organization that opens doors for women to get involved with multimedia. According to Hill, members range from writers, artists, programmers, and producers to the inexperienced.

> It's a very welcoming group, therefore making it easy for even the novice to approach without trepidation. The multimedia industry can be daunting because of the jargon and the industry walls created by the old boys network. We see ourselves creating an answer to this: an all-girls network. Letting women out there know there's someone there to lend a hand is what we're all about.

On Site info—Women in Multimedia—is basic info on site right now and some stuff about the previous month's meeting. I found links to membership info, links to news info, links to the newsletter (industry info, the notes from previous gatherings), links to info from members (some new Web site or announcements), links to resources sections, such as software, multimedia, and Web sites (a huge list of sites), and general info on WiM itself. Call (415) 312-7200 for more.

Virtual Cabaret
www.datalounge.com

The fans of Trudy's Data Lounge want all the women, even "Saturday girls," in the world to know Trudy. And because Data Lounge may be gone soon, what with so much being swept away by the lack of advertising funding, we decided to show how wonderful she is and let you see (and perhaps support) her for yourself.

Because of the prominence of this lounge, we checked in with Trudy, who runs the femme part of the Mediapolis site, home of **hx.com, qsanfrancisco.com,** and other sites worthwhile looking at once. (Mediapolis, a Web service company, runs this place—and more details about Data Lounge may be found in Chapter 7.)

But that's not important. What is, is Trudy's babee. She is an assured hostess with the most going on. The Virtual Cabaret!

> My day has come!'' she explained recently. ''Old white zinc oxide is making a come-back and surfers who are gay and lesbian should know that. Nobody knows how excit-ing my life is. I am a sculptress, girls, and a necessary evil. Everyone who meets me online knows that once they fall into my grip, they have no choice. I must have a drink before I tell you more. . . . Okay, I think this site contributes in a fuller way to world peace. Overwhelming ecstasy—not the drug, my little club kitten! I cannot abide by the ''cyber world.'' I will NOT take on advertising. At least six people e-mail me a day looking for ad rates. Girls, I rarely have time for a rinse and a set. Is this not obvious? See the pic, deary. Would Clinton [have] vote[d] for Dole? Hmm? But the girls at the lounge do such a delightfully charming job with the magazine, Out-dot-something or other, that I usually am there very often, looking at e-mails, bothering clientele. The whole works.
>
> I receive countless calling cards from gracious visitors. The oddest contact was Miss Peggy Lee's grandson, who contacted me to let me know that ''herself'' had seen the site [the Cabaret holds no one in too much high esteem] and was not dis-pleased. Sip, sip. Have you ever had a Sazerac, honey?
>
> Let's see, what will happen to the Cabaret? Two years—world domination. Ah, don't print that. Write my favorite: ''Do what you do and your do will do what it must.'' Such sweetness. And light.

Our advice is Trudy's advice: See the Virtual Cabaret before it slips away from your little fingers.

P.S.: Trudy ain't no *lady*.

All the Young Droll Stories
odyssey.lib.duke.edu/women/pulp.html

Herer's where lesbians can get remembrances from times past. If I were a writer of droll tales I would *live* here with this collection of (free on the Web) fifties bedtime stories, little pulpy paperbacks from the Golden Days when being a lesbian was strictly chic.[2]

---

[2]What is it today? I'm hoping an out-of-the-closet thing. In other words, not so clandestine.

> Come here, Laura. . . . She looked unearthly as she spoke, with her black hair tumbled, her cheeks crimson. They stood motionless, so close that they touched. . . . Laura shook all over. She couldn't talk except to repeat the other girl's name over, as if she were in a trance . . . Neither of them heard the phone ring, felt the chill of the rainy night, knew of anything. [3]—Pulp Web Site

I know, I'm a tease. But from the Collection at Duke link (a look into the Special Collections Library of Duke University) to How to Add Pulps [of your own] to the Collection, women/pulp is where it's at for early pulp fiction.

Let me tell you, the site tells quite a story of a sordid history that was started by Pocket Books in 1938 (!). Also included is the series called "Twilight World"—I mean, who comes up with titles like these?—from Fawcett Books, also published in the fifties. According to the text I pored through on an altogether fascinating site, ladies in the fifties could choose from among these *types* of reader-friendly icons:

- LESBIANS IN INSTITUTIONS
- THREE WAYS WITH GUYS
- GALS "SAVED" BY STRAIGHT MEN

That's it. While the site points out secondary sources, including some bizarre scholarly material, it is firmly a part of lezzie history, a part of homosexual history! I should point out that many women will not like the lurid prose and (now) camp cover art, a text that includes some very sick subtleties in order to ensure that straight readers are, well, satisfied.

The site says that, when there was a huge cry for such books, they were re-released into the *mass market* through the 1970s. *I* never saw one of them in my Kmart.

If you e-mail **specoll@mail.lib.duke.edu,** the Listserv of pulp lesbian fiction, you will no doubt be kept abreast. The Women's Studies Archivist is looking for hard copy, too. E-mail them to pour your heart out, open your collection up. Yeah, I may be pushing it with the puns. Go get 'em, girls.

---

[3]Taken from Ann Bannon's *I Am Woman* (way before "hear me roar"), a sensational fifties pulp novel about sex and romance.

SEX REFERENCE SITES

For lesbian soft- and hardcore porn, see:

Bad Attitude
166.82.150.105:80/lesbian/

Lesbian Links
www.best.com/~agoodloe/lesbian/

Queer Ring
www.cs.auc.dk/~zennaro/queerring.html

Homosexual Agenda/sex
www.ouragenda.com

Girl Jock
www.tezcat.com/~ksbrooks/index.html

Lezzie Smut
prometheus.digital-rain.com/~lezzie/

Sexy Body Jewelry
www.sexy-jewelry.com/

Diva Net
www2.zoom.com/divanet

·10·

HEALTH

Is your day job giving you migraines? Are you wondering if hanging out in the locker room until everyone is gone means you're gay or lesbian? Sprain your ankle at the disco? Depressed because your boyfriend likes gin gimlets more than he likes you? Did your girlfriend forget to tell you about her extracurricular activities at Girl Camp? Then you must check out any and all health resources on the internet!

The information age has granted the public easy access to an abundance of medical and health literature, facts, ground-breaking research findings, and alternative health resources that were previously only shared by small communities. In fact, many site administrators would have you believe that they fall just short of providing everything but a prescription pad and a lollypop.

Caution. *Don't* believe all the hype! Just because the information is available, doesn't mean that it is worth reading or can even help you with your health concerns. People are looking for advertising, publicity, and money, and, considering the experiences of the gay, lesbian, transsexual community with the HIV/AIDS epidemic, our gay and lesbian community is a perfect target for entrepreneurial desires. The quality of health information on the net is a crucial issue. This is not to imply that indiviudals are not able to make their own decisions, but it does imply that everyone needs to be more cautious in discerning what is truly healthy and not false and potentially harmful.

Gays, lesbians, and transsexuals have an extremely diverse set of health sites targeted at them and need to discern the validity and helpfulness of the information. The majority of sites that cater to gays, lesbians, and transsexuals are associated with sexual health, mental health, or fitness. Yeah, fitness. These three areas are not narrow in scope, either. Yet, if your health concern is not considered part of one of those three general areas, you may feel motivated to create your own WWW site that can address your concerns as a gay, lesbian, or transsexual. You can use many of the bulletin board systems on online services (see Chapter 4), or create your own channel on the IRC (see Chapter 6).

To make this easy, I have listed sites that cater to the general population and exemplify the best of the cyberhealth interventions, in addition to listing sites designed specifically for gays, lesbians, or transsexuals. Cyberhealth interventions are a type of public-health intervention that uses the fairly new medium of the internet to improve the health and well-being of people. Many cyberhealth interventions are, however, totally disorganized, contain irrelevant information, are boring as hell to use, and do not abide by any of the foundations of public health, such as accountability, sustainability, and effectiveness.

In order for a cyberhealth intervention to demonstrate quality of its design, it must have:

1. A target audience
2. Goals and objectives that can be understood by the target audience
3. Contents within the site that were designed, programmed, or reviewed by someone in a target audience to assure that the "message" is indeed getting across
4. Documented evaluations that demonstrate that the goals and objectives were or are being obtained
5. Set in place a system of continually evaluating materials to ensure the most timely and accurate information and beneficial outcomes

What does all of this mean for you as a consumer of cyberhealth? If a particular health site has all of those qualities, your chance of getting the information or help you want (if you are a member of the target audience) is greatly improved. However, if a cyberhealth site did not have any of those qualities, then you are at risk of hurting yourself or others. You may even end up with the latest sold-on-TV, abdominizerlike apparatus in your living room!

It's a rough world and we're going to try to make you better. The sites reviewed in this chapter, except for the ones mentioned in the section, Dangerous Surfing Water, have shown an intention to fulfill the general philosophy of helping the public by including the public in the *design* of the site. Read on and feel safe in knowing that the cyberhealth interventions reviewed in this chapter are concerned with enabling you to alleviate your health concerns.

TEST TIME!

Time to assess your risk or determine your problem. What are your chances of being physically and emotionally scarred during a mugging in the next month? What are your chances of acquiring chlamydia? The internet is filled with sites that proclaim to assess your risk for an event, good or bad. These sites are the same as those popular culture magazine questionnaires that purport to determine your boyfriend's sexual intentions or your pet's culinary preference. The conclusions of these risk-assessment tests are about as reliable as a psychic 900 number, and about as fun too.

Many questionnaires on the internet—even those designed by health professionals—are not designed for gays and lesbians. I do not recommend using these cyberhealth tests if you are feeling confused about your mental or physical problem. The best advice is to get help from close friends, a personal health-care professional, or surf the internet's specifically gay and lesbian health sites reviewed still later on. Remember: These cyberhealth interventions are great fun, but potentially *harmful* if you take them too seriously! So don't.

Nashville Net-Police Department
www.nashville.net/~police/risk/index.html

Take one of these tests!

"Are you going to be raped, robbed, stabbed, shot, or beaten?"
"Are you going to be murdered?"
"Is someone going to break in and burglarize your home?"

Simply click one of the appropriate boxes provided, and send your message off by following directions. After you are done, you will understand how sensationalist this damn site is. According to this test I should be preparing my will! (Nonetheless—on a personal note—everyone should have a will.)

Of course, I am not nervous because this basic program (*very basic program*) was built on general U.S. statistics that draw generalizations about individuals. It does not take into consideration where you live, what sexual partner you prefer, and on and on.

Cocaine Anonymous World
www.ca.org/test.html

Hm. You. Think people talk about you or watch you? You could be addicted to cocaine. "I don't think so." These predictable twelve-step questions are not effective on the internet. If you have a cocaine problem and are surfing the Web world looking for cocaine addiction sites, you will find that there are many undesirable advertiser-driven sites that purport to educate people on how not to take drugs.

This quiz is not a place to start. It annoyed me and I have never experienced addiction crash. I suggest that cocaine-addicted surfers head to **www.ca.org/index.html#HOME,** get the hell away from the computer screen, and—see it there?—dial the **help** number. (Partners of cocaine-addicted persons should check out this helpful site too.)

Perhaps you would like to explore your addictions further? Check out this super addicted site that covers all of them: **users.aol.com/na4napa/na10.html.**

Blue Cross/Blue Shield
www.abcbs.com/health/questions.html

A quiz concerning your general knowledge about health that is sponsored by an HMO (Health Maintenance Organization). Beware: Their answers may be the ones with the most cost-benefit.

NYU Department of Psychiatry
www.med.nyu.edu/Psych/public.html

> Online Depression Screening Test (ODST) (NYU)
> Online Screening for Anxiety (OSA) (NYU)
> Online Sexual-Disorders Screening for Women (SDS)
> Online Sexual-Disorders Screening for Men (SDS)
> Online Attention-Deficit Disorder Screening Test

After taking these tests, I was ready to commit myself.

The validity of these tests is in question, and you should be asked to caution yourself before discussing any of NYU's overhyped advice with someone you know. Taking tests online is different from taking tests in the doctor's office. If you have just finished visiting sex sites or doing a variety of naughty (or nice) things on the internet, the results of an anxiety test may be measuring something entirely different from perceived anxiety at the workplace!

Longevity Game
www.northwesternmutual.com/games/longevity/longevity-main.html

Tell us your cholesterol level and driving record and we will tell you how long you are going to live. This is a slightly sensationalist site, playing off of everyone's fear of death. Creepy! Now I "know" what year I will die! I think this site is interesting to visit, but if you believe the results, you should check out the addiction sites and then deduct ten years from your so-called final age because you have other issues not reviewed in this deficient questionnaire.

SURFING IN DANGEROUS WATERS

Health and Medicine What's New
www.arcade.uiowa.edu/hardin-www/mednew.html

Here's an example of a site that is absolutely no help whatsoever. In this book, we wish to point out the good, the bad, and the ridiculous. Welcome to the last category in all its glory.

This site is simply a download of Yahoo! searches on the word "health." Whatever!, as the girls from *Clueless* said. This is no help to anyone, and will only confuse you. You need to know right off the bat that there are much better resources than those sites containing downloads.

Go back to safer surfing waters immediately!

A Man's Life
www.manslife.com/

A magazine for men, particularly straight men. Why is it here? Well, they're gorgeous straight men, okay? However, it *is* conscious of health and fitness concerns of men in general. This site is really strange, though; taking a cheap shot at women, trying to attract the same group of guys that watches *Home Improvement* (they even use an image of Tim Allen as their opening screen). Look, cheap shots at women could cause health problems—the advice it gives men on women is lacking in valid health information. It asks men to objectify the ladies in their lives: "Give your woman a number," for example. What? Are they kidding?

Planetout Health Resources
www.planetout.com

What is going on here! This type of confusion at a site professing to have thousands of subscribers and (now) millions of users is detrimental to the health and well-being of the gay and lesbian community. All I could find were a few documents under umbrellas such as Women's Health and Mental Health. If there is information here, it is not easily accessible. This site tells me over and over that it is the major source for gay and lesbians (see Planetout in Chapter 7); I say it's misleading. Here we have an example of a site that is more interested in its advertising dollar than in the health of its constituents.

INTRODUCTORY CYBERHEALTH INTERVENTIONS

Now that you know what waves to stay away from, let's begin surfing safer waters. If you are asking where you should begin, then see the introductory cyberhealth interventions. The list below will help you to get started in understanding how your health is as diverse as the other people, places, and experiences you have had in your life. If you know what you want, read ahead to find the more specific sites.

Healthwise
www.columbia.edu/cu/healthwise/

This site is run by the Health Education and Wellness program of Columbia University Health Service. The opening page states, "We are committed to helping you make choices to contribute to your personal health and happiness, well-being of others, and the planet we share." This is one of the most accessed sites on the internet, and for good reason. This site has professional guidance and is attuned to the specific needs of individuals seeking cyberhealth interventions.

Centers for Disease Control and Prevention (CDC WONDER)
wonder.cdc.gov/

CDC WONDER provides a single point of access to a variety of CDC reports, guidelines, and even statistical public health data. These data include everything from prevention of disease, injuries, and disabilities to information on nearly any ailment. You can even consult one of the world's largest databases to search for public health information on AIDS/HIV, cancer, and many other topics.

Family Health
www.tcom.ohiou.edu/family-health.html

A site of a daily series of two-and-a-half-minute audio programs designed to reach a general audience with practical, easy-to-understand answers to the most frequently asked questions about health and health care. The series deals with a wide variety of health-related subjects. Rarer diseases are occasionally covered, but the focus of the series is on those common health problems people are likely to ask family physicians about.

MedAccess
www1.medaccess.com/home.htm

This site, in its ads, promises to fill you with all the latest in sensationalist health care. Reports on drugs and their side effects, risks that will prevent you from living a normal life, and the possibility of choking on your chicken soup. The reports here are entertaining and completely unfounded. However, this site has used popular culture metaphors of health to draw a great number of people in and provide them with resources after they have become involved in the pithy little health stories. Remember: These are all *stories*.

AIDS/HIV CYBERHEALTH INTERVENTIONS

The gay, lesbian, transsexual community has made tremendous strides in raising the public's awareness of AIDS/HIV. San Francisco was one city that had, and still does have, a unique position in the HIV/AIDS political environment. Today, coincidentally, San Francisco is also one of the two leading internet technological centers in the world. That city's history as an early epicenter of the AIDS epidemic and its relation to Silicon Valley has fostered an abundance of AIDS materials on the net.

Most of the material is exceptional and takes unprecedented strides at promoting the most recent philosophies of public health. Concentrating on assessing needs, the implementation of ideas, and evaluating materials to assure that knowledge is being translated into action are the focus of many West Coast-based sites. But have no fear, East Coasters (who I see pouting in the corner): Your coast is close behind because of the rising tide of HMOs on the internet.

Until the overflow, let's take a look at some of the revolutionary cyberhealth interventions and read on to find those sites that are (still) full of drivel and potentially harmful.[1]

---

[1]These are definitely not the only dangerous sites; use them as examples to guide you through the hazardous surfing waters of HIV/AIDS cyberhealth interventions.

Safely Surfing HIV/AIDS Resources

The STOP AIDS Project
www.stopaids.org/

The mission of the STOP AIDS Project is to develop and implement a community-organizing project for self-identified gays and bisexuals in San Francisco, who are seeking to reduce HIV transmission and lessen the adverse effects of the epidemic on the community.

The STOP AIDS Project evaluates all programs, using several different sorts of evaluation. Formative evaluation includes focus groups, opinion leader interviews, and materials pretesting. Volunteers debrief staff after most program activities. They collaborate with researchers from the University of California at San Francisco's Center for AIDS Prevention Studies in designing and implementing preintervention and six-month follow-up questionnaires evaluating changes in behavior, knowledge, and attitudes for all discussion groups.

Comprehensively designed to help the community as it defines its own issues, the Project is impeccable at fact checking and eliminating well-intentioned yet ineffective cyberhealth interventions. Use this if you want the best in cybercare! We refer to this when vetting other health-related sites.

Gay Men's Health Crisis (GMHC)
www.gmhc.org

A hardly equaled site in the distribution of knowledge and resources, GMHC's site is a wonderful demonstration of the effectiveness that an internet site can have in organizing and disseminating information to all interested parties. With the most years' experience of any AIDS organization around, GMHC is conscious of every aspect of AIDS/HIV-related health.

European Information Center for HIV and AIDS
hiv.net

One of the leading resources for current advances in and the experiences of Europeans with the AIDS/HIV epidemic.

Estate Project for Artists with AIDS
www.artistswithaids.org

Finally, a health site with an overwhelming amount of creativity woven into its information. This site is presented with the knowledge that reading from a screen, well, sucks! Remove some of these images and download some of the files before you jet out of this site to one of its many listed links. Artists, please check this page out. The invaluable resources available here are not to be believed.

United in Anger
www.panix.com/~boyfren

Internet activism found here. This site has committed itself to the voices of those who have been denied during the fight to bring AIDS into the political spotlight.

The voices of women ring true here. Women are all over this site: I would have hated to have been the CDC official who said to one of the very bright and talented women highlighted at this site that he did not know what cunnilingus was.

Rural Prevention Center
www.indiana.edu/~aids/

The major focus on the Rural Center for the Study and Promotion of HIV/STD prevention (Rural Prevention Center, or RPC) is the promotion of HIV/STD prevention in rural America, with the goal of reducing HIV/STD incidence.

The RPC develops and evaluates educational materials and approaches, examines behavioral and social barriers to HIV/STD prevention that can be applied to prevention programming, and provides prevention resources to professionals and the public.

CDC AIDS Clearinghouse
www.smartlink.net/~martinjh/cdcnews.txt

An invaluable resource for the individual who wants to stay on top of the political developments concerning the latest scientific rhetoric. Find out what the doctors who wear military uniforms (and the CDC doctors *do* have military uniforms) think are the steps you and I should take to wage war against AIDS.

AIDS Treatment Data Network
www.aidsnyc.org/network/index.html

This is it. Do you have a question about any AIDS treatment? Find the answer here! Get the info on alternative treatments, specific concerns of women and children, or find out about the latest research by drug companies that shows promise.

Positively Living
www.paonline.com/phiv/home.htm

This site is truly a joy to visit. It takes some time to make the graphics fun and then inspires you to peek around a bit more than you might have thought you wanted to (average time on a site is thirty seconds, recall.) An invaluable resource for people who are living with AIDS and interested in chatting with other PLWAs. The boards are always lit.

ACTUP New York
www.actupny.org

Although the numbers at meetings may be dwindling, the efforts to educate the community about the AIDS epidemic and the politics surrounding it just won't fade. Check this to learn everything about activism from one of the leading organizations, the mother of AIDS activism.

SEXUAL HEALTH CYBERHEALTH INTERVENTIONS

Society for Human Sexuality at the University of Washington
www.comeout.com/health/index.html

The goal of this guide is to give people of all genders, orientations, and preferences the info they need to perform a wide variety of sexual acts safely, pleasurably, and comfortably. An excellent spot to find the general terms to turn you into your own caretaker, an admirable goal for a cyberhealth advocate. A lot of text here; it has the semblance of a school. The authors' academic background is clearly an influence. Get your definitions here!

Human Rights Campaign
www.hrcusa.org

As gay people in America, our rights seem under siege, but politically we can influence the powers that be to help us defend and maintain those rights. The Human Rights Campaigns (HRC) does just that by mobilizing this energy into one force to ensure basic equal rights, end discrimination, and protect the health and safety of all lesbian and gay Americans—a well-worth-visiting stopover featured in Chapter 7.

The SafeGuard
www.critpath.org/safegrd2.htm

Not the soap, darling. The SafeGuard is a volunteer-driven organization dedicated to promoting the overall good health of gay and bisexual men, especially in regard to the practice of safer sex and the reduction of HIV and STD (sexually transmitted diseases) transmission. Some insightful gorups designed to confront STDs and HIV on the SafeGuard page are (with in-house descriptions):

Twenty Something
This new group is for those of you who have been affected by HIV, though not infected. You're looking to find support to remain HIV negative? Here's the place to venture to.

Negative Reinforcement
Here's the group for gay and bisexual men of all ages who are looking to build community and commit to remaining HIV negative. Join us for discussion and friendships.

Opposites Attract
Two new groups for gay and bi men who are in a relationship with a man of opposite HIV status. Explores ways to strengthen your relationship.

New: Anything Butt
A six-session group exploring the ins and outs of anal sex and how it fits into gay and bisexual men's overall health. Learn about your own body, learn how to prevent STD and HIV transmission, and learn about the meaning of anal sex for gay and bi men.

CYBER MENTAL HEALTH INTERVENTION:
From Depression to the Enjoyment of Truly Coming Out!

The advent of interactive media has introduced the concept of the virtual therapist. We have discovered online interaction "services" with a number of trained professionals. Imagine: no 140-dollar-an-hour price and you can ask your most serious and kooky questions without the fear of being exposed![2]

Dr. Jesse Miller, a virtual therapist and clinical psychologist for CompuServe's much-maligned and usually uninspiring Pride Forum, is receiving e-mail messages every day from disconcerted gays and lesbians, and cyberheads who are locked in what Dr. Miller calls the "virtual closet." Dr. Miller concludes that the majority of these virtual closet inhabitants are people living in areas other than the twelve metropolitan areas in the United States. Dr. Miller told me, "The level of misinformation and complete lack of knowledge about the most basic concepts of sex and health is unbelievable. It doesn't seem possible that these people have ever been to San Francisco."

One of Dr. Miller's statements considerately addresses the many members of the virtual closet he communicates with every week:

> Those of you who are still asking yourselves "Am I gay?" need to seriously question what you mean by that question. If you are having same-sex fantasies, you may be just like zillions of other "straight" folk who spice up their lives and loves with fantasy. As I've said before, If this doesn't cause YOU distress or disability it's nobody's business—and have fun. Straights play with each other's bottoms too, you know. So that isn't it. It's ultimately about PREFERENCE. Who would you PREFER to be with—if there was NO social stigma attached to your choice? Start thinking about it there.

Dr. Miller, in conjunction with working therapists on the internet, has taken on this so-called virtual closet in hopes of educating this greatly "unurbanized and undereducated" population. However, he states, neither he nor other online professionals is ready to start delivering *real therapy* on the internet. Developing the technological medium to deliver such services as an interactive medium will be difficult in the initial states, he told us, because rarely has therapy been conducted with individuals who are not accountable for their words or actions in the moment.

Another problem with these sites returns to Basic Psych 101: Social scientists have proven that, in nontraditional therapeutic approaches, knowledge does not equal behavior. Knowledge can assist in the decision making process.

---

[2]This isn't really therapy, though. Keep saving up.

Most, if not all, virtual therapist resources do not provide one-on-one therapy simply because it is so difficult to allow for the lack of accountability and how it plays into the therapy sessions. What you find instead are general answers to your questions posted on the site—without your name of course.

As many virtual therapists are located in cities, they aren't accustomed to dealing with many of the problems faced by individuals in rural settings who are questioning their sexuality. Although some therapists may have moved from a rural setting and be able to guide you, it's something you need to find out. Chances are, if you are a member of the "virtual country closet," you will need to qualify your experiences in order to obtain information and guidance that can actually assist you. Here are a few guidelines to help you describe your lifestyle to your virtual therapist.

- Specifically, how do you see yourself in a different position from that of other gay, lesbian, or transsexual people you have heard of or interacted with on the internet? Do you have more or less freedom? Do they have more access to information than you do?
- Do you think your geographical location plays a part in dealing with your sexuality? Explain why.
- How have you felt about the gay, lesbian, or transsexual resources you have used on the internet? Why, or why did they not, help you?
- Tell your virtual therapist the types of sites you frequent on the internet, both sexual and nonsexual in nature. And best of all, tell the therapist why you go there.

As a rural gay, lesbian, or transsexual, you need not be worried about anyone chastising you or belittling you for lack of a "typical" gay, lesbian, or transsexual lifestyle. Many virtual therapists are honestly concerned with the well being of others—even those in the far away country! Says Dr. Miller, "Prefacing your concerns with a description of yourself will be the best way to get the answers appropriate for you."

Otherwise you may just get some West Coast dude doctor who doesn't realize that "pulling your shit together" may mean potentially losing not only your family, but also your job, your home, your town, your state, and a style of living that could never be experienced in a city.

If you are a city mouse and think that you have got a grip on your closet but still have concerns that have affected your life in unacceptable ways, then you, too, should take advantage of all the internet has to offer.

Check out the mental health resources and use the virtual therapist too. Explaining yourself in the same manner as someone not as familiar with city gay, lesbian, or transsexual lifestyle may also be helpful. State why you feel you are alone or feeling lost, and how you believe your environment affects your state of mind. Using virtual therapists is one facet of gaining a grip: ascertaining what your problem is ("owning up to it") and working toward achieving a healthier being.

INTRODUCTORY CYBER MENTAL HEALTH INTERVENTIONS

Miller's Way
www.pride.com/millerth

Our friend Dr. Jesse Miller has one of the first sites to concentrate solely on issues relating to gays, lesbians, and transsexuals and others who do not consider themselves entirely straight, or to people who may be straight but have concerns about someone who is not. This site is a must for people questioning their sexuality!

Mental Health Net
www.cmhc.com/

According to several health professionals we spoke to, this is the big one. You need only see the introduction to know its goals: ". . . to provide you with an easy-to-use, friendly resource in which to access all the mental health topics on the Internet. And it's all for free, in keeping with the Internet's nonprofit tradition. . . . We do this in a casual but interesting format, so as to not bore the pants off you!"

This is as good a way as any we know to find links to other specific sites related to your health concerns, or to make a posting for a unique request. "Does anyone have any information on brain size and heterosexuality?" we asked. Yes, as a matter of fact. They have answers.

The Ackerman Institute: Gay and Lesbian Family Project
www.behavior.net/orgs/ackerman/gay.html

The overall goal of the project is to normalize the gay and lesbian experience. More specifically, it seeks to understand and validate lesbian and gay families, teach and train the mental health community about gay and lesbian family issues, and aid in the validation of gays and lesbians within their families. An excellent resource and guide to a better understanding of gay and lesbian family issues.

Mental Health Education
www.metrolink.net/~jquimby/mentill.htm

This site is dedicated to educating the public about mental illness. This is great for both surfers who have concerns of their own or are concerned about the mental health of a friend. This site provides much of what is missing from many of the general mental health sites.

You must complement any of your mental health site visits with a jaunt to Mental Health Education in order to better understand what it means to live with a mental illness and the obstacles to achieving good mental health care.

Melissa's Therapy FAQ
abulafia.st.hmc.edu/~mmiles/faq.html

Melissa has had a few problems of her own and shares some of her positive and negative experiences with you in order for you to make better decisions. This is a great place to cruise around if you are wondering if you even need to be looking for a therapist, or wondering why you are looking for one in the first place. She is not preachy and is considerate of the fact that we are all a little crazy!

Dr. John Grohol's Mental Health Page
www.coil.com/~grohol/

Everything you need to know, and didn't need to know, is located on this page. Once again, this is a great springboard from which to bounce off and discover information about millions of mental health concerns. Don't plan a leisurely cruise around this site though; it is simply too vast and bogged down with information. Use this site to access others to guide you.

Psychology Self-help Resources on the Internet
gasou.edu/psychweb/resource/selfhelp.htm

Want to chat with someone else who is thinking about the same topics? This is the resource for those living away from the cities. You can use the many chat environments listed on this site to meet others as isolated as you are, or those contemplating the same emotional questions.

We found that this site helped us connect with others who ask lots of questions; we found many people with likeminded mental challenges.

The Social Worker Networker
pages.nyu.edu/~mfh0446

Are you about to get involved in something a little beyond your own world, or possibly considering activism in relation to your mental health concern or that of a friend? This link, unlike many of its boring counterparts, blows you away with some graphics and gives thousands of links to sites that give advice and information on how to get involved.

Dr. Bob's Mental Health Links
uhs.bsd.uchicago,edu/~bhsiung/mental.html

Let Dr. Bob screen the sites for you. Avoid the quacks and ensure that the information that you get is comprehensive, up-to-date, and relevant. Use this site to get what you want; it has some promise of addressing what you are seeking from the mental health Web.

National Alliance for the Mentally Ill (NAMI)
www.nami.org/

They are on your side. This org has an excellent reputation as a great resource for the mentally ill and their saner friends. The mission statement, to ". . . eradicate [sic] mental illness and improve the quality of life of those affected by these diseases," makes NAMI an excellent evaluator of the many materials on the internet. Use this site for obtaining the best internet information, and finding that much-sought-after sense of community.

SURFING THE WAVES OF EMOTIONAL INSTABILITY

The Depression Homepage (DHP)
www.isca.uiowa.edu/users/david-caropreso/depression.html

Meant to be an index to some of the more informative and useful Web sites for depression, the sites listed on the DHP are broken up into four distinct categories: user groups, education, commercial, and miscellaneous. Each independent site has a brief description about its contents and its usefulness. If you would like more information than what's listed on this site, you may search the Web using their page as a home base. We approve.

Bipolar Planet
www.trenton.edu/~ellisles/BipolarPlanet/

Feeling as if you're on another planet because of your mental disorder? You are not alone. Please go find some camaraderie at the Bipolar Planet. The experience and stories of hundreds of others like yourself await. Read and devour. (Everything's a "Planet" . . .)

The Walkers of Darkness
www.primenet.com/~jtp/walkers.html

Here is a group of people who are using the internet in an intuitive, interpersonal manner in the health world. The Walkers of Darkness work through the buddy system. The Walkers support one another primarily through e-mail and you can join up through a net feature that joins you to their list. This group is diverse; yet through it all has proven itself to be sensitive to issues of sexuality.

!OutProud!, The National Coalition for Gay, Lesbian and Bisexual Youth
www.cyberspaces.com/outproud/

As discussed in Chapter 7, OutProud is *the* org for youth seeking to meet up. Need a pen-pal or someone to discuss someone issues about being young and contemplating sexuality? This is the place! And many more resources for the young, only the young.

SURFING THE WAVES OF SUBSTANCE ABUSE

Alcohol, Tobacco, and Other Drugs Resource Guide for Lesbians, Gay Men, and Bisexuals
www.drugs.indiana.edu/publications/ncadi/radar/rguides/ lgb.html

This is what we found out: It is believed that factors such as stigma, denial, alienation, discrimination, and the cultural importance of bars *place* lesbians, gay men, and bisexuals at higher risk of developing problems with alcohol, tobacco, and other drugs. Although we need more research before we can substantiate this, one thing is true: Many issues need to be understood and addressed by prevention professionals working with lesbian, gay, and bisexual communities before they can deal with the destructive consequences of drugs. Use this site to access information that addresses your sexuality in conjunction with your dependence or addiction.

SURFING THE WAVES OF ABUSE AND SUPPORT

Male Rape
www.nvc.org/ddir/info37.htm

About sixteen years ago, the counterculture magazine, *Soho Weekly News,* published an article about male rape and it shocked the so-called New York literary community. Nothing has changed about this, the last taboo in polite society. And it is a problem well addressed on the internet, thankfully.

Use this to get help, or to assist a friend who has been assaulted. This is one of a few sites addressing solely the problem of male rape, but other crisis intervention sites (see GMHC, Community United Against Violence, and **www.cs.utk.edu/ ~bartley/saInfoPage.html**) have sections within their pages on the topic.

Truths About Domestic Abuse: Gay/Bisexual Community
www.xq.com/cuav/truths.htm

If you are interested in this topic, read what they have to say on the front page: "It is not simply a lover's quarrel or a fight. Domestic violence involves one man using intimidation and force against his partner. While the victim may defend himself, this does not mean the violence is mutual." Use this site to get information on homosexual domestic violence. This is a tough site to see because it boldly discusses a subject many gay men do not want to face.

Community United Against Violence
www.xq.com/cuav/index.html

Community United Against Violence (CUAV) is a fifteen-year-old nonprofit agency preventing hate violence expressly directed at lesbians, gays, bisexuals, and transgender persons. CUAV also provides services to gay men who are battered by their partners. CUAV offers crisis intervention, short term counseling, advocacy with the criminal justice system, support groups, and a "24-hour Crisis Line." In addition to documenting and publicizing antilesbian and gay violence, CUAV offers speakers for schools and community groups and safety monitoring for community events.

"We routinely distribute safety information, and provide whistles and self-defense classes as preventative measures," says the page. This site is truly an example of a comprehensive cyberhealth intervention. Take advantage of it, if you have questions about violence or need help.

SURFING CYBER WOMEN'S HEALTH INTERVENTIONS:

Women-Identified Health Care

See Chapter 9, Lesbian Light, for more sites related to general overviews of and information about women's health.

Ask a Woman Doctor
www.healthwire.com/women/ask.htm

Exactly what it says it is. Are you interested in getting your information from a women doctor who has experience in more than just gynecology and breast cancer? At this site, your questions concerning all aspects of health can be answered by a staff of female physicians.

PEN Women's Health and the Women's Health Forum
America Online, Keyword: Women's Health

Get your articles and information at PEN, and check in with all the women in the Women's Health Forum who discuss issues pertinent to a female human being's life.

Make sure, before you log on, that you are indeed interested in diet or exercise. I was almost tempted to place the Women's Health Forum in the Dangerous Waters category until I realized that women's voices were being heard. These are the views of women. Yet, and this is something AOL has a lot of problems getting across to the content provider, *they need to stop editorializing the facts.*

I would have liked to see some interventions that address some underlying causes of women's obsession with fitness and figure. The girls here talk about it endlessly, but there is no solution to "the problem" in sight.[3]

FeMiNa Women's Health
www.femina.com

"We created FeMiNa in September of 1995 and put it online for one reason only: to provide women with a comprehensive, searchable directory of links to female-friendly sites and information on the World Wide Web."

An array of sites on not only medical health, but also that can help promote health and enable women to make informed decisions about their health. This site represents a broad-based definition of health that encompasses those things that are not medical or biological in nature. Take advantage of the many women's connections at this site and improve the quality of your life—something that we hope will undoubtedly affect your health.

Women's Health Interactive (WHI)
www.womens-health.com/

Women's Health Interactive provides a holistic view of women's health. Where there is fragmentation, we intend to bring the whole picture into view as each disease, condition, or symptom is examined. Where there is failure to recognize the unique differences of gender, we intend to advise. And where there are unanswered questions about the health problems concerning women, we intend to make available

---

[3]To be fair, fitness and diet are an extremely important part of anyone's life. But the messages left on the boards seemed to be more gossipy than helpful.

the opportunities to get answers from healthcare professionals—as well as from the experiences of other women.

As far as we can see, it's a modern approach to medicine that will be taken to the care of men before too long.

Feminist.com Women's Health Issues
feminist.com/health.htm

This site offers a listing reviewed by a group of empowered, activist women. Use this to find out *before you make mistakes* that you are checking into a previously screened site. Thanks to this ingenious screening device, feminist.com has become an excellent resource for an abundance of literature, contacts, and advice unrelated to the biology of health, but rather to it's maintenance: how to lead a healthy life and ensure you will always be able to.

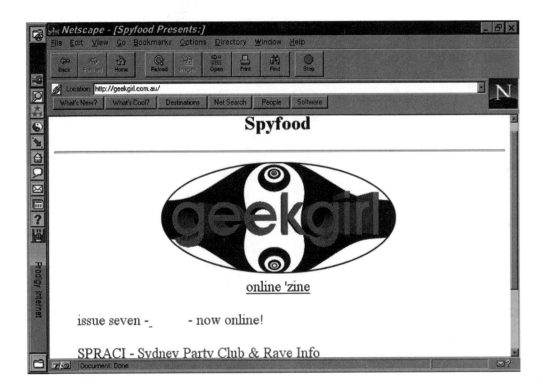

GeekGirl
geekgirl.com.au/

Though Geek is not really health-oriented, I couldn't leave this cool girlie magazine out. (No, not that kind of girlie!) This magazine from Australia is so popular, it made GeekGirl from Details magazine change her name! Surfing through this masterpiece is bound to make you giggle and feel healthy. Check out the funky graphics too! And another thing: The name's a misnomer. More like GreatGirl.

SURFING THE DANGEROUS WAVES OF CYBER WOMEN'S HEALTH INTERVENTIONS

Women's Health Center (WHC)
wellweb.com/WOMEN/WOMEN.htm

Here you find a relatively new and commercialized approach to the medicalization of women. Be careful. Advertisers on WHC certainly don't care if you are a women but do care if you are a woman with money! Go check out Ask a Woman Doctor first, before purchasing anything on this site. It's all about spending money on products.

ALTERNATIVE HEALING METHODS

The sites listed below are merely resources to learning about alternative methods of healing. Find something within them that is appropriate for you. Take a site and link to something that interests you from that location. A site alone is not helpful.

Ayurveda
Aurvedic Foundation: **www.ayurvedic.org**

Chinese Medicine
Chinese Herb and Health Homepage: **www.geog.hkbu.edu.hk/health**
China Med: **ourworld.compuserve.com/homepages/chinamed**
Acupuncture: **www.acupuncture.com**

Chiropractic
Chiro-Web: **pages.prodigy.com/CT/doc/doc.html**
Chiropractic Online: **www.cais.net/aca**
Chiropractic Page: **www.mbnet.mb.ca/~jwiens/chiro.html**

Herbal Medicine

Algy's Herb Page: **www.pair.com/algy**
Herb Web: **www.herbweb.com**
Reference Guide for Herbs: **www.realtime.net/anr/herbs.html**

Holistic Medicine

American Holistic Medical Association: **www.doubleclickd.com/about_ ahma.html**

Homeopathy

Homeopathy Education Center: **homeopathy.com/~educate**
Homeopathy Homepage: **www.dungeon.com/home/~cam/homeo.html**
Homeoweb Homepage: **antenna.nl/homeoweb**

Massage Therapy

International Massage Association: **www.nationweb.com/business/ima/ ima.html**

The Center for Reiki Training: **www.reiki.org/**

Shiatsu, Therapeutic Art of Japan: **www.doubleclickd.com/shiatsu.html**

Meditation

Foundation for Spiritual Unfoldment: **www.cityscape.co.uk/users/ea80/ fisu.htm**

Practicing the Presence: **netnow.micron.net/~meditate**

Naturopathy

American Association of Naturopathic Physicians: **healer.infinite.org/ Naturopathic.Physician**

Naturopathic Medicine Network: **www.pandamedicine.com**

Osteopathy

American Association of Colleges of Osteopathic Medicine: **www.aacom.org**

Overall, the internet is a plethora of resources that can both enable you to take control of your health and well being, or waste your time and potentially present outdated or false information.

Finally, a reminder from a health expert: Health is one aspect of health and the topic *health* is in itself an extremely broad concept. Spending time surfing entertaining sites can be a very healthy experience.

Research for Chapter 10 was contributed by Kenneth Legins, MPH. A public health researcher, he is currently controlling outbreaks of infectious diseases in New York City, a daunting task, and freelancing as a writer about health. This is Legins's first book project.

11

GET OFF THE
INTERNET...OKAY?
(A Selection of Tourist Cybercafes)

Sure you can travel. But, everything you've done while traveling, you can do on the net. Then again, why not do both: see some places in living color, and still do the surfing. The recent phenomenon of cybercafes popping up in every major city has gotten tremendous media exposure, and I decided to show off some of the destination spots in this country and others. Follow the road!

In effect, the presence of cybercafes is more than just a fad, because they have developed into a new generation of fast-food chains and eateries established by big-time corporations. In late 1996 Apple Computer and Intel Corporation each developed a chain of cybercafes, with licensed products and merchandise available in these venues. Intel, for example, formed an alliance with Starbucks, the Seattle-based company already known for its coffee, and proves that these cafés are no joke.

The cybercafes aren't for the jet set but, rather, for the Jetson set. These are places to "go interactive" and get "wired," as many come to surf or become acquainted with the net in the familiar environment of a coffee shop. It is a great place to go and pretend you know the Web.

The coffee shop or espresso bar, as we all know, is the place where conversation goes like this: "I'll have a double mocha, heavy on the whip, but light on the water content." Cybercafes now have the added benefit of this line: "Oh, you have the internet too!!! I'll have to try it." They have also become, in this information age, a rest area for travelers who must maintain appearances by telnetting to the office and checking an e-mail or six. Whatever your take on this, cybercafes have found their niche in this global village.

As I write this I am sitting in the Sip 'n' Surf Café at 48 West 20th Street in

Manhattan (212) 242-0825, above the Ditto Copy Shop.[1] This is a place with more antiques than beautiful computers, but the owner—who is not a net nut—believes that art and commerce can coexist with computers and will do anything to prove it. He's a copy shop owner and this is a café for internet fanatics (or newbies) and, in order to go further than mere conception, the owner is aware he's going to have to *think fast*.

So he went out and installed a bar for milk freaks! And one for steamed milk! (Mind you, I have to suggest that will probably not be in business for *that* long. Milk?) Still, he's gone so far as to install a Web page (**www.dittointernetca-fe.com**) so that people can e-mail him on site . . . and tell him what else to do with this space. This guy has it right: In order to bring people *off* the net, you have to make it superappealing.

That's why so many libraries have installed Freenet systems. They want people to remember them when they think *information*. Remember in grammar school when they told you that the library was really a media center? And you scoffed then? Now the media centers in major cities and many small towns, too, are equipped to run you to the internet systems of the free world!

Freenet is free internet, the café system, where you can join the many so-called queer cybercenters that great people like Matt, the co-owner of **www.gaywired. com** (see Chapter 7) are putting together in places like the LA Gay and Lesbian Community Center, which can be seen in all its glory online at **www.qcc.org**. At the Center, and at the Web site, you can set up a free e-mail system (yeah, you have to be gay but not necessarily prove it!) and receive assistance with "connectivity"! Meanwhile, the best part is that you can come in and greet other gay men in person *and* on the web. It's a hoot.

Schools are the most famous providers of this service and that's why colleges give kids free internet access—especially in universities where it's considered a perk yet costs nothing to provide. (The net started at the university and governmental levels, both groups mastered and invented it, respectively; who's going to charge them now?) I read that, in Seattle, a bunch of homeless men discovered the library Freenet system and now call themselves network geeks because they spend their free time roaming the net. The library officials were, according to a local reporter, *amazed* and perhaps a little chagrined that they would be wasting the library's precious single computer resource. The reporter, Stephen L. Nelson, said in his handbook, *Field Guide to the Internet*, that, "The geeks explained: 'We're homeless but we're not stupid.' "

Although I do not include cafés in all of the states, and there are *many* cybercafes across the nation, I wrote about the ones gays and lesbians would travel to while in

---

[1]See New York cybercafes listed below.

vacation mode! According to our interviews and inquiries, the following cafés have been frequented by gays and lesbians. Many of these cafés serve more than coffee and they offer activities and attractions for the whole family. Keep in mind the information may change as the places decide to upgrade.

CYBERCAFES IN THE UNITED STATES

Travelers, please note that not all cybercafes have Web addresses, unlikely as that might sound. You can, however, call them and insist that they get one; maybe they'll get the obvious picture.

CALIFORNIA

Almost Paradise, 4148 ½ Viking Way, Long Beach CA; (310) 429-2066; **www.cyberplace.com/paradise_ext.html;** contact John Shull; Monday–Saturday 10 A.M.–10 P.M.; Sunday, 12 noon–8 P.M.

Almost Paradise is the kinda place where you can do the hula and not get laughed at. The café has a tropical theme interior and a staff clad in tropical gear— Hawaiian shirts and shades.

John Shull, the manager, says that he can get you an e-mail address wholesale, and download or print "whatevers." (He has great printing devices unlike places like Kinko's, which charge you for sitting there!) This guy gives great local internet access. Plus *free* classes on internet, particularly for the young 'uns. John sponsors soccer leagues, dance studio programs, comedy, and music, and is embarking on a promotional series that started in late 1996). Café owners are from the theater world. He can get you a seat at one of seven stations, all IBM PCs. Although there is no hula dancing here, the idea has crossed their minds; clearly, it's near paradise.

CyberState Café, 1224 State Street, Santa Barbara, CA; (805) 899-3723; **cyber-state.com/;** Monday–Thursday, 8 A.M.–10 P.M.; Friday, 8 A.M.–11 P.M.; Saturday, 9 A.M.–11 P.M.; Sunday, 9 A.M.–9 P.M.

High-speed PC computers, word processing, desktop publishing programs, graphic design programs, color and laser printing, e-mail accounts at $10 a month, faxing, T-1 access . . . all in Santa Barbara. (Not the soap, y'all.) Joe Mazur, the manager says that he has no interest in classes because the space is being rented now to Cox Cable for use in MSNBC cablecasts! The machines, says Mazur, rent for $8 an hour with a fifteen-minute minimum, "for normal customers." They go down to $6 if you can prove that you're a student.

California's Coin-operated Internet Terminals

The latest in the cybercafe craze coming out of California is the advent of coin-operated internet machines. These no-fuss, no-problem systems act much like pay phones. Drop in a quarter and you are on your way to cyberspace. An example:

Buzz Coffee, 8200 Santa Monica Boulevard, West Hollywood, CA; (213) 650-7742; (no Web site); contact Chris; Sunday–Thursday 7 A.M.–12 midnight; Friday and Saturday, 7 A.M.–2 A.M.

If you are star-struck and star-bound, you can check out the scene at Buzz, where the buzz is not just in the coffee but also in the customers! Famous actors, models, and musicians are said to frequent this joint, and they keep coming back because Buzz has a policy of not letting the public nor the media know who's who in java news. Built like a gallery, but reminiscent of coffee houses in France, the café has some stunning counters, which look like marble but are not. It specializes in gourmet coffees and foods like cakes, pastries, and pastas. You can access the one coin-operated computer terminal for three minutes for a quarter or $5 for every hour "on the surf."

Equator, 22 Mills Place, Pasadena, CA; (818) 564-8656 (no Web site); contact Norbert Furnee; Monday–Thursday, 7 A.M.–12 midnight; Friday, 7 A.M.–1 A.M.; Saturday, 8 A.M.–1 A.M.; Sunday, 9 A.M.–12 midnight.

The Equator may divide the earth into two hemispheres, but this upscale rustic café separates the men from the boys. Furnee says that, since 1992, his business has been the realest of the real in coffee. Among the popular drinks are the mochas, such as the Black Forest Mocha, which is as tasty as it is warm. Be sure to have a pocketful of change though, a handful of quarters, that is, to use the two coin-operated internet terminals, because the café doesn't administer them: a quarter for every three minutes and $5 per hour.

More Internet Cafés in California

Al Cappuccino Coffee House, Fullerton California; (714) 870-7588; **www.expresso.com/alcaps/**
Brewnet, Gardena, California; (310) 538-2491; (no Web site)
Coffeetopia, Santa Cruz, California; (408) 338-1940; **www. cyberiacafe.net/cyberia/guide/ccafe_uw.htm#santa_cruz**

Connected.Café, La Verne, Los Angeles, California; (909) 593-1188; **www.cyberg8t.com/coffee/**

Cyber Java, Venice, Los Angeles, California; (310) 581-1300; **www.cyberjava.com/**

DP's Coffee House, Costa Mesa, California; (714) 722-9673; **www.deltanet.com/users/taxicab1/**

eCafé, Santa Barbara, California; (805) 897-3335; **www.ecafe1.com**

ICON Byte Bar & Grill, San Francisco, California; (415) 861-2983; **www.matisse.net/files/bytebar.menu**

Los Gatos Coffee Roasting Company, Los Gatos, California; (800) 877-7718; **www.los-gatos.ca.us/los_gatos_coffee.html**

SurfNet Café, Ventura, California; (805) 658-1287; **www.surfnetcafe.com**

The World Café, Santa Monica, California; (310) 399-6964; (no site)

COLORADO

Jitters Internet Café, 1523 18th Street, Denver, CO; (303) 298-8490; **www.jitters.com;** contact Matt Haggstrom; Monday–Thursday, 6:45 A.M.–12 midnight; Saturday, 9 A.M.–2 A.M.; Sunday, 4 P.M.–12 midnight.

This Colorado mainstay is home to the Digital Artists Workgroup (DAWG), which meets monthly in the café. Matt is your host. Most computers are Macintoshes and can be used for a half hour for $4; students who can prove it are not charged anything. Only one online computer. Since Denver made it law in late 1996 to give city workers domestic-partner benefits, all is forgiven.

Café@Netherworld, 1278 Pennsylvania on Capitol Hill, Denver, CO; (303) 861–8NET; **www.netherworld.com;** Monday–Saturday, 11 A.M.–2 A.M.

The only café in Denver that has a liquor license, this one holds parties for neighborhood groups who help clean up the community and for the *Gay and Lesbian Pink Pages*. They let you check your e-mail for free. You can use four Power Macs for $4 an hour and cruise the Web in an eclectic crowd.

More Internet Cafés in Colorado

Caroline's Coffeehouse, Dillon, Colorado; (970) 468-8332;
www.colorado.net/coffee
Majordomo's Net Café, Denver, Colorado; (303) 830-0442;
www.majordomos.com

GEORGIA

Redlight Café, 553 Amsterdam Avenue, Atlanta, GA 30306; (404) 874-7828; **www.redlightcafe.com;** contact Mark and Bill Hoover; Tuesday–Sunday, noon to whenever; closed Monday.

Located in the heart of Atlanta, Redlight beckons the wild, the tamed, and those who fall in between. Drink, eat, and surf and be spirited, this café serves beer and wine! Redlight's menu, which includes *allachecca,* a dish of tomato and basil simmered in olive oil and served over angel hair pasta, and German chocolate brownies, is the talk of the town. They have an ISDN connection, with one Mac and 2 IBMs for $5 per hour and two ports for anyone to plug in. This café specializes in "flexibility." With an outward concern for their community, they allow their space to become anything they want it to become: concert hall, art gallery, etc. Redlight also builds virtual reality worlds where users can see into their café when an art exhibit is in progress, for example. Classes are taught on an individual basis on Sunday and Thursday and vary in price depending on complexity.

HAWAII

The Internet C@fé, 559 Kapahulu Avenue, Honolulu, HI; (808) 735-5282; **www.aloha-cafe.com;** contact Michael Seeney **(surfbum@aloha. net)** and Donna Austin, general manager; open twenty-four hours a day, seven days a week.

If you don't keep regular hours, this café won't care, because it's open all night! Centrally located near the zoo and golf course, the café is a microcosm of picturesque Hawaii. Its beautiful interior of plants, reclining and leather chairs in forest green, furniture in blond wood and deep plum carpet make for a down-home and loungy feel. Ten Macintosh Performas capable of speaking Japanese are $6 an hour to rent for surfing the Web, designing Web pages, or for e-mail. Home to many students, the café offers "hacker" foods, which include Ho-Hos, Twinkies, and drinks like Fukola, a not-from-Brooklyn quick pick-me-up for those burning the midnight oil. Pity the college student—after 1 A.M., word processing is just $2 an hour and 10 cents a copy. The café hosts many events that are not of the mundane, such as commercial castings for MTV. Forget the hula music, the C@fé features live acoustic music from a computer station with a MIDI[2] interface preloading the songs.

More Internet Cafés in Hawaii

Coffee Haven, Honolulu, Hawaii; (808) 732-2090; **www.aloha. net/~mawi**

ILLINOIS

Interactive Bean, 1137 Belmont, Chicago IL; (312) 528-2881;**www. Ibean.com;** contact Andy Laing; Tuesday–Friday, 8 A.M.–11:30 P.M.; Saturday, 9:30 A.M.–12:30 A.M.; Sunday, 9:30 A.M.–9:30 P.M.

This classy place is host to groups such as Webgirls and the Chicago Mac Users Club. Andy, the master of this domain, says that on Monday they close down for private renting when corporate education groups meet. From Tuesday through Thursday, it costs 16 cents a minute for the use of one of their ten PC jobbers. (Sixteen cents is real, that is no typo here.)

Urbus Orbis, 1934 West North Avenue, Chicago, IL 60622; (312) 252-4446; (future Web site TBA); contact Tom Handley; Friday and Saturday, 9 A.M.–1 A.M.; Monday–Thursday, 9 A.M.–12 midnight; Sunday, 10 A.M.–12 midnight.

For a neighborhood and cozy feel, this café is it. Urbus Orbis, bastardized Latin for city limits, is in central Chicago in Wicker Park—an area known for musicians, art, and theater—and the café evokes the quality this district warrants. Urban Orbis lends itself to many "in-play" concerts given by music and record companies, as they have a performance space in the back built for these kinds of gigs. Ben Harper, Jewel, and Laurie Carson have been some of the acts coming through the café. They also have one computer terminal on a self-promotion basis,[3] which can be rented for $6.95 an hour. They plan to upgrade their system to allow teleconferencing and other internet services. Patronizing Orbis, aside from the local residents, are international

---

[2]MIDI is a standard interface for the creation and playback of electronic music. With a program that provides this interface, you can create music using a standard keyboard or other imput device. You or others can then play your MIDI-conforming creation with the same or another program and a sound card as a music synthesizer. The MIDI program may come with a graphical user interface that looks like a sound studio control room. Many sound cards come as a package with MIDI software (for example, Media Vision's Pro Audio Studio 16).

[3]They have one, so they can call Orbis a cybercafe.

folks who enjoy a good cappuccino—a shot of good espresso and milk foamed at the right temperature offers the satisfaction that brings them right back.

Another Internet Café in Illinois

The 3rd Coast Café, Chicago, Illinois; (312) 664-7225; (no Web site)

MASSACHUSETTS

Cybersmith Café, 42 Church Street, Cambridge, MA; (617) 492-5857; **www.cybersmith.com;** staff are helpful; Monday–Wednesday, 10 A.M.–11 P.M.; Thursday, 10 P.M.–1 A.M.; Friday and Saturday, 10 A.M.–12 midnight, Sunday, 11 A.M.–9 P.M.

Here, on forty-eight machines, every new computer technology is available at your fingertips. Not only can you try out virtual reality games or videoconferencing over the internet but also all types of Web browsers are at your disposal, including America Online, Prodigy, and Netscape Navigator. MIT's Nicholas Negroponte makes sure that all the emerging technologies are available for your use. Create your own custom-art screen savers, digital greeting cards, or your own image on a T-shirt. For only twenty-two cents a minute, you can surf all day.

Maura, the self-titled Net Head Read, tells us she can help any cybercafe junkie in Boston. Meanwhile, *NetGuide* (see Chapter 12 for the scoop on that magazine) declared, "Forget the Hard Rock Café and Planet Hollywood . . . the place to be seen is Cybersmith."

Internet Café Nantucket, 2 Union Street, Nantucket Island, MA; (508) 228-6777; **www.nantucket.net;** hours depend on their seasonally altered moods.

At hours varying depending on season, as Nantucket is not really open for visitors except in summer, Suzanne Daub runs what is known as a public-access group and local Web provider. She offers classes on the internet, has ten computers, provides e-mail services and access to internet, writes and posts Web pages, hosts virtual domains (where people go and chat—it's a big party), offers consulting services for page making and to other internet service providers, occasionally hosts open houses, has a "reflector," and, thankfully, owns both Mac and PC machines. (A reflector is a client/server "relationship" allowing you to talk to and see people (CU-SeeMe); see the reflector Web site **(www.cu-seeme.com)** for even more information.

More Internet Cafés in Massachusetts

Café Liberty, Cambridge, Massachusetts; (617) 492-9900;
   cafeliberty.com/Liberty.html
Designs for Living, Boston, Massachusetts; (617) 536-6150;
   www.mynet.com/
Sheffield Pub, Sheffield, Massachusetts; (413) 229-7770;
   www.tiac.net/users/longleyr/spizza/

NEW YORK

Koko Bar, 59 Lafayette Avenue, Brooklyn, NY; (718) 243-9040; **www.
kokobar.com;** open at odd hours and when they feel like it.

Koko is run by Tanisha Walker, the daughter of Alice Walker (*The Color Purple*),
and is located in a not-very-cyber Fort Greene, Brooklyn. Koko's partners are a bunch
of youngsters who think they know it all about cyberspace and unfortunately have
put in a very disorganized print shop and so-called classes for e-mail with a few
computers with DNS servers that continually go down. It's a great experiment for
Brooklyn, though, because this borough has nothing like a cybercafe in its precincts.
The Web site seems to be down all the time, a sign that the place is either not staffed
or not kept up.

Also in New York are what you'd expect from a city that has it all: ultimate
cliché spots, such as the @-Café, which recently underwent a sorely needed renova-
tion and holds tons of launch parties or cyber-silly events (not to be confused with
Silicon Alley Events, code for the downtown scene). The @ is a place people go to
hobnob with the so-called cyberelite in the city and on the internet.

@café, 12 St. Marks Place, New York, NY; (212) 979-5439;
www.fly.net/; contact Nick Barnes; 5 P.M.–4 A.M. every day.

Cybercafe does the same, though it's not hyped to the same extreme:

Cybercafe, 273 Lafayette Street, New York, NY; (212) 334-5140; **www.
cyber-cafe.com;** contact Robert Angelone; Monday–Thursday, 11 A.M. to
10 P.M.; Friday–Saturday, 11 A.M.–1 A.M.; Sunday, 11 A.M.–11 P.M.

Alt-Dot-Café—pronounce it to get it—is nearby in the East Village on
Avenue A between St. Marks Place and 9th Street (**www.altdotcoffee.
com**); open till 3 A.M. on Saturdays and Sundays. The Cyberchill gathering
for local computer industry types assembles here.

Nothing fancy or too impressive takes place at any of these. There are some computers and a few lectures, rarely a free beer, sometimes (as in Koko Bar) a class in how to "do internet." Koko has signed up more people for Freenet e-mail than any system in Brooklyn. At last count, a local library in that borough was racing to beat them! Kids were coming out of the woodwork to be a part of it.[4]

New York City is filled with places that think they're the hippest; the list of cafés herein proves that the rest of the nation is far and above beyond that. And if you get off the net for any reason, go there.

More Internet Cafés in New York

Common Grounds, Buffalo, New York; (716) 633-4589; **www. cgicafe.com**

Cyber Caf@l@, Manhattan, New York; (212) 334-5140; **www. cyber-cafe.com**

Cybersmith, White Plains, New York; (914) 686-3570; (no Web site)

The Hub Café, Rochester, New York; (716) 461-4850; **www. hotliquid.com**

Internet Café, East Village, Manhattan, New York; (212) 614-0747; **www.bigmagic.com/**

Surf's Up Internet Café, Rochester, New York; (716) 473-7873; **www.surfsupcafe.com/**

OKLAHOMA

InterEarth Café, N.W. 49th and Western, Oklahoma City, OK; (405) 840-0502; **www.soonernet.com/earth/;** contact Tempie Nichols; Monday–Friday 8 A.M.–9 P.M.; Saturday, 10 A.M.–6 P.M.; and Sunday, 10 A.M.–5 P.M.

With a nod to free internet connection, this space has a single terminal, lots of managers, and, uncannily, emcees "the local vegetarian society" meetings. Tempie tells us that she is into nutrition and advertises as such. The Earth does not offer classes because it would rather have speakers who discuss their learned research.

---

[4]Talk about competition. A public library is going all out to impress kids.

However, right along with those lectures on the environment, it does feature specific lectures about the net, which you can attend on the Web or in person.

More Internet Cafés in Oklahoma

Main Street CyberHall, Norman, Oklahoma; (405) 364-0071; **www.cyberhall.com**

PENNSYLVANIA

Cyber Loft, 1525 Walnut Street, 2nd floor, Philadelphia, PA; (215) 564-4380; **www.cyberloft.com;** contact Mostafa Eldefrawy; Monday, Thursday, and Friday, 9 A.M.–6 P.M.; Tuesday and Wednesday, 9 A.M.–8 P.M.; Saturday, 9 A.M.–1 A.M.

If internet cafés with informal settings are your thing, then this cybercafe is your place to hang. Cyber Loft is set in busy downtown Philadelphia where you can bring your own body (BYOB)—eats, drinks, etc. At twelve terminals (ten Macs, two PCs) for $9 an hour, users have internet access, virtual domains, and Web design and development. The café has a T-1 connection built for speed and offers memberships for $45 a month that are good for thirty hours of doing anything you please. Web design classes are also offered on an individual basis and vary in level of instruction for the very beginner to the very experienced.

TENNESSEE

The Edge, 532 South Cooper Street, Memphis, TN; (901) 272-3036; **vdospk.com/edge/index.html;** contact Stephanie and Frank James; daily, 5 P.M.–1 A.M.; 2 A.M. on special occasions (e-mail them your ideas on where Elvis is: **edge@vdospk.com).**

Strangely, in Memphis (say "meumphees") the cybercafes open at night, and that's it. This one, which has been open just under three years, is definitely one hot cup of joe, filled with fun ideas. This is Memphis's midtown cool spot for surfers and the elite. "Owned and operated by real people," they say. We say, Just great. Stephanie and Frank, the marrieds who run it, show off themselves and their staff (some quite cute) with a slide show on the Web page. Inside the café, find my favorite mini-site, The Edge's Caffeine Page, which can be found by itself at **ubd2. vdospk.com/edge/caffeine.**
 I want to go to Memphis (as Joe Jackson said), taste the java, and run the script at Edge.

The menu is awesome. The couple who serves us guarantees that you get good food or your cash back. The fact they "respect [the] demand for the quality and service that is . . . The Edge," makes us think this is damn good. And, if you can't handle the millions of frames on their Web site, you can click a frame-free area and go to one . . . single . . . page. Ahhh. I can sleep *bettah*.

More Internet Cafés in Tennessee

Bean Central, Nashville, Tennessee; (615) 248-3803; **www. bean.isdn.net/bean/**

WASHINGTON

The Speakeasy Café, 2304 2nd Avenue, Seattle, WA; (206) 728-9770; **www.speakeasy.org;** contact Mike Apgar or Chris Osburne; Monday–Thursday, 9 A.M.–12 midnight; Friday, 9 A.M.–2 A.M.; Saturday, 10 A.M.–2 A.M.; Sunday, 10 A.M.–12 midnight.

All the amenities of a café and more; this café is as serious about the internet as it is about coffee. With a soup-and-salad kind of menu, their specials change weekly depending on Seattle's taste buds. Set in a converted warehouse, Speakeasy has twenty terminals that are available at $8 an hour for graphical terminals, $10 an hour for the one PC or the one Mac, and free for the text-based terminals. Memberships are $10 a month, with up to 10 megs of server space for Web pages, e-mail, and discounts on the terminal rentals. Speakeasy is a one-stop facility fulfilling every need, craving, or job, and offers virtual hosting and Web design for commercial clients. Classes on effective e-mail writing and Web-page building are offered for $35. Pioneers in innovative services, Speakeasy has set up RAIN (Remote Access Internet Node), a system of "Speakeasy" terminals in various cafés sprinkled throughout Seattle. Tied back to the mothership, they allow members to connect to the Speakeasy to check e-mail or whatever.

More Internet Cafés in Washington

Café Internet®, Port Townsend, Washington; (360) 385-9773; **www.daka.com/cafe_inet/front.htm**

Higashi Kaze (Eastwind Espresso), Bremerton, Washington; (360) 377-4170; **www.telebyte.net/center/center-fitness.html**

Internet Caf@] @, Seattle, Washington; (206) 323-7202; **internetcafe.allyn.com/**

More Internet Cybercafes Throughout the United States

To be fair, we tried to include every state we possibly could but some were left out.

ALASKA

Kaladi CoffeeNet, Anchorage, Alaska; (907) 344-5483; **www.matisse.net/files/bytebar.menu**

ARIZONA

Congo Internet Café, Phoenix, Arizona; (602) 209-1947; **www.congo.com**

CyberCafé, Flagstaff, Arizona; (520) 774-0005; **www.infomagic.com/~cafe**

FLORIDA

Cybernation, Fort Lauderdale, Florida; (954) 630-0223; **cyber-city.net/cybernation**

Infohaus, Tampa Bay, Florida; (813) 878-2233; **www.haus.net**

Cafe Kaldi, Sarasota, Florida; (941) 366-2326; **www.cafekaldi.com**

IDAHO

Metropolis Bakery Café, Twin Falls, Idaho; (208) 734-4457; **www.magiclink.com/pro/metnet**

IOWA

Internet Café, Des Moines, Iowa; (515) 279-9357 or (515) 288-7268; (no Web site)

KENTUCKY

Online—The Internet C@fé, Louisville, Kentucky; (502) 456-0912; **earth.maverick.net/**

MARYLAND

Funk's Democratic Coffee Spot, Baltimore, Maryland; (410) 276-3865; (Web site TBA)

Ze Mean Bean Café, Baltimore, Maryland; (410) 675-5999; (no Web site)

MICHIGAN

Four Friends Coffeehouse & CyberLounge, Grand Rapids, Michigan; (616) 456-5356; **www.grfn.org/~4friends/4friends.html/**

Big Surf Cyber Café, Birmingham, Detroit, Michigan; (810) 433-3744; **bigsurf.com/**

Caffè Bravo, Detroit, Michigan; (810) 344-0220; **www.cybercaffe.com/**

MINNESOTA

Techno Village Internet Coffeehouse, Mankato, Minnesota; (507) 386-2665; **www.techno-village.com/**

Cahoots Coffee Bar, St. Paul, Minnesota; (612) 644-6778; (no Web site)

Cyber X, Minneapolis, Minnesota; (612) 824-3558; **www.cyberx.com**

MISSOURI

The Grind, Central West End, St. Louis, Missouri; (314) 454-0202; **www.artsci.wustl.edu/~hussain/STL/CWE/**

The Grind, SLU, St. Louis, Missouri; (314) 454-0202; **www.icon-stl.net/~grind/**

MONTANA

CU Café, Whitefish, Montana; (406) 862-5824; **www.cucafe.com**

NEBRASKA

13th Street Coffee Company, Omaha, Nebraska; (402) 345-2883; (no Web site)

NEW JERSEY

Hoboken Coffee Warehouse, Hoboken, New Jersey; (201) 792-0707; **www.netcorner.com/hcw/**

NEVADA

Cyber City Café, Las Vegas, Nevada; (702) 737-4918; **www.cybercitycafe.com/**

NORTH CAROLINA

On-Ramp, Matthews, North Carolina; (704) 898-8900; **www.webserve.com/clients/onramp/**

Caffè Driade, Chapel Hill, North Carolina; (919) 933-4161; (no Web site)

Cup@Joe, Raleigh, North Carolina; (919) 828-9886; **www.nando.net/ads/cspot**

ESCape Computer Center, Jacksonville, North Carolina; (910) 347-2800 or (800) 446-7259; **www.toddalan.com/tacc/ escape/escape.html**

OREGON

The Habit, Portland, Oregon; (503) 235-5321; **www.teleport. com/~habit**

Paper Moon Espresso Caf@]@, Ashland, Oregon; (503) 488-4883; **www.opendoor.com/PaperMoon.html**

Garo's Java House, Ashland, Oregon; (503) 482-2261; **java-house.mind.net**

PENNSYLVANIA

Internet Café, Scranton, Pennsylvania; (717) 344-1969; **www.scranton.com/**

Cornerstone Coffeehouse, Camp Hill, Pennsylvania; (717) 737-5026; (no Web site)

Rhino Coffee Company, Philadelphia, Pennsylvania; (215) 923-2630; **www.cyberdelphia.com**

TEXAS

Java Island Coffee Roasters, Plano, Dallas/Fort Worth, Texas; (214) 491-1695; **www.java_island.com/**

The Raven & The Sparrow Gourmet Caf@]@, Corpus Christi, Texas; (512) 887-7778; **www.wantabe.com/ccmall/ra-ven.htm**

PJ's Coffee & Tea, Houston, Texas; (713) 521-2002; **www.iah. com/coffee/**

The Discovery Incubator, Austin, Texas; (512) 495-9448; **www.eden.com/~incubatr/**

VIRGINIA

Bogen's, Blacksburg, Virginia; (703) 953-2233; **www.bnr. com/~bogens/**

Mudhouse, Charlottesville, Virginia; (804) 984-6833; **www.mudhouse.com/**

CyberCafe & Training Center, Staunton, Virginia; (540) 887-8402; **bashful.cybercafe.cfw.com/**

CYBERCAFES IN EUROPE

AUSTRIA

DAS Computerhaus, Rainbergstrasse 3a A-5020 Salzburg; 43-662-844-377; **www.dascom.or.at;** Monday–Sunday, 9 A.M.–12 mdinight.

I don't know a hill of, well, hills, about Austria, but it was fascinating to sit down and read through their site. DAS specializes (via classes) in teaching people how to use the internet. For $2.50 for fifteen minutes, you can use one of thirty Pentium (Windows 95!) computers.

BELGIUM

1101 Cybercafe, 1001 Chausse de Wavre, Brussels, Belgium 1160; 32 2-646-0364; **www.cyber1101.ontonet.be;** contact Stephen Bouvard; Monday–Saturday 7 A.M.–12 midnight.

1101 Cybercafe is the way-cool-for-Brussels spot[5] featuring live music. Get on the net. The first hour is free and then it costs $7 for each additional hour you surf the Web. The seven computers are Pentiums with Windows 95, and you can use both Netscape or Microsoft Internet Explorer. As if.

ITALY

Virtualia Cybercafe, Pastrango 68, 10024 Moncaleare, Torrino, Italy; 39-116063070; **www.mulpex.com;** contact Franco Cassardo; Tuesday–Sunday, 9 A.M.–6 P.M.

Virtualia Cybercafe has both PCs and Macs available for your use for $5 an hour. There are four computers and two of those are connected to the internet. Another 100 computers there are linked by a UNIX line that enables one to chat with others in the café and with users in other cafés of the Virtualia Cybercafe. The café is closed on Mondays. And closed at nights. Hmm.

SPAIN

El Café de Internet, Avenida de las Corts Catalanas 656, 08010 Barcelona, Spain; +34 3 4121915; **www.cafeinternet.es;** contact Daniel Ferrer; Monday–Thursday, 10 A.M.–12 midnight; Friday and Saturday, 10 A.M.–11 P.M.; Sunday and holidays, 5 P.M.–11 P.M.

---

[5]Old Belgian joke: Why did the chicken cross the road in Brussels? He had nothing better to do.

What more do you want in beautiful, scenic Barcelona, Spain, than the internet—when you want to Telnet to your server back in the states, and maintain your life! El Café is a modern venue where the restaurant is downstairs and the computers and bar are upstairs. Low lighting and a yellow and green interior set a modern and comfortable atmosphere at this café that attracts many of the young, old, and curious. The twelve PCs are rentable at 600 pesetas per half hour, or you can purchase a card good for ten hours at 5,000 pesetas. El Café has been likened to an international airport because many tourists visit. Most of the staff speaks English; they feel that, if they are dealing with the internet, they must speak English. Many of their customers are Americans living in Barcelona to learn the language of love, and they come to check their e-mail. Those with AOL accounts can't check their mail, but they're working on it, Ferrer says; they get so many requests that they have to.

SWEDEN

Kajplats, 305 Kajplats, 305 Norra Neptunigatan, Malmo; 46-40-342574; **www.Kajen.com;** Monday–Friday, 2 P.M.–10 P.M.; Saturday, 2 P.M.–10:30 P.M.

This two-part café, is says the manager, Jorgen Svensson, "very unique and provides a model for other cafés to emulate." One room has computers and café; another is strictly for educational purposes such as learning 3-D applications or how to make pics. Fifteen online MACs or PCs are available as is Netscape and Internet Explorer, with more of the same expected by the end of 1996. The going rate for time online is $4 per half hour.

SWITZERLAND

Café Parterre, Mythenstrasse 7, Lucerne, Switzerland CH-6003; 41 41 210 40 93; **www.parterre.ch;** contact owner, Sacha Welj, or Stephen Fuch; open every day, 7:30 A.M.–1 A.M.; extended for performances.

Well, it's the funcoland of Europe! Café Parterre is a restaurant nestled in Lucerne, Switzerland, and offering more than the usual food and drinks. The place is equipped with two Macs and one PC internet terminal available for rent for between 8 and 15 francs. As Parterre is a main hang-out for the young and sometimes the old, live music performances ranging from the blues to hip-hop and Swiss dj competitions take place regularly on Friday and Saturday. The space is also used for fashoin shows promoting young designers. The café also houses an exhibit of obscure collectibles, such as items associated with the UFO phenomenon that is currently sweeping Europe—where alien dummies used in movies are on display. This multifunctional land is popular among American tourists in the summertime, and has become terminally hip.

UNITED KINGDOM

Internet Express Web Café, 1B Central Station, Queenstreet, Exeter, England; 44 1392 201544; **www.nxpress.co.uk;** Monday–Friday, 10 A.M.–10 P.M.; Saturday, 10 A.M.–8 P.M.; Sunday, 12 noon–6 P.M.

The cheerily named I-EX hosts pages for *Friends of the Earth* (a British Greenpeace charity that uses the synthetic paper, Polyart, environmentally correct and quite cool, for invitations to events). Find eight Pentium computers for £4 an hour. On Monday, Wednesday, and Friday, happy hour is between 7 and 10 P.M. and then the computers cost £3 an hour. There is a discount for students and the disabled.

Globally Found, based in the United Kingdom, with many chains all over; **www.cyberiacafe.net;**[6] times vary—always open late at night.

With a fabulous Web site, this Russian-sounding conglomerate is combining a worldwide addiction to caffeine with a wannabe-tech-head world's fascination with all things Web. (The Web address—for Channel Cyberia—is complicated, slow to open, filled with frames, and made all the more exasperating by containing more ads than any page for a café's homepage I have seen to date.) The Cyberians have opened what they term the first "global chain of cybercafes" including online chat, hosted music, and fashionable sites that stay open late-late in London and Manchester, England, Kingston, Tokyo, and Paris. New York and Eastern Europe are being discussed; at last look they were planning a union of cafés. A Teamster coffeehouse?

CYBERCAFES IN SOUTH AMERICA

BRAZIL

Café Café, Senador Area Leao, 1399 Jockey Club, Tereina, Piaui, Brazil; 55 (86) 223 4418; **cibercafe@servo.com.br/;** Cafe Cafe Av. (Dos); Campos Sales, 2084 Centro Teresina, Piaui Brazil.

One computer in each location. And a subtle gay theme throughout!

---

[6]Just like 800 numbers, the web is running out of originals! If you try **www.cyberia.com,** you will find, instead of this classy site, a jumble of noncoffee information such as how to use newsgroups and download handy software such as Freeagent. Be careful when addressing.

The point of all this is to have fun while traveling. Gays and lesbians are very much welcome in cybercafes as users of new and established technology—and, of course, we are also welcome as spenders of new and retained income. If you don't enjoy coffee, have no fear. Water is indeed universal, with or without "gas."

12

PAPER (THE MEDIA)

Everything from *Entertainment Weekly* to LA's *Buzz* magazine to *Newsweek* to the *AMA Journal* covers the Web or the net. I read the *Boston Herald*'s Friday column sometimes and especially appreciate the friendly column in the *San Jose Mercury News* on all things Web (sometimes twice a week). There is a lot of information on cyber-stuff in local papers and magazines and on specifically gay- and lesbian-related cyberitems in local gay and lesbian publications. I read them because, well, I'm a news junkie. *I read.* It's a difficult thing to admit but you and I have to do it. I like the feel of paper, no matter how light, and I like newsprint all over my hands and face (people *can* read me like a book).

It doesn't make sense for me to list every imaginable publication that covers the internet; there are some good ones to start with.

GAY AND LESBIAN PUBLICATIONS

New Yorkers have *LGNY* (a newspaper); Seattle-ites have *Seattle Gay News;* in Orlando, look for *Watermark;* Indianapolis residents go for *Word;* Boston has been sitting pretty for years with *Bay Windows;* San Francisco's recent addition is *Q San Francisco;* Chicago has the weekly *Windy City Times,* and *Gay Chicago* appears regularly; Philly does *Philadelphia Gay News* and *Au Courant* weekly; there's *Network* out of Edison, New Jersey; *In the Life* from Wappingers Falls, New York; *Baltimore Alternative* in you-know-where; the much-needed *Houston Voice* in Texas; the magazine *Curve,* formerly *Deneuve,* for the nation's lesbians, out of San Francisco; *Our Own* down in Norfolk, Virginia; *Nightlife* in Hollywood; *In Step Milwaukee; Blue Nights* (and black days?) from way over in Charlotte; *Homo/Denver; Columbus Free Press* (Ohio); *Of a Like Mind* in

Madison, Wisconsin; and, our favorite title, the *Lesbian & Gay News-Telegraph* weekly in St. Louis. All these places cover cyberspace when it's newsworthy.

As mentioned in the Chapter 7 sidebar, The Advocate Strikes Out.com, the *Advocate* and *Out* have covered the cyberscene on the Web. **Www.advocate.com** is the only site among them now. In print, however, they cover the world of gay cyber with a page here and a page there. It's important, but not crucial to them. And very often it seems to be like logrolling, people helping people they know.

OFFLINE MAGAZINES

Many of the magazines herein claim to offer "secrets" to the internet. Guides, you should realize soon enough, are offered in every format—online service, Web site, magazine, comic book, TV segment, radio show, funnily named guidebook from Broadway, you name it. In this game, you need something you can look at while you're online. Here's helping you. Interestingly, although these magazines all serve a purpose, hardly any of them gets the point: If you present clear, concise directions and relatively few opinions, people will gobble up the information. Note: Not much is gay or lesbian in the following because the gay print media only cover the salacious and slightly controversial, leaving the current events to these paper colleagues:

Byte calls itself the global authority for computing technology, and that is a pretty big boast, especially with the glut of magazines on computers and computer technology available. At first glance this magazine out of Peterborough, New Hampshire, may seem a little scary if you're inexperienced. The technological terms and photos jump off the pages and are a bit more advanced than I can handle. For the computer novice or intermediate (I'm the latter guy), this may scare you at first, but there is something so interesting about the way facts are laid out that you want to get on the Web and learn everything. I mean, you got to keep up with (Mr. and Ms) *Byte* Jones.

Computer User is a "future of computing" magazine given out free in cities on the eastern seaboard (and soon, more widely). Freebies usually suck, but in this case I have learned more about (1) the remaining BBSs, (2) telephony on the net, (3) how to develop a headache-free site cheaply, and (4) where the best New York-area deals are on fixing, buying, and even leasing equipment. That kind of material makes this paper, housed in New York's Flatiron district, quite a helpful pitcher-in. Macintosh users like me are treated not only well but also fairly. (I know the Mac isn't perfect and it helps to be reminded!)

Digital Creativity. I know, by now you're going, "Whahh?" But, really, if you want to find out about what's happening with the most creative side of or sites on the Web, check into this mag, subtitled, "Business Solutions for Imaging Professionals," of which I admit I know none. This magazine from the stable of Cowles Business Media products—publishers of *Inside Media* (my favorite weekly)—allows *people* you and I have no idea of, gurus of the net, to talk about the future of design and where we're headed as we turn into a Web'd world. I had never heard of Paul Saffo[1] but in 1996, Paul, who is famous in some circles, told me: "Creativity is a collaborative group process that stretches horizontally among colleagues and vertically through time. With an ongoing interaction between the subject and the observer, we might finally blow away the distinction between the two." Also, reviews, and a look at products nobody except Bill Gates's best friend can afford.

Dynamic Graphics. Why is this here? Desktop and the Web go together like gloves and hands. You can put your scanner to work and become a publisher, if you wish. And this magazine (based in Peoria) can help you find the way. Not a cheapie pub, by the way; but beautiful and goal-oriented. "**MASTER TERRIFIC HEAD-LINES**" is a chapter I got into. The section, "Desktop Toolkit," is for anyone seeking to turn time on the Web into a biz.

Home Office Computing is a slick mag that has won lots of awards, and holds the record, as far as I can see, as the mag with the most departments (such as "Log On: The Latest Way to Collaborate with Clients and Colleagues," and "Legal Matters: Ways to Slash Your Bills") than most glossy rags. My experience with these magazines with misnomers for names—see the list you're reading—is that most have columnists who drone on and on, and a few original ideas for lead stories. HOC (no pun intended) is doing quite well as a magazine, according to its press, and that's because any user of the net who has time on his or her hands is sure to want to know how to use that time more efficiently. *Home Office Computing* fits the bill.

Inc. Technology is a special *Inc.* quarterly that helps you understand how to make money online as a entrepreneur. For surfers, there is a section on "selling with multimedia" tools, reviews of deal-making disks, and an Industry Watch (a bit trite). All in all, they take managing on the Web seriously—particularly when referring to intranets (see Glossary), making this publication worthwhile for execs at no matter what level who want a quick fix on their worldview.

---

[1]He's a person who predicts what's going to happen online for Fortune "100" companies. Nice work if you can get it?

Internet Underground. The cool artwork on the cover promises that this publication won't be one of these nerdy computer mags that I often see computer geeks shoving their faces into on the subway. Still, I was hesitant. When I finally summoned enough courage to open it, boy, was I pleased with the inside. This is a very entertaining magazine, let alone computer magazine. Coolness and quirkiness abound on every page. The point here is that, while these guys from Lombard, Illinois, take their work seriously, they certainly prove that humor can help the cause. (Here's hoping they get a cover designer who does seriously quirky—rather than merely serviceable—work.)

There are cool sections, such as Culture Watch, where you'll be able to find not only Tori Spelling's Web address, but also Captain and Tennille's. (Yeah, love kept them together.) Other sections in the magazine include Weird on the Web, where you can find the addresses and descriptions of the Spam Web site or The Smelly Socks Sweat Shop side by side.

The articles are smartly written, reflecting an out-of-college yet (still) youthful insight into the subject. Whether writing about religion on the Web, those pesky legal ramifications of downloading music online, or the act of meeting potential partners online, the editors' analytic-yet-funny approach is what makes this a good read. Combine that with a nice layout and you have a magazine that is both mega-informative and well-worth keeping on the coffee table beside your tasteful porn.

Byte. The problem with this publication is its savviness. If you're a Web novice and you want to know mere facts, forget it. Articles are more apt to scare new Web users than to encourage exploration into the Web. In other words, you don't become a good driver by getting behind the wheel of a Porsche on your first day out. You need to get into a VW Bug or a Chrysler K car first. *Byte* is the top-of-the-line Porsche, and although it looks so pretty, you might not be able to handle the beast if you don't know how to drive properly. Beastly!

Interactive Week. This magazine stands out among the others. The first time I saw it, the cover was plastered with the titles of articles about legal and corporate issues on the Web. The articles themselves actually caught my attention, because they were not only intriguing, but also, and more importantly, they were understandable.

This is a good magazine for anyone going onto the Web for the second time. Readers get a thorough and clear overview of the latest issues on the internet, on intranets, and on infrastructures. Terms are clear and the tone of the articles is informative rather than condescending! What a relief. Pieces on the Web and miscellaneous legislation and business issues affecting the net also give the novice user a better grasp of the internet's scope. Then there's all that technical information they include, always explaining each term. Ah.

This magazine, based in Garden City, New York, gives readers a complete and thorough education on tons of net issues. It is definitely one of the better computer magazines out there.

Internet World. Don't let the flashy artwork on the cover fool you. This Westport, Connecticut, publication is a very serious magazine for the internet explorer. Articles here cover the whole spectrum surrounding the internet. Again, most importantly, the langauge here is simple yet informative. There are millions of Web sites listed here to be checked out for both pleasure and information. This is the consummate guide to the internet. An easy read with a leisurely pace, *Internet World* provides the reader with everything the net can offer and then some, without headaches.

MacWeek comes from New York and is a newsweekly for Macintosh managers. I love Macs, and this magazine gives me a warm glow. As far as learning the Web, it's useful only if you own a Macintosh. There are a few articles here pertaining to the Apple machine and the Web, nothing that's too informative such as reviews of new browsers or Web addresses to check out. Articles focus on broader ethical and legislative issues on the net. Codicil: If you're serious about the Web, this is probably one magazine you might not want to pick up. There are many magazines out there that are far better and not as singularly focused on one kind of computer, the Mac!

NetGuide is one of my faves. Another very good magazine for the Web, arguably (even though it's based on Lung Eye-Land) one of the best. The language here is simple yet informative. You'll find everything from how to build a better and more effective Web site to how to get on sites. The ratings of sites here are honest and useful. There are many helpful hints and nuggets of information that are often skipped over in other publications. Its dedication to the Web will keep this magazine light years ahead of its competitors and safely in the bags and libraries of Web junkies.

PC Computing. Out of the high peaks of Boulder, Colorado, like other Web magazines (see *Yahoo! Internet Life*, below), comes the crème de la crème of computer magazines. This is by far one of my favorite magazines for its Web coverage. There are numerous articles about the Web, how to get on, news services available on it, reviews of browsers, stories exploring the possibilities of the Web, etc. The langauge here is easy to understand and the magazine itself exudes an aura of insider knowledge that I rarely find in other magazines. I learned a lot from my first reading and feel that any user, whether old or new, will have much to gain by reading it. A definite must for the library of the aspiring computer geek and net jockey.

PC Magazine, hailing from the Apple and billed as The Independent Guide to Personal Computing, is a good read for someone who's interested in the net. There are well-thought-out articles here ranging from how slow downloading info off the Web can be to critiques of the latest browsers available. The level of net experience needed here is medium to high, but the amateur needn't worry because information is unbelieveably clear, although slightly pedantic. This is an important addition to the collection for reference and for learning.

PC Week. A dinosaur that has been around a while, seems slow, old, and creaky, and yet somehow, the material is here. Though it's not as slick as the new boys are, and though it is sometimes hard to follow, *PC Week* is going after Web types in a big way. Reviews of Web servers, reports of news of the day—very deadline oriented— and special reports on new products by everyone from the mainstays, IBM and Adobe, to chat-client software providers, such as iChat and WebMaster, are being written up here for *the industry.* I like the ads, too, because the people (even newcomers) who make products for people like us, advertise here because they know it! Last addition is a column called Reality Check, which discusses products, services and companies on the Web and takes tips on what to cover. (They took one from me at **david_berlind@zd.com.**)

PC World. It like this, one of the oldest magazines of its ilk, because it is, basically, ALL INTERNET ALL THE TIME. In one issue last year, someone wrote a lengthy article titled "Free Help Online," which gave so many ideas. I used it, asked questions, and got a real-people response. I asked, "How come I can no longer see color on my monitor?"

Someone replied, "Your browser may not be able to allocate enough colors. For instance, if you use UNIX you should try the -install command line option, which lets Netscape allocate a private color map." Amen.

If you're a computer junkie, everything is covered: filtering search engines, info about upgrades on software, internet overload, what's outdated in net hardware, sneak peeks, a look at the best, and, some respected critics who tell you how to use your PC to get what you need on the internet. (You can even use this magazine to buy a darn great printer.) This *World* encompasses articles that some of its advertisers might not like: "Are You for Sale?" answered the question by showing how marketers find out everything about you every time you're online. Thanks.

But, when flipping through *PC World,* which is published in San Francisco, don't ever look for Mac information—it's plum gone.

Video & MultiMedia Producer. A White Plains, New York-based publication that's seriously reader friendly, cool, *and* necessary. Readers will get a lot of solid information about the Web, its functions, new additions, and new developments surrounding it. Articles on video and multimedia are recommended for beginners who are interested in learning more. Written in simple language, this is a very nice-looking magazine as well, which is a definite plus. A good addition to reading lists of ye who are interested in learning about my buddy, The Web.

(The) Web magazine, a newish publication, is a mag I have tried to like but don't get. Who knows . . . perhaps they don't get us.

Wired, for the San Francisco-based mag's column, "Net Surf," gets into the gritty of the Web sites it chooses to laud or ridicule. Thanks to clever editing by Kristin Spence, the column covers everything from the obscure to the unbelievable, and a lot in between. *Wired* is now a coffee-table magazine with a satisfying Web site of its own (**www.HotWired.com** features some nail-biting fiction serials), and it is a pleasure to tell you that, after all these years, "Net Surf" still covers Web upstarts uncynically and with something notably new to say each time.

Yahoo! Internet Life is up there too, with its Web-happy columnists who offer a strangely-titled-but-organized monthly strung together in Boulder, Colorado. I have already told you to spend time on the gifted and notorious Yahoo! search engine looking up gay topics as obscure as Lezzie Peanut Butter. (Well, why not?) But the "Pretty Strange" and "ed by the Net" columns in the magazine are pure fun compared with the yawn-inspiring Web area titled "Incredibly Useful Sites." Seriously, how many useful sites can you look at before you want to slit your throat? (Like, have you seen **www.charged.com,** the wacked-out, extreme sports Web site?)

"Touched" is an amiably readable column that begins with, "Some ordinary people are doing extraordinary things on the Information Superhighway" and "Pretty Strange" (I *love* barfOrama) is downright funny. Many Web magazines scorn humor because they think it distracts the reader.

Incidentally, while you're reading this, remember that people who write for magazines or produce radio and TV shows often toss out Web addresses as reference. (PBS and National Public Radio are famous for this.) Keep a small notebook around to jot down the Web addresses. In writing this tome, I discovered that finding, holding, and losing crumpled scraps of paper annotated with URLs is a great way to remain frustrated. For Web fans, it's the best 49-cent investment to make.

AUTHOR'S NOTE
For updates and breaking news, go to **www.yeahwhatever.com,** the *Get On with It* site, with links to our online service compendium.

GLOSSARY

56k Line

A digital phone line connection (a leased line) capable of carrying 56,000 bits per second (bps). At this speed, a megabyte will take about three minutes to be transferred. This is almost four times as fast as it would travel on a 14,400 bps modem. But don't get too excited. Nothing's been *proven* on regular phone lines.

Access

The means of getting into an online system, or any internet "space" in general.

Access Provider

A company that lets you connect to its internet host, usually for a fee.

Account

You usually need an account to use big computer networks and systems, such as those owned by universities or large businesses.

Address

Where someone can send mail or files to you at an online site. Can also mean where you live, but we're really not interested in your real-world goings on!

Address Specifications

The rightmost segment is the type or location of the site (.com for commercial, .edu for educational, .uk for the United Kingdom, etc). Outproud.org is the national association of gay youth groups. Harvard.edu is Harvard University's domain name. The address can tell you what country a person is from or if he or she has an online account—you are talking to a hacker, in which case, you'll never know. :)! (See Chapter 3 for details.)

ADN (Advanced Digital Network)

Usually refers to a 56k leased line.

America Online (AOL)

A commercial online service—a way of getting access to the Web. Exploiters of the gay population and very good at it.

Anonymous FTP

Simply means that someone without an account on the internet host can still FTP. In other words, if an internet host allows anonymous FTPs, you can connect to the host (no matter who you are) and start FTPing. But don't forget that an anonymous FTP site allows people to be anonymous. We like that, so don't be a butthead and ruin it for everyone else!

Applets

With the use of small Java programs called *applets,* Web pages can include functions such as animation, calculators, and other fancy tricks. Microsoft Explorer and Netscape Navigator can get you many of the applets you need. I prefer getting them off small Web sites such as **www.cyberia.com,** which has a FAQ for users that includes many "cool" software pieces (ditto from **www.shareware.com**).

Archie

A tool (software) for finding files stored on anonymous FTP sites. You need to know the exact file name or a substring of it. You can find this stuff at any net browser's homepage.

ARPANet (Advanced Research Projects Agency Network)

The precursor to the internet. Developed in the late sixties and early seventies by the U.S. Department of Defense as an experiment in wide-area networking that would survive a nuclear war. This was the daddy or the mommy of it all!

   See also internet.

ASCII (American Standard Code for Information Interchange)

This is the de facto, worldwide standard for the code numbers used by computers to represent all the upper- and lower-case Latin-alphabet letters, numbers, punctuation, etc. There are 128 standard ASCII codes, each of which is represented by a seven-digit binary number, 0000000 through 1111111. You will be tested later.

Baud

In common usage the *baud rate* of a modem is the number of bits it can send or receive per second. Technically, it is the number of times per second that the carrier signal shifts value. For example, a 1,200 bits-per-second modem actually runs at 300 baud, moving 4 bits per baud (4 × 300 = 1,200 bits per second). And that is the truth!

BBS (Bulletin Board System)

A computerized meeting and announcement system that allows people to carry on discussions, upload and download files, and make announcements without all the participants being connected to the computer at the same time. There are many thousands (millions?) of BBSs around the world; most are very small, running on a single IBM-clone PC with one or two phone lines. Be careful, they can be addictive, and before you know it you will be receiving 1,000 mail messages a day . . . ugh!

Binary Files

A file containing arbitrary bytes or words, as opposed to a text file containing only printable characters (e.g. ASCII characters with codes 10, 13, and 32-126) Usually files containing graphics or programs.

Bit (Binary Digit)

A single-digit number in base-2, in other words, either a one or a zero. The smallest unit of computerized data. Bandwidth is usually measured in bits per second.

Bookmark

Using a World Wide Web browser, a bookmark is a saved link to a Web site that has been added to a list of saved links. When you are looking at a particular Web site or homepage and want to be able to quickly get back to it later or in a future session, you can create a bookmark for it. You can think of your browser as a book full of (millions of) Web pages and a few well-placed bookmarks that you have chosen. The list that contains your bookmarks is the "bookmark list" (and sometimes it's called a "hotlist").

BOT

A (ro)bot is simply either a collection of /on commands that are loaded from a script (text) file into the irc client, or a C program. They appear in two forms:

ircIIscript Bots

These are simply a bunch of /on commands that are triggered by specific events. The "bot" is programmed to react to certain events, such as mode changes, kicks, etc.

C Bots

These are a C program that either uses the IRC client or connects directly to the IRC server. It is programmed to watch for certain events and to react as programmed when the event happens.

Browser

A client program (software) that is used to look at various kinds of internet resources. The browser also controls the information you have access to, so don't always take what you are, or are not, seeing for granted in the future. (We have no proof that anything is going on now, but we did catch all those notices on Netscape that warned users of "gay content" . . . evil, evil, evil!)

Bulletin-board Service (BS)

Insanity. It may not get you on the Web, but it lets you post messages and bond with like-minded subscribers all over the world. But don't sign up for too many newsgroups or you might find your e-mail account shut off for B.S. overload.
See also BBS.

Byte

A set of bits that represents a single character. Usually there are eight bits in a byte, sometimes more, depending on how the measurement is being made.

Cache

This is a place to store something more or less temporarily. A browser's cache directory stores Web pages. This alleviates the need for duplicate downloading when you revisit an internet site.

cgi-bin

The most common name of a directory on a Web server in which CGI (common gateway interface) programs are stored. The *bin* part of cgi-bin is an abbreviation of "binary" because, once upon a time, most programs were referred to as binaries. In real life, most programs found in cgi-bin directories are text files—scripts that are executed by binaries or programs located elsewhere on the same machine.

Chat

Real-time online conversation conducted when two or more people type to one another. This is where it's at, boys and girls.

Chat Room

An online "window" where lots of people (up to thirty) can all type into the same space and read one another's comments. Just as rooms in a house are designated by their primary function, such as bedroom, laundryroom, so are online chat rooms, e.g., Lethrluv or Men4Men.

CIS

One of the services run by CompuServe Corporation. CIS provides a wide variety of information and services, including bulletin boards, online conferencing, business news, sports and weather, financial transactions, electronic mail, travel and entertainment data as well as online editions of computer publications. CompuServe Information Service should not be confused with CompuServe Corporation's other sectors, which offer many other services besides the consumer information service.

CompuServe also offers gay content in the form of Pride and Café Q.

CIS is a large international conferencing system (albeit with a heavy U.S. bias). It provides an access to the Usenet news (GO INTERNET). Forum UKCOMP topic Acorn/Z88 is the place to find Acorn users.

CompuServe's main competitors are AOL, Prodigy, and now MSN.

Client

When you're talking about the internet, a client is a software program running on your personal computer that lets you do internet stuff. Examples of client options are: FTP, Telnet, and Netscape.

Cookie

A cookie is a mechanism by which operations on the server side (such as CGI scripts; *see* cgi-bin, above) can store and retrieve information from the client side of the connection. In practice, this means that information submitted by a Web browser to a Web server via a forum or other interactive method can be stored on the browser machine and resubmitted when the Web-server URL is accessed at some point in the future. Examples would include login or registration information, the contents of online "shopping carts," or user surveys. Cookies can store user information (on the user's own computer), so they are used to personalize the WWW experience by recognizing and acknowledging the user when he or she reenters a Web site. Cookies are typically set to expire after a predetermined time. Cookies *do not* read your hard drive and send your life story to the CIA.

CU-SeeMe

A program for multiuser, desktop video- and audioconferencing over the net. Requires a video input source to send video. Has taken cybersex into a new dimension. Can be very scary, or quite a treat, depending on who's sent you an image.

Cyberpunk

Cyberpunk was originally a cultural subgenre of science fiction taking place in a not-so-distant, overindustrialized society. The term grew out of the work of William Gibson and Bruce Sterling and has evolved into a cultural label encompassing many different kinds of human, machine, and punk attitudes. It includes clothing and lifestyle choices as well.

Cyberqueer

That would be you and me.

Cybersex

You figure it out, and if you still can't, you bought the right book!

Cyberspace

Term originated by the author, William Gibson, in his novel *Neuromancer*. The word *cyberspace* is currently used to describe the whole range of information resources available through computer networks.

DCC

DCC allows the user to overcome some limitations of the IRC server network and to have the ultimate in secure chat connections while still in an IRC-oriented protocol.

Digerati

Modeled on the term *literati,* this is a description of the people seen to be knowledge-able, hip, or otherwise in-the-know about computers.

Domain Name

The unique name that identifies an internet site. Domain names always have two or more parts, separated by dots. The part on the left is the most specific, and the part on the right is the most general. A given machine may have more than one domain name but a given domain name points to only one machine. Usually, all of the machines on a given network will have the same thing as the right-hand portion of their domain names, or as I like to say: "If you're on the IRC, the domain can give you a hint about who the kids are." For example, .edu, as in the address mail.cmu.edu, shows that "the kids" are logged on from an educational (e.g., university) site.

It is also possible for a domain name to exist but not be connected to an actual machine. This is often done so that a group or business can have an internet e-mail address without having to establish a real internet site. In these cases, some real internet machine must handle the mail on behalf of the listed domain name.

See also Address.

DNS

The unique name that identifies an internet site. Domain names always have two or more parts separated by dots. The part on the left is the most specific, and the part on the right is the most general. A given machine may have more than one domain name, but a given domain name points to only one machine.

Download

Move files from a remote computer to your own.

E-mail (Electronic Mail)

Messages, usually text, sent from one person to another via computer. E-mail can also be sent automatically to a large number of addresses (*see* Mailing List, below). If you don't know this, you need to read this book very slowly and then, when you are done, go buy a computer, and read the book again.

See also Chapter 3 (all about e-mail).

FAQ (Frequently Asked Questions)

FAQs are documents that list and answer the most common questions on a particular subject. There are hundreds of FAQs on subjects as diverse as Pet Grooming and

Cryptography. FAQs are usually written by people who have tired of answering the same question over and over. In other words, read any available FAQs before you start bitching.

Finger

Besides being an appendage that has been places no one should know about, it is an internet term for address. Fingers are also used to give access to nonpersonal information, but the most common use is to ascertain whether a person has an account at a particular internet site. Giving the finger is a popular U.S. sport.

Fire Wall or Firewall

A combination of hardware and software separating a LAN into two or more parts for security purposes.

Flame

Originally, *flame* meant to carry on in a passionate manner in the spirit of honorable debate. Flames most often involved the use of flowery language and good flaming was an art. More recently *flame* has come to refer to any kind of derogatory comment, no matter how witless or crude. Spelling flames, obsessed with correcting spelling errors and printing them over and over, are the most ignorant, annoying crackheads on the internet.

See Gay Words for *flame.*

Forum

A gathering place based on a theme, specifically in CompuServe and Prodigy Internet, where this is an art form (a-hem). Another word used to establish some semblance of reality in cyberspace.

Freenet

The term *freenet* refers to an internet host that people can use for free and thereby connect to the internet for free. Schools, community groups, and libraries are often providers of freenet sites.

See also Chapter 11.

FTP (File Transfer Protocol)

A way to transfer files between computers on the internet. When you retrieve something via FTP, you are basically transferring from hard drive to hard drive. Many internet sites have established publicly accessible repositories of material that can be obtained using FTP by logging in using the account name <anonymous>; thus, these sites are called anonymous FTP servers.

It is one of the most common formats for getting free stuff (such as shareware) off a public network (a library or university), for retrieving pictures (typically gifs or jpegs), for downloading Netscape's free Web software, and so forth.

Gateway

Technically, a gateway is a hardware or software set-up that connects two dissimilar protocols by translating one to the other. For example, Prodigy has a gateway that translates its internal, proprietary e-mail format to the internet e-mail format. Another, sloppier meaning of the term, *gateway,* is to describe any mechanism for providing access to another system, e.g., AOL might be called a "gateway" to the internet.

GIF (Graphics Interchange Format)

Licensed by CompuServe, gif is a common format for compressing graphics files. Most Web browsers and other graphical interfaces for the internet will display gif (or jpeg, the other common picture format used on the net) files as pictures on your monitor. There are others, but these are the most common. This is the format that most of the dirty stuff you're probably looking for comes in.

A gif (pronounced "jif") is one of the two most common file formats for graphic images on the World Wide Web. The format is actually owned by CompuServe, and companies that make products that exploit the format (but not ordinary Web users or businesses that include gifs in their pages) need to license its use.

Gopher

A widely successful method of making menus of the material that is available over the internet. Gopher is a client-and-server–style program, which requires that the user have a Gopher client program. Although Gopher spread rapidly across the globe in only a couple of years, it has been largely supplanted by hypertext, also known as WWW (World Wide Web). There are still thousands of Gopher servers on the internet and we can expect that they will remain for a while.

Host

Any computer on a network that is a repository for services available to other computers on the network. It is quite common to have one host machine provide several services, such as WWW and Usenet.

Hotlink

1. Using hypertext, a link is a selectable connection from one word, picture, or information object to another. In a multimedia environment such as the World Wide Web, such objects can include sound and motion video sequences. The most common form of link is the highlighted word or picture that can be selected by the user (with a mouse or in some other fashion), resulting in the immediate delivery of an associated page of information. The highlighted object is referred to as an anchor. The anchor reference and the object referred to constitute a hypertext link.
2. A mechanism for sharing data between two application programs where changes to the data made by one application appear instantly in the other's copy.

HTML (HyperText "Markup" Language)

The computer-coding language used to create hypertext documents for use on the World Wide Web. HTML looks a lot like old-fashioned typesetting code, by which you mark a block of text with codes that indicate how it should appear. Additionally, in HTML you can specify that a block of text, or a word, be linked to another file on the internet. HTML files are meant to be viewed using a World Wide Web client program, such as Netscape or Mosaic.

HTTP (HyperText Transport Protocol)

The protocol for moving hypertext files across the internet. Requires an HTTP client program on one end, and an HTTP server program on the other end. HTTP is the most important protocol used in the World Wide Web (WWW). In the old days, circa 1933, people referred to the WWW as "HTTP files."

Hyperlink

A reference (link) from some point in one hypertext document to (some point in) another document or another place in the same document. A browser usually displays a hyperlink in some distinguishing way, e.g., in a different color, font, or style. When the user activates the link (by clicking on it with the mouse), the browser will display the target of the link.

Hypertext

Generally, any text that contains links to other documents. The links may be words or phrases in the document that can be chosen by a reader and that cause another document to be retrieved and displayed. Words or images that appear different on the screen (e.g., they appear in blue when the rest of the text is in black) are the links that, clicked on, take you to another site.

IM (Instant Message)

This is a one-on-one private chat online, where two people are typing live into the same window. This is big on AOL, and is not recommended for those who require privacy.

Internet

The vast collection of interconnected computer networks that all use the TCP/IP protocols and that evolved from the ARPANet of the late sixties and early seventies. The internet now connects roughly hundreds of thousands independent networks into a vast global internet. The word is also used in describing the connection of two or more networks together: an inter-net, as in inter-national or inter-state. Either way, I feel that it's up to you how you capitalize it, or don't bother; I always go for the lower.

Internet Explorer

You use it to explore the World Wide Web. After downloading IE, you get a free subscription to the *Wall Street Journal* online—**www.wsj.com**—but only while Explorer is warming up.

Intranet

A private network inside a company or organization that uses the same kinds of software that you would find on the public internet, but that is only for internal use. As the internet has become more popular, many of the tools used on it are also being used in private networks. For example, many companies have Web servers that are available only to employees. The distinction should be made between a network and an intranet. This is tricky stuff.

IP Address (Internet Protocol Address)

This address is a unique string of numbers that identifies a computer on the internet. These numbers are usually shown in groups separated by periods like this: 123.123.23.2. All resources on the internet must have an IP address—or else they're not on the internet at all.

IRC (Internet Relay Chat)

Basically a huge, multiuser live chat facility. Around the world there are a number of major IRC servers that are linked to one another. Anyone can create a channel and anything that anyone types in a given channel is seen by all others in that channel. Private channels can (and are) created for conference calls. And it is pretty much an anything-goes world, where you can send your favorite pics to newly made friends.

ISDN (Integrated Services Digital Network)

Basically, a way to move more data over existing regular phone lines. ISDN is rapidly becoming available in much of the United States and in most markets. It is priced very comparably to standard analog phone circuits. It can provide speeds of roughly 128,000 bits per second over regular phone lines. In practice, most people will be limited to 56,000 or 64,000 bits per second. This ain't cheap.

ISP (Internet Service Provider)

The name for the organization that connects you to the Web (for a fee) and usually offers other services, such as e-mail. Usually the cheapo version of getting connected . . . bettah find one if you are going online because of the high prices of commercial online services.

Java

Java is a programming language invented by Sun Microsystems that is specifically designed for writing programs that can be safely downloaded to your computer through the internet and immediately run without fear of viruses or other harm to your computer or files. Java That—or Hot Java, as some of its applications are known—is a new programming language that may transform the Web with enhancements such as real-time audio and video, continuously updated data (such as sports scores or a financial ticker), and group interactivity (multiplayer games or live, online auctions). It may finally make the net look like it does in movies about hackers. However, stay tuned for the battle of the programming languages.

Also, really good coffee.

jpeg

A jpeg is a graphics file format. Basically, the jpeg file format was created because people felt that other graphics file formats, including the ever-popular gif format, were too big.

Listserv

Listserv is one of the more popular mailing list-manager programs. (The other two mailing list programs you often see are LISTPROC and Majordomo.) So what does a mailing list-manager program do? Simple. It adds users to and removes users from a mailing list.

Don't join too many of these Listservs. Quality—not quantity.

Login

Noun: The account name used to gain access to a computer system; not a secret (contrast with Password).

Verb: The act of entering into a computer system, as in, "I suggest that you login to the 'WELL' and then go to the 'GBN' conference."

M4M (Male 4 Male)

E.g., gay.

Mailing List

On the internet, a mailing list is just a list of people who want to receive information via e-mail about a particular topic.

Majordomo

A program that allows you to maintain an e-mail-based mailing list.
See also Listserv.

Modem (MOdulator/DEModulator)

A hardware device that allows computers to talk to other computers through the phone system and computer users to send files and messages over the phone lines. Basically, modems do for computers what a telephone does for humans.

MOO (Mud, Object Oriented)

One of several kinds of multiuser role-playing environments, so far only text-based. A computer geek word, definitely, this MOO.
See also MUD.

Mosaic

The first WWW browser developed the early 1990s in the innocent days of the Web. It was available for the Macintosh, Windows, and UNIX all with the same interface. Mosaic really started the popularity of the Web. The source code for Mosaic has been licensed by several companies. Now there are several other pieces of software as good or better than Mosaic, most notably Netscape (made by the same company.)

mpeg

Mpeg is a graphics file format for video or movies.

MUD (MultiUser Dungeon or Dimension)

A (usually text-based) multiuser simulation environment. Some are purely for fun and flirting, others are used for serious software development or education purposes and all that lies in between. A significant feature of most MUDs is that users can create things that stay after they leave and that other users can interact with in their absence, thus allowing a world to be built gradually and collectively. This is groovy stuff! For more on MUD, see *Mazes and Monsters,* a bad film, starring John Candy and Tom Hanks, made in 1982. Leonard Maltin didn't give it any stars.

See MOO.

Multimedia

A broad term that encompasses CD-ROMs, the Web, 3-D animation, or anything that combines sound, text, and graphics.

Netiquette

The etiquette on the internet. Yeah, right. It really depends on who you are, what you want, and how you plan on getting it. Hackers really don't subscribe to this nonsense.

Netizen

Derived from the term *citizen,* referring to a citizen of the internet, or someone who uses networked resources. The term connotes civic responsibility and participation. If you are interested in forming a nice little community, then you have found your term. *Not* a geek word, this is some businessman's word.

Netscape

A WWW browser and the name of the company that makes it. The Netscape™ browser was originally based on the Mosaic program developed at the National Center for Supercomputing Applications (NCSA).

The main author of Netscape, Mark Andreessen, was hired away from the NCSA by Jim Clark, and they founded a company called Mosaic Communications and soon changed the name to Netscape Communications Corporation. Andreessen is smart enough to know a good deal when he gets one. (He put in some of the money to start up Planetout, discussed in Chapter 7.)

Remember, don't get scared by their product-laden homepage. Check around their Web page before you pay their outrageous prices. SURF ON!

Network

Any time you connect two or more computers together so that they can share resources, you have a computer network. Connect two or more networks together and you have an internet.

Newbie

A computer geek word that describes someone who is a virgin in cyberspace.

Newsgroup

The name for discussion groups on Usenet. Here you can find all the latest chitchat from some redneck who is obsessed with Jane Pauley and has signed up for four hundred newsgroups. In other words, people have been hanging out here a little too long, and need to move on to the WWW or MUDs.

Node

Any single computer connected to a network; as in, "CompuServe has nodes in every major metropolitan area in the United States."

Online

Any situation when two computers are talking to each other.

Online Service

An online bulletin board-like commercial service that provides an array of services for a fee. These provide the most popular gay and lesbian forums on the internet today! AOL, Prodigy, CompuServe, and MSN are the biggies. MSN, meanwhile, is morphing into something *huge* in 1997.

Password

A code used to gain access to a locked system. Good passwords contain letters and symbols and are not simple combinations, such as the word *virtue*. A good password might be 12!92. If you've problems with password recollection, see the description of Site for Sore Passwords in Chapter 7. It can help.

POP

1. A Point of Presence (POP) usually means a city or location to which a network can be connected, often with dial-up phone lines. If an internet company says it will soon have a POP in Belgrade, that means that it will soon have a local phone

number in Belgrade and/or a place from which leased lines can connect to its network.

2. Post Office Protocol (POP) refers to the way e-mail software such as Eudora gets mail from a mail server. When you obtain a SLIP, PPP, or shell account, you almost always get a POP account with it, and it is this POP account that you tell your e-mail software to use to get your mail.

Port

1. Most generally, a place where information goes into or out of a computer, or both; e.g., the serial port on a personal computer is where a modem would be connected.

2. On the internet *port* often refers to a number that is part of a URL, appearing after a colon (:) right after the domain name. Every service on an internet server listens on a particular port number on that server. Most services have standard port numbers, e.g., Web servers normally listen on port 80. Services can also listen on nonstandard ports, in which case the port number must be specified in a URL when accessing the server, so you might see a URL that starts with gopher:// and shows a Gopher server running on a nonstandard port (the standard Gopher port is 70).

3. *Port* as a verb, denotes the translation of a piece of software from one type of computer system to another, e.g., a Windows program must be translated before it will run on a Macintosh. IMPORTANT THING TO REMEMBER: This really is not important, unless you are a sysadm or sysop, and if you are, you probably already know it.

Posting

A single message entered into a network communciations system; e.g., a single message posted to a newsgroup or message board. Be careful, though, if you post to everyone, you may get bombed by mail, and thus your memory or hard drive can stall or *overload!*

PPP (Point-to-Point Protocol)

Most widely known as a protocol that allows a computer to use a regular telephone line and a modem to make TCP/IP connections and thus be really and truly on the internet.

Prodigy

A commercial online conferencing service, codeveloped by IBM and Sears, Roebuck, Inc. Prodigy's main competitors are AOL, CompuServe, and now MSN. (Prodigy is now owned by International Wireless.)

Screen Name

Your alias online. If you use a screen name that's different from your name, nobody will know who you really are. You can use several names; same as a nick. Mine is nativeguy.

Server

A computer, or a software package, that provides a specific kind of service to client software running on other computers. The term can refer to a particular piece of software, such as a WWW server, or to the machine on which the software is running, as in "Our mail server is down today, that's why e-mail isn't getting out." A single server machine could have several different server software packages running on it, thus providing many different services to clients on the network.

Shareware

Shareware is software that is given away free. *If* you like the software or intend to use it, you are supposed to send a small fee to the programmer who created it. Yeah . . . right. It is a good idea to do it for people who are creating "kewl" stuff, but—not to mention any names—not everyone deserves a donation.

Shell Account

With a shell account, you use a communications application to connect to an internet-access provider and possibly receive limited mail messages. Useful for someone who just wants access to the WWW.

SLIP (Serial Line Internet Protocol)

Like PPP, it is a method of connecting directly to the internet. When you make a SLIP connection, your PC becomes a host computer on the internet for the duration of the connection. Once the standard for using a telephone line (a serial line) and a modem to connect a computer as a real internet site, SLIP is gradually being replaced by PPP.

Spam

An inappropriate attempt to use a mailing list, or Usenet, or other networked communciations facility as if it were a broadcast medium (which it is not) by sending the same message to a large number of people who didn't ask for it. Spamming sucks.

There is in circulation the belief that the term *spam* was derived from the classic skit in *Monty Python's Flying Circus* wherein a person in a shop can order nothing but

Spam. That may not be true. Spamming is so derided that the term may well have be a reflection of someone's low opinion of the food product with the same name, Spam being generally perceived as a generic, content-free waste of resources. For more on Spam, the trademarked product of the Hormel Corporation, see the site that has the URL **sp1.berkeley.edu/findthespam.html.** And spam spam spam.

Sysop (System Operator)

Anyone responsible for the physical operations of a computer system or network resource. A system administrator (sysadm) decides how often backups and maintenance should be performed and the system operator performs those tasks. The author (me) acts as sysop at CompuServe Information Service. For examples of my work, the go word is Native. Go!

T-1

A leased-line connection capable of carrying data at 1,544,000 bits per second. At maximum theoretical capacity, a T-1 line could move a megabyte in less than 10 seconds. That is still not fast enough for full-screen, full-motion video, for which you need at least 10,000,000 bits per second. T-1 is the fastest speed commonly used to connect networks to the internet.

T-3 is a leased line capable of carrying data at 44,736,000 bps. Whoah! Big time!

TCP/IP (Transmission Control Protocol/Internet Protocol)

This is the suite of protocols that defines the internet. Originally designed for the UNIX operating system, TCP/IP software is now available for every major computer operating system. To be truly on the internet, your computer must have TCP/IP software.

Telnet

The automatic command and program used to log in from one internet site to another. The Telnet command and program get you to the login, the prompt of another host. Don't underestimate the power of a cool Telnet site, which is simply an independently run computer. Who knows what you will find? Who cares?

See Chapter 6 (TRC stuff).

Terminal

A device that allows you to send commands to a computer somewhere else. At a mimimum, this usually means a keyboard and a display screen and some simple circuitry. Usually you will use terminal software in a personal computer—the software pretends to be (emulates) a physical terminal and allows you to type commands to a computer somewhere else. (It's a glamorous TV.)

UNIX

A computer operating system (the basic software running on a computer, underneath applications [programs] such as word processors and spreadsheets). UNIX is designed to be used by many people at the same time (multiuser) and has TCP/IP built in. It is the most common operating system for servers on the internet. The language is definitely not user friendly, unlike all the Windows crap you have been using. This stuff is hardcore and is the basis of computer system languages today.

Upload

To send a file from your computer to a remote system, such as a commercial online service, an internet FTP site, or a BBS file storage area.

URL (Uniform Resource Locator)

A standard way to give the address of any resource on the internet that is part of the World Wide Web (WWW). A URL is any address whatsoever that gets you to where you want to go on the net. The most common way to use a URL is to enter into a WWW browser program, such as Netscape or Lynx, type this address at the "Open Location" command of your browser, and the stuff you want will be displayed on your computer in a moment, e.g., http://www.cyberboy.com.

Usenet

An international meeting place where people gather (but not in real time) to meet their friends, discuss events, keep up with trends, discuss politics or other issues, seek information, or just talk. Over ten thousand newsgroups exist on Usenet, which resides primarily on the internet. You'll find discussions on engineering, environmental issues, television shows, college classes, OJ Simpson, boys who like Twinkies or Yodels, or any other subject about which more than one or two people have a passing interest. Two? Who said two? I started a newsgroup called Dyke.On.ABC and only one lady named Ellen joined me on it. She was nice.

See all of Chapter 2.

Username

When you log in to a network, the network wants to know your identity. To identify yourself, give your name or username. Your username is also the first part of your internet e-mail address. Also, someone who only wants your body.

Veronica (Very Easy Rodent-Oriented Netwide Index to Computerized Archives)

Sugar, sugar. From our buddies at the University of Nevada, Veronica is a constantly updated database of the names of almost every menu item on thousands of Gopher servers. The Veronica database can be searched from most major Gopher menus. You are my candy, girl.

See also Archie.

Web, WWW, or World Wide Web

1. Loosely: The whole constellation of resources that can be accessed using Gopher, FTP, HTTP, Telnet, Usenet, and some other tools.

2. The universe of hypertext servers (HTTP servers), which are the servers that allow text, graphics, sound files, etc. to be mixed together. If you still don't get it, then you had better "Get On with It."

Web Site (Website)

That's a destination on the user-friendly World Wide Web section of the internet. It can be a teenager's homepage—a bunch of pictures and words—or it can be an intricate array of text, images, audio, and video put together by a company.

Zip

A data-compression technique that rearranges the data so that more can fit in less disk space.

GAY WORDS

Actup Clone

That guy who can't stop talking about his activist group and wears combat boots, dog tags, and close-cropped hair.

Basket

The bulge in his pants—look at the fly.

Bears

Furry gay men.

Bondage

Being tied up and whipped; S&M practice.

Bull Dyke

A woman who is tough and butch and maybe scary.

Butch

A tough-acting guy, or a masculine woman, or a man or women in a toughie outfit.

Clone

Typical queer and not the Absolut Vodka version! The seventies: mustache, tight jeans, longish hair, if any, some kind of bandanna in pocket, cigarettes, plaid shirt. The nineties: Actup or similar statement button, moussed hair and one earring, tight jeans, and, probably, a leather jacket.

The Community

Who we are, really.

Community Spirit

The essence of our collective souls.

Companion

Lover, boyfriend, friend, girlfriend, partner, significant other, as in *"I'm with Stupid."*

Cross-dresser

Someone who dresses like the sex he or she isn't.

Cross Training

Cardiovascular workouts that get the heart beating. Very good for you, unlike weight training, which is very good for your looks and inner strength. This is in the book for no known reason.

Cruise Bar

A place that sells liquor and allows you to look for a man or a woman to have sex with.

Daddy

Some men call their lovers this if that person is someone they look up to. Quite literally.

Direct Action

Something people do when they want the world to change, such as when Actup fights City Hall by staging a march or an indiscreet sit-in.

Domestic Partnership

The new law on the books all over America which, I think, patronizingly states that a couple who are not heterosexual are married in respect to insurance, hospital visiting hours, and leases.

Drag Queen

A man who dresses up like a woman and performs (where the phrase "Sing it, girl" comes from); also Drag King.

Fabulous

A truly overused term; means absolutely nothing.

Faggot

Horrible way of describing one of us.

Fag Hag

A woman who seems to adore gay men.

Fetish

My favorite sexual thing: When you can't get enough of something—such as feet, or whips, or using globs of Cool Whip!

Flamer

An effeminate man (homophobic term). Not to be confused with flame.

Girlfriend

The person who is the dating partner of a woman (the lesbian definition).

GMB

A gay black man.

Guppie

A gay urban professional—"very BMW scene."

GWM

A gay white man.

HIV

Human Immunodeficiency Virus, the virus known to cause AIDS, which is not a disease but a deficiency in the autoimmune system that allows diseases to go unchecked.

Homophobia

The fear or hatred of a homosexual for some inane reason; a social disease that is curable.

Hunk

See Stud.

Lipstick Lesbian

A fancy lesbian; look for a purse; femme.

Mary

A term of address first popular among gay men born before 1960 and now enjoying a resurgence.

Miss Thing

A weird, old-fashioned term for friends—boys say that to other boys about other boys.

Unnecessary term, *Mary!*

Outing

A picnic. No, actually it's when someone is described publicly as a homosexual (when he or she has been telling people otherwise). Made famous by Michelangelo Signorile years back (in *Outweek*).

Partner

A lover, companion, or significant other. Some people say that such terms as *partner* and *significant other* are wimply misnomers. I prefer *"that guy."*

Passing

Pretending to be straight.

People of Color

African Americans; Latinos and Latinas; Asians.

Stud

See Hunk.

Top

The penetrator in intercourse.

Training

What people in gyms do; requires no manual.

Trick

A sex partner; usually means for one night and rarely even cab fare after that night.

Two-stepping

A really nice country-western dance.

Transgender

A mixture of the two. Transgender areas online are thought to be warm, safe places. (And *cuddly?*)

> *See* Chapter 7—*throughout.*

Transsexual

Someone who was one sex and is now another.

Transvestite

Someone who wears women's clothing when he is a man; not necessarily a gay man (The word is not used for a woman in men's clothing.)

INDEX